trisha

AS I AM

TRISHA GODDARD

trisha

AS I AM

JB

JOHN BLAKE

Published by John Blake Publishing Ltd,
3 Bramber Court, 2 Bramber Road,
London W14 9PB, England

www.blake.co.uk

First published in hardback in 2008
First published in trade paperback in 2008

ISBN: 978 1 84454 562 9
Trade paperback ISBN: 978 1 84454 597 1

British Library Cataloguing-in-Publication Data:

A catalogue record for this book is available from the British Library.

Design by www.envydesign.co.uk

Printed in the UK by CPI William Clowes Ltd, Beccles, NR34 7TL

1 3 5 7 9 10 8 6 4 2

Papers used by John Blake Publishing are natural, recyclable products made
from wood grown in sustainable forests. The manufacturing processes
conform to the environmental regulations of the country of origin.

Every attempt has been made to contact the relevant copyright-holders, but
some were unobtainable. We would be grateful if the appropriate people
could contact us.

Dedication

To 'Bertie', 'Bearwig', 'Moosie', and doggies:
Alf and dear departed Razzie.
With you I'm always loved and safe because you
truly accept me – as I am.

Acknowledgements

First and foremost, my sincerest thanks to Mark Hanks who's been with me every step of the emotional journey that was writing this book. Your empathy and power of intuition is truly amazing!

Also Michelle Signore at John Blake Publishing for being just about the gentlest, most understanding editor-in-chief I've ever come across! John Blake himself deserves a mention for being a fabulous lunch companion and should definitely form a comedy/business double act with publicist Phil Hall!

As ever, I'm grateful to my friend and business partner Malcolm Allsop for his energy, support and unfailing belief in me from that first day we met in Sydney back in 1987.

This book would not have been possible without my 'emotional coach' helping me confront and deal with the hornet's nest of issues it stirred up, thus it would be churlish not to thank my psychotherapist (you know who you are!)

John Redshaw, Sarah Barrett and my brilliant producers and researchers at Town House Television productions have my admiration and appreciation for helping me compile a list of some of the more memorable-than-usual I've come across on my television chat show. Also Leyla Sadr and Laura Halls for their loyalty and organisational skills.

To the thousands of people I've met through my chat show: so many of you have triumphed in the face of adversity. You reinforce my belief that shining light into a dark corner can scare that Monster called 'Misfortune' away. I continue to be inspired...

Thanks to both Norwich MIND and Norwich Home Start charities for making me their patrons, allowing me to put a little back into my local community.

My de facto 'sister' Claire Wilkinson and her husband, Peter, Kevin Farmer, Madison McCoy, my sister-in-law Maureen Garrett, Brian Burgess, Ian and Collette Gooderham: all of you have been there, ready with unconditional love, when the poo was being freely dispersed by the air-conditioning! 'Thanks' isn't strong enough a word. I love the lot of you.

Thanks to all of you whose honesty, suggestions or kind words of support and praise have spurred me on over the years, either personally and/or professionally. Michele, Judy, Fozzie, Rosie, the Dunn and Ciccone families are just some who've done just that at some time in my life.

And, lastly, I even appreciate those who've either accidentally or purposely given me hell!

Why? Because, as a powerhouse Aussie businesswoman called Jan Murray used to say, 'The best form of revenge is to go out there and be successful, baby!'

Contents

Introduction

For years, people have been going on at me about writing a book and for ages I've resisted. When I was about to hit the big Five-O last year, those voices got even louder. 'You've had such a life,' people would say, 'and your show is all about people's lives. Why not tell everyone about yours for once?' And, for the first time, I began to think about it. After all, I thought, writing a book would be my turn to do what I hope I give my guests the chance to do: to tell *my* version of *my* life and try to make sense of it all while I do so.

Besides, I've always believed that things happen for a reason. Having your fiftieth birthday, the one that unequivocally announces you're halfway to one hundred, tends to make you want to tie up loose ends, to deal with things once and for all and free yourself up to enjoy the next fifty years.

So I began to put pen to paper. I was terrified about what going over my past and letting the world in on it might unleash – what Pandora's box might I open? But, hey, I thought, around fifteen thousand of my guests have trusted me enough to bare their hearts and souls, so it would be a bit hypocritical for me to make a bolt for it now!

As I wrote, I had to dig deep into a lot of memories, good and bad. I pulled the diaries I wrote from my childhood to my mid-thirties from the bottom of my filing cabinet. In the past, whenever I'd looked at them I would be overwhelmed with emotion – each time I opened one and began to read I would promptly close it and throw it back in the drawer. But this time, I *had* to read on in the name of 'research'. It was painful. Maybe this sounds dramatic, but the diaries *are* packed with dramatic things, events that were terrible at the time. I had to dredge up so much of what I thought I'd put behind me, and, as anyone who's tried to move on from painful experience knows, it's not exactly a laugh raking over old memories.

As many people know, I'm a great believer in therapy. Without it, I wouldn't be the person I am today; I'd be stuck in the past and I probably wouldn't be able to try to help others as I do. It's been a long time since I've called upon a therapist, but I knew that writing this book would only be possible if I had support mechanisms in place. So I went back into therapy. And you know what? It helped me write. I didn't think it would be possible, but talking not only helped me find the strength to recount my past, but the act of writing helped me in therapy. I went deeper into myself than I've ever been before, and it wasn't easy. I'm glad it's over, I'm glad it's done, and I'm pleased I did it. I'm also glad the sleepless nights are over!

I'm pleased that my fiftieth birthday party was one of the happiest days of my life. My wonderful husband Peter organised a fabulous Hollywood-themed party. It was no celeb bash; it was family and friends, plus a few surprises. Peter flew in old friends from Australia, and a whole host of beloved faces from right back to my teenage years turned up. How surreal it was to be shaking hands and kissing some of the very people I'd been writing about. Early boyfriends, schoolmates, ex-colleagues and best friends formed a Who's Who of my life. It was a roller-coaster of emotions and gave me a chance to reflect back over the years and remember the happy and the unhappy times under the glow of a room filled with love.

I only hope reading this book interests and entertains anyone who picks it up, and that my story may help others with their lives, just as over the years so many people's stories have helped and inspired me.

1

Daddy's Girl

It's a bit of a cliché, but I always felt different. Different from my three sisters, all of whom were much lighter-skinned than me. Different from my school peers, who were white. And different from those who seemed happier with their families and didn't share my burning desire to escape, find adventure and, above all, succeed.

When I say different, I don't mean better. Just different. So many things affect the way a person turns out, but nothing more than their childhood. Mine had its ups and downs, and my memories of it bring both happiness and pain, as well as confusion and questions that will never be answered. There are naturally plenty of gaps in what I recall, but what the hell, I'll try to start from the beginning and see where it takes me!

I'm a bit hazy about the events surrounding my birth. I do know that, about three years before I arrived on the

1

scene, my mum had come to England from Dominica on a boat packed with hundreds of other West Indians eager to start a new life. She'd been invited by the then Minister of Employment, Enoch Powell (who, it seems, later regretted his kind invitations to immigrants). To my mum, the streets of England were paved with gold. Or so she'd been told. She'd also been told that England was a home from home, which is why she only brought a cardigan with her. Inevitably, the British climate came as a bit of a shock. From then on, the cold weather was to be one of her favourite little whinges. Amusingly, though, when she eventually travelled back to the West Indies years later, she whinged that it was too hot. Unlike Goldilocks, Mum never found a temperature that was quite right.

Dad was white, a Norfolk boy born and bred. He too had done a bit of travelling with the Army Medical Corps. Judging from an old photo of him with the service boys and another photo of his, of a stunning Japanese girl, he was an adventurous type and maybe a bit of a flirt – just the sort of bloke Mum would always warn me to steer clear of, in fact! I used to consider a lot of Dad's qualities as things that were peculiar to him, but since I've been living in Norfolk I have discovered that in many ways his personality was shaped by the place. People around here can be generous, but there's a certain thriftiness about them that is in some ways good, in other ways bad.

When he needed something for his car or his bike, Dad would happily go down to the local tip to see if he could find it there first before reaching for his wallet. We used to joke that presents were no exception. Looking for a special gift? Just head down the tip! It's a little mean to say

Norfolk people are tight, but some are and my dad certainly was. Inasmuch as he was careful to never spend unnecessarily, and to never throw anything away, I have definitely inherited his frugality. Not that you'll ever see me lurking around the local tip, mind you, but I'm a real hoarder.

Also, Dad was always critical of everything. At the risk of generalising, I'd say that's a Norfolk thing too. Everybody has heard the song 'Always Look on the Bright Side of Life'. Well, the Norfolk version might well be 'Always Look on the Shite Side of Life'.

Mum and Dad met while training to be nurses in Hackney, London. Mum was 29, Dad five years younger, when the problem of me arose. As a result, they took a trip to the registry office and got married – during Dad's lunch break, the story goes. I was born in December 1957 in the local Salvation Army maternity hospital, and Mum and Dad must have been pretty taken with my resemblance to a Cabbage Patch Kid (either that or the fact that contraception was not as readily available back then) because by my fourth birthday I had three sisters, Pru, Paula and Linda.

By this time, our family had moved about a bit. First, there had been a little flat in Hackney, then a very modest caravan on a site in Kent, and we had moved to a semi-detached hospital house in Brentwood, Essex – by then Dad was a psychiatric nurse – when I began primary school in 1962.

I was taller than most of the other kids and this proved a disadvantage to an unfortunate little boy named Geoffrey. When I was running about one day, I crashed

into him and my goofy teeth cut his head and made it
bleed. He screamed like mad and I was convinced he was
about to die. Of course, he survived – it turned out he was
just a wimp. I loved being at school, and until that point I
hadn't really known I was black, or at least hadn't seen
myself as any different from others. What changed all that
was a certain writer – frigging Enid Blyton!

Good old Enid's books were read out loud in class. The
first time, I just sat there and listened with everyone else,
but soon enough I started to notice people looking at me.
What about the story? I thought, and then it dawned on me
pretty quickly – they were looking at me because I looked
like one of the naughty little golliwogs in the stories. I was
the only black kid, and at break time the other kids seemed
to enjoy calling me a golly and telling me I was bad. The
fact was, you just didn't see black people around in those
days, not where I was living anyway. So the only time I
came across them was in stories we read at school. And it
sure made me feel different.

Forget whatever kids love about Enid Blyton's writing, all
I knew was that Enid equalled shit treatment for me in the
playground! Every time one of her books came out, my
stomach just started flipping. Thanks to her, life was hellish.

But Dad told me a great story to make me feel better
about it all. Thousands of years ago, he said, God called
everyone in the world to get together so he could talk to
them. So people came and formed an immense crowd,
stretching in every direction as far as the eye could see.
The trouble was that, mid-sentence, God had a bit of an
accident and pooed on everyone from above. They all got
covered in God's business, but some were hit worse than

others. Dad told me that the ones who were closest to God, the most important ones, were the brownest people and that the ones farthest away from Him were the white ones with their little freckles made by God's you-know-what! This, Dad told me, is the way things remained from then on. Not exactly politically correct, but it worked a treat in helping me deal with things.

Funnily enough, one of the kids who teased me most was Geoffrey, the guy who ended up with my teeth in his head. Geoffrey had his own little accident in class one day. Oops. But it was me who got into trouble, for running around singing, 'Geoffrey pooed his pa-ants, Geoffrey pooed his pa-ants.' It was worth it, of course, and I enjoyed it all the more because of Dad's poo story.

Dad was great at making me feel good. When it was thundering, it was God stamping around – nothing to worry about too much. We would often sing together – I remember changing the words to a song called 'Bobby's Girl' to 'I Wanna Be Daddy's Girl', I felt so close to him. Another vivid memory is sitting around while Dad was decorating his and Mum's bedroom, singing away to 'Tell Laura I Love Her' and 'The Night Has A Thousand Eyes', and just feeling warm, safe and happy.

My dad was my hero then.

Oddly, I have virtually no recollection of my mother before the age of 11 or so. The memories I have are merely snapshots, and I can't make sense of why it is these particular ones have stuck. I mean, why do I remember some radio report about Yuri Gagarin and her being in the background? Or her telling me about performing first aid on a man who had walked through a glass door in East

Africa? Or being made to write 'I must not be bad' a hundred times on my seventh birthday (all because I'd been honest with someone and unintentionally dropped my mother in it) but very little else? Surely there must have been more between us than that.

Who knows, but most of my young days with Mum are lost to me. There may be some huge psychological reason for this, but I believe the fact that Mum had four kids in four years meant that Dad spent a lot of time looking after me while Mum tended to my younger sisters. Also, she seemed cagey about things and didn't like to talk much about herself. This made it hard in my early years to get close to her. My belief now is that her stiff upper lip had something to do with her brother dying in a fight when she was young. I think it shut something down in her, made it hard for her to open up. I mean, we didn't even know her age until I was 15, and I must have been 9 before I eventually found out her full name, Mary Agnes Fortune. That says a lot about how open we were.

I remember Mum using French patois, encouraging me to use words and sayings which helped hugely when I came to learn French, and also her teaching me to dance. Because of her background, people always assumed she would be into reggae, but she hated it, and so do I. Bizarrely, Mum loved country and western, and songs like 'Ride De Donkey', which she would often sing loudly, sometimes to my great embarrassment.

In those days, Mum was very, very slim and had a real Carib look, with a hint of Asian. She had a lovely West Indian lilt (except when out in public) and used to call me 'Tootsie' – don't ask me why! My sisters and I used to take the mick out of her when she greeted anyone she didn't know. We used to say she'd greet them like the Queen. 'Oh hello,' she would say down the telephone in the most regal of voices, and if she knew who it was she'd go right back into her West Indian accent. My kids say I'm exactly the same, telling me I posh it up when I answer the phone. They love baiting me for putting it on.

Something Mum did for which I am eternally grateful was instil in me a need to work hard. Later on, she would tell me that if you were black you had to be twice as good to be half as good. She taught me to think of myself as an ambassador for my colour – if I behaved well, people would make up their own minds about black people instead of believing the stereotypes. Not that Mum had some kind of black solidarity thing going. No, in truth, she almost wanted me to transcend my colour and assimilate into the white world.

Again, it's not politically correct, but Mum seemed to have very little time for black men. I often heard her suck her teeth at the stereotypical black man, recklessly fathering kids and, in our private chats, she never seemed very positive about them in general – unless they were friends or relatives. Years later, she made it clear she wanted me to 'marry out'. I'll never forget when my sister brought home a black boyfriend; Dad had no problem with this, but Mum simply said, 'Watch your handbag!'. Even if she was joking, it shocked me.

Other than these few odd recollections, as far as the early years are concerned, I think of Mum and my memory draws a blank. I simply remember more about Dad.

Life in those early years was easy. It may sound odd, but I loved primary school despite the teasing and, from what I recall, home life was good too. Nevertheless, times were tough for Mum and Dad, and the offer of a new nursing job for Dad must have been a good one, because before I was six years old it was bye-bye, Brentwood, hello … East Africa!

2

Paradise

As kids, you just get on with things. What may present itself as a massive, nerve-racking challenge to an adult is merely a walk in the park for a wide-eyed child. I don't remember leaving England to move to Africa being a big deal for me. In fact, I didn't quite understand where we were going, or why. But I do remember being on a boat and having my eyes opened to a completely foreign, exciting world, and I loved it.

The trip from Southampton to Dar es Salaam took six weeks, and during my time aboard the mighty *Rhodesia Castle* I saw sights I'll never forget. We called in at Naples, passed along the Suez Canal – being woken up by the stench of the port of Aden is a memory I will never shake – and stopped off at Cairo. It was an overwhelming experience, but one of the best events on that trip was my discovery of something very, very special indeed – ice-cream. I remember I was on a rocking horse and was given a tub and a little wooden spoon, and that was it – I was hooked. I was given one tub of ice cream every day at 11am, and, rocking back and forth on that horse, I thought, Life doesn't get much better than this. Sometimes I find myself sitting in my Jag thinking, How does this rate on the ice-cream scale? And, you know what, I'm not entirely sure it rates at all.

I loved that ship, and seeing those places and experiencing all that would happen once we arrived opened my eyes to the thrill of travelling. Even then, it made me appreciate that Britain really isn't the only place in the world, which is what some folk in this country would have you believe. Britain's not necessarily 'the bollocks' – there are plenty of other places with just as good, well, balls! Every place has its beauty and I could never be patriotic to just one country.

Just as a father can never give his attention to just one child. As I said, my dad was my hero and, up until that trip, as the eldest, I'd always felt I was number one. But things were about to change, and it began on the boat. For a start, I remember feeling slightly resentful about the sleeping arrangements. I had to share a cabin with Dad, which was fine, but Pru was in with us and I didn't like it one bit. Yet there was something more than possessiveness going on, something hard to describe. I sensed a change in Dad's attitude towards me that, looking back, was definitely a sign of the way things would come to be between us in the not-too-distant future. For now, it was just a sense of losing someone's attention, having the tap turned off a little. Later, it was to get a lot worse.

Paradise

We arrived in Dar es Salaam and were thrust into an intense atmosphere – the events surrounding the formation in 1964 of Tanzania from Tanganyika and Zanzibar, both of which had struggled to achieve independence from Britain, meant that the area around the hotel we were staying in was packed with British troops. I remember all the family sitting in a cafe, and I was wearing what we called a 'twist dress', which was violet and a bit like a tutu. I loved that dress, and when 'Speedy Gonzales' came on the jukebox I jumped up on the table and did the twist for all the soldiers. It must have provided an antidote to some of the tension because I received a huge round of applause and it was great. I always loved dancing and wasn't shy when it came to getting up in front of strangers and potentially making a fool out of myself. Not much has changed there.

One day, there was a lot of noise coming from outside, so I looked over a window sill in the hotel to see what was going on. Amid a lot of chaos, I recall seeing a man with a big microphone and a big camera. From having watched telly back home, I could tell they were filming the news, but I'd never seen it actually being *made* before. I was transfixed. All the noise seemed to drop away and my attention was focused entirely on this man – a journalist – at work. I didn't really know anything about it, but what he was doing seemed such a courageous, honest and necessary thing – it was such a strong image. That moment changed something in me, made me want to do what this man was doing. Up until that point I had wanted to become a bus conductor. After all, nearly all the black people I'd seen back in Brentwood were bus conductors, so I'd assumed that's what black people did.

Thanks to Dad's job, we moved into hospital housing in Dadoma. Built by Germans who had colonised East Africa, ours was a typical colonial house – a bungalow with a stone floor. It wasn't posh compared with other houses in the area, but we loved it. All four of us kids were in one bedroom, but that didn't matter because we only spent time in there when we wanted to sleep. Playtime was always outdoors, and there was a lot of playtime – Mum and Dad just left us to it, which was great. We had paw-paw and mango trees in the garden. We'd make dolls out of mango seeds, keep chickens, wear ribbons in our hair to use as tourniquets for snakebites and go on adventures with our sausage dog, Saucy. Everyone had sausage dogs because they were great at 'snaking' – finding snakes and getting rid of them.

Saucy was always hanging around us, like a mate who never leaves you, and we loved him. We repaid his friendship by flinging him into a reservoir dam and watching him paddle like fury with all his sausage-dog might back to the bank – only to then get flung back in again. Poor Saucy. The RSPCA would have loved us for that. But Saucy stuck by us, watching as we played in the mud and built our little huts, so it can't have been so bad for him.

Africa felt so free and exciting, and I think it toughened all of us up. You didn't cry over a grazed knee when there were vicious apes a hundred yards from your garden.

We went to expatriate schools run by New Zealand ma'ams – tight-lipped, tight-fisted, tight-laced and vicious when it came to enforcing punishment. If you swore, you had your mouth washed out with soap and water. To this day, I can still taste the soap in my mouth whenever I swear. A minor misdemeanour would result in a thwack with a ruler across the back of the legs, while the reward for total disgrace was a cane across an open hand with the whole class looking on. We were being shown a film about New Zealand one day and I got two across the hand for pointing at a Maori with a big white beard and exclaiming, 'Oh, it's Santa,' which made all the kids laugh. Obviously, the teacher wasn't so amused.

They were hard but fair and it was a great school. In one class, you had 30 pupils ranging from 7 to 17 and only one teacher. Despite this, the level of education was way ahead of the British system, as I would later discover. We learned French and Swahili, and I discovered a love of poetry that has never left me. I was also lucky enough to get caught mucking around on the piano by one of the teachers, Miss Allen. From then on, I received lessons, and so began another lifelong passion. Extra music and drama was always a feature of life with Mum and Dad, and it's something that in turn I've passed on to my own children.

Outside of school, all the kids used to hang out and all the parents knew one another. We were all from such diverse backgrounds – there were Brits, Germans, Dutch, Kiwis and Aussies. The thing everyone had in common was that they were all trying to make a go of it in Africa. There was a real pioneering spirit among the expats, a can-do, go-get-'em attitude that I loved and would encounter again in Australia many years later. Tanzania was an emerging state in Africa and it was tough, as were the people who lived there. Everyone worked hard, and when work was over social events took place at the golf course. While the adults did their thing, us kids would find our own mischief. It was wonderful making our own fun and being so free.

I had a few friends, but often felt the odd one out in bigger groups. When it came to the picking of 'gangs' for games, I was always the last one to get picked. It was weird because on the face of it I was a bit of a clown and was growing adept at making people laugh, but I found it hard making close bonds with people. To me it just didn't come easily. During one gang-picking session, there were two laburnum trees at the end of the drive, one for each gang. I recall running between each tree, knowing I wasn't particularly wanted in either gang, and feeling embarrassed that, whichever one I was accepted into, they would only be taking me out of charity. At that age, the way you look has a lot to do with how you are received by others, and I knew I wasn't pretty. I was plain, and until I was 12 I was frequently mistaken for a boy.

It was my sisters, Pru and Paula, who had the looks. When we walked into a room, all eyes would swivel towards them. It didn't make me jealous, but it didn't make me happy. Through that, I eventually learned that my 'allure' – for want of a better word – was my personality. Sometimes it can be a blessing not to be too pretty, since you have to rely on other things to get ahead. And, as I learned then, you're never going to get picked for any team if you just sit back. Or run from tree to tree. It's a lesson I've never forgotten.

Dad also kept us busy when he had the time. One of our favourite things was to go walking, though at first Dad's 'walks' felt more like forced marches. Off we'd go every Sunday and cover stupid distances, and, boy, did Mum bitch about it in the car on the way to wherever we were planning to start our walk. But soon enough I had begun baking all sorts of cakes and snacks to take with us and we all had a fine time of it. Those excursions are where I got my love of walking from, and now I walk or run every day. It's a bit of an addiction.

We'd go on wonderful safaris around Lake Tanganyika, on the border between Tanzania and Congo. Dad loved a bargain, and I remember one trip where an African at the roadside offered us a ludicrous amount of bananas for next to nothing. 'We'll have them!' said Dad. But, as we got to the entrance to one of the game reserves, a ranger spotted all these bananas hanging out of the car and warned us not to take them into the campsite because the elephants would sniff them out and come in looking for them. Rather than throw them away, Dad made us eat all these frigging bananas as he drove on. So there we were, scoffing bananas and tossing the skins out of the car as we went. Typical Dad, he'd rather eat bananas and chuck up than throw them away! So we arrived at the campsite banana-free, but pretty damn sick, and went to bed.

In the middle of the night, we awoke to the sound of a great commotion – shouting, yelling and elephants trumpeting. We rushed out of our tents to see what all the fuss was about. Dad asked a guy what was going on, only to be told, 'You won't believe it, some idiot left a trail of banana skins leading right to the campsite.'

Luckily, there wasn't too much damage done, but we

just kept quiet. Though it was about 30 years before I could stomach another banana.

The African people were accepting and warm, and at the same time so strong. I was often in awe of them. I remember seeing the Masai warriors at a huge festival – the power of their singing and the noise of their feet as they jumped up and landed was truly awe-inspiring. As a little girl, watching them left me gobsmacked. Tough people, they'd run a hundred miles across the desert in full war dress. I'm not quite up to that, admittedly, but the strength of the Masai remains an inspiration to me in my daily training. To this day, I know who I'll run to when the bomb goes off! If anyone crawls from the wreckage, it'll be the Masai.

Dad's involvement with his work was admirable. So often he would go beyond the call of duty. For instance, I remember he hired a cine-projector one day so that he could show films to the patients at Isanga Mental Institution near our house. During the day, we'd see these patients and prisoners chained together and singing as they shuffled up the hill, where they were set to work mining and breaking rocks, and it was a special moment watching such poor, enslaved people enjoying old black-and-white cartoons. I admired Dad so much for his sense of social inclusion and I definitely learned my social conscience from him. He did a lot to improve conditions for the mental patients, and through his actions he taught me not to have an 'us and them' attitude to criminals and people with mental-health issues.

I'm proud to say that, when I returned to Africa in 1984 and visited Isanga, 'Goddard', as everyone called him, was still remembered. Someone my dad had trained there all those years ago has gone on to become the country's health minister. But when I told Dad about this he found it hard to swallow. He has always been tough on himself and can't really take a compliment. He's critical of himself, just as he is of others.

However, as I mentioned, my relationship with Dad began to change even before we reached Africa. Increasingly, I felt like I had to seek his attention, but I never seemed to get it, and there were times when he made me feel like he just didn't care. More hurtfully, he started to punish me for things that I felt weren't my fault at all.

One such incident has stuck in my mind for years. Because our school friends all lived so far away from us, Mum and Dad set a rule that we had to get prior consent if we wanted to bring someone home to play. One day, we were waiting for Dad to pick us up and Pru told me she was going to bring her friend Elizabeth Taylor home with us. 'But we're not allowed, Pru,' I said.

'I don't care, I'm bringing her home.'

Elizabeth's parents turned up and Pru waved them off, saying my parents would drop her home later, but when Dad turned up he took one look at Elizabeth and started reading the riot act. Not to my sister, though, but to me.

'No, Dad, you've got it wrong. I told Pru we're not allowed...' I pleaded.

But it was no good. Dad lost his temper with me while Pru and Elizabeth stood by.

'Right!' he shouted at me. 'You can walk home.' And with that, off they went.

It was dusty and hot, and I sat there for what seemed

like an age, assuming Dad would come back to get me, that he was just teaching me a lesson. But he didn't come back. Eventually I got scared and began to cry as I realised I really was going to have to walk home.

It was a long walk. I had to go past the cemetery, which terrified me, and I was howling with tears. Eventually I cried myself out and steeled myself for the rest of the journey. I had to walk past the grounds of the mental hospital, which was another scary place for a young girl, and then past the leper colony. I'll never forget passing all the lepers and walking on to a hill that was being mined. I knew it was safe to cross it because the red flag was down and that meant there were no explosions taking place. I walked for what seemed like ages.

As I approached the house, the first thing I saw was Pru and my other sisters playing happily, running around with Elizabeth. It seemed as if they didn't have a care in the world and I just thought, How could my dad just leave me? Why is he doing this? I was confused, upset, jealous even.

I got home and my father said nothing.

For years I pondered this memory, and often questioned whether I was right to be angry about it. Am I making a fuss over nothing? I thought. Perhaps it hadn't been such a long walk after all. Maybe it just seemed a long way to a scared little girl.

Any doubts were put to rest during my 1984 visit. I retraced my steps – this time in a car – and to my horror discovered the distance I'd trekked that afternoon was around five miles. And we're not talking English countryside here – we're talking frigging *Africa* and all its potential dangers! I was shocked and, when I next saw my dad, I confronted him with my anger. 'That was fucking awful of you,' I said. 'I would *never*, *ever* do that to a child, and it wasn't even my fucking fault!' I exploded.

'Oh, I didn't think you would walk,' he replied.

'Well, what did you expect? What did you think I was going to do?'

'I would've come back for you'

'How was I to know that?' I shouted. 'How did I know that, Dad?'

To this question he had no answer. And for his actions he had no apology.

Whatever the reasons for Dad beginning to treat me differently from my sisters – he used to tell me that as the eldest child I should be responsible – to an eight-year-old girl his behaviour was not the way a hero behaves.

But, despite my confusion, I loved Africa, and I still loved my father.

Dad's contract came to an end in 1967. I was so sad to be leaving, but excited to be getting on a plane for the first time. The fact that we were going back to England didn't mean much to me, as I didn't really have any memories of the place. I wasn't sure what to expect. All I knew was that the Goddards were moving on again.

3

Nigger, Nigger!

The cry rang out as Pru and I arrived at the schoolgates: 'The blackies are coming, the blackies are coming.'

We paused for a second but knew we must carry on. To run would have been to admit defeat, so on we went, bracing ourselves for the worst. As we passed through the gates, a welcoming crowd of 20, perhaps 30, kids crowded around us, pressing in and chanting, 'Nigger, nigger, nigger, nigger!' as their punches rained down. As each blow landed, we pushed harder to make it through. The crowd dispersed – they'd given us their first thought for the day. We knew how they felt, and we also knew to expect more as the day went on, and another warm welcome the next morning. Perhaps they didn't think we'd ever get the message that we weren't welcome. No one needed to tell me to go home – I would have given anything to be back in Africa, back where I'd come from.

From the moment my dad's brother, Uncle Maurice, picked us up from Gatwick, I had a bad feeling about England. It wasn't just bad, in fact. It was terrible, an awful sense of foreboding. Something was *wrong*. Jolly Uncle Maurice was pleased to see us, but no amount of good humour could dispel the dread I felt as I peered out of the window of the old minibus we'd borrowed as he drove us towards Norfolk. Everything I saw seemed grey – the sky, the rain, the roads and buildings, even the people – and the contrast with beautiful, colourful Africa was almost too much to take.

In particular, I remember my horror when I was told that what I assumed were lovely big houses all around us were actually terraces of tiny homes. That may sound snobby, but when you've come from a place where you can't see the next house from yours, you don't expect people to be on top of one another. All of us, Mum and Dad included, were very quiet on the journey to Uncle Maurice and Aunty Mary's house in Heacham, near Hunstanton.

This place was everything Africa wasn't. We all felt as flat as pancakes.

We moved into a little cabin in the woods that Uncle Maurice had found for us. Our own little house in the woods, I thought. Great! Famous last words. The romance lasted about a day, until I realised that, after the wide, open spaces of Africa, the six of us cooped up in a tiny cabin was simply not going to work. In Africa, we had run free, all doing our own thing, then suddenly we were all in one another's faces and the stress started to mount. Looking back, it must have been hard on Mum and Dad. Both of them were in need of work, and with four kids to look after it can't have been easy. But, whatever tensions were developing in the house, they were nothing compared with what awaited us when we stepped outside.

School was a nightmare from the start. Up until then, I thought I'd heard every 'coloured' joke going. In fact, my dad had always told them to us so that we would laugh at their ignorance. But there were plenty of new jokes, and real punches to accompany the punchlines. We were the first blacks in the village, and the kids didn't take a shine to us, to put it mildly.

But there was one exception – Julie! Not long after the punches and chants at the school gates had become the norm, this girl emerged and did something amazing. What she did for Pru and I will stick with me for the rest of my life. Tomboyish, with long blonde hair and a high ponytail right down her back – oh, and she was *white*! – Julie appeared by our side one morning as we were about to run the gauntlet of abuse from our schoolmates. (Our white cousin, who walked to school with us, would scarper at the gates, and I didn't blame her.) She started shouting in her cockney accent at our tormentors, 'Come on, girls, I'll fight wiv ya! Come on, get that one! And that one!' And fight she did.

From then on, Julie was there for us. She was incredible and really saved our skin. It would have been so easy for her to fall in with the crowd and throw abuse at us with the rest of them, but she actually *chose* to be on the loser's side, which was truly astounding. I'd love to know what happened to her. People who fight for the underdog deserve good things in life, and Julie was a fine example of such a person. She made a horrible situation a little more bearable. With her around, the nasty world we had found ourselves in didn't seem quite so bad.

Lunchtimes were never easy. In the canteen, I would always find my cousin and sit with her. She was a friendly face in a crowd of kids who looked at me like I was an alien. I was about to sit down with her one day when a boy on the same table said to me, 'Ugh, we don't want you on our table!'

Immediately I felt like crying but I knew better than to show I was upset, so I just ignored him and went to sit down. Before I knew it, the boy turned and pushed me hard, sending me flying, along with my tray of food. Everyone in the room turned to look. As I fumbled on the floor, desperately trying to hold back tears and to get my food back on to my plate, all I remember is the sound of laughter filling my ears. The humiliation was awful. Nobody came to help and, as I began to cry, everyone just looked on and laughed. The food I had dumped back on to my plate was inedible, so I composed myself as best I could and went back to the dinner queue.

'Can I have some more dinner because they've thrown mine on the floor?' I asked a dinner lady.

'No, you've had yours and that's that,' she snapped with a look that I wouldn't call sympathetic.

And that was when I lost it. I threw my tray down and ran from the canteen. Once outside, I collapsed in tears on the nearest steps.

I noticed someone approaching me. At first, I assumed it was some kid coming to rub my nose in it even more, but was relieved to see it was my form teacher. Someone gives a shit, someone cares, I thought. But, as this goofy, blond-haired teacher began to talk, I quickly realised I was wrong.

'Come on, Trisha,' he told me, 'you've got to toughen up a little and not let the other kids get to you.'

I didn't know what to say. What could I say? I probably nodded as I cried.

He carried on, 'You've got to realise that you're different and that some people don't want you in their country, but you've got to be tough. That's the way to deal with it.'

So it was *my* fault. My fault that this bunch of arseholes were making my life a misery. My tears stopped because suddenly I had it sussed – I knew I could trust nobody. What chance did I have if the teachers condoned what was going on? I realised that if you were black you were on your own.

I had Pru, of course, although we were in different classes. In the playground, however, we were always together. We'd always meet up there. But one day I couldn't find her. After some time, I asked after her, running around appealing to anyone who might have seen her. Eventually someone told me she'd been made to stay behind in the classroom. We weren't allowed into the school buildings during break, so the only way for me to look into Pru's classroom was to climb up a buttress in the wall. It was a difficult climb and my fingers bled and my knees scraped against the rough concrete as I hauled myself up using the bars that covered the windows.

Looking into the classroom, I saw Pru. She was sitting alone in the middle of the room, a book open on the desk in front of her. Her long hair covered her face and her shoulders were shaking violently. She was sobbing her heart out. I wanted to reach out to her, but my efforts to knock on the window were in vain, as the bars kept me from reaching the glass. 'Pru,' I shouted, 'Pruuu!' Nothing. I felt helpless watching the sister I was so fiercely protective of suffering alone. She was hungry, dejected and scared, and I knew that, whatever she had done, she didn't deserve to be treated this way.

I don't remember anything else about the incident, but for 20 years the episode recurred in my dreams to such an extent that I began to wonder if it was only a dream in the first place. About 15 years ago, I asked Pru about it, and she confirmed that it was no dream. It turned out that she had been told to remain in class because she had been accused of talking to another pupil without permission. It was true, she had been talking, but only to help a classmate with something they did not understand.

The fact of the matter was, because we had been lucky enough to receive such a high degree of education in Africa, we were streets ahead of the rest of the class in almost every lesson. We didn't show off about it, but it certainly made lessons boring, and, when asked questions in class, more often than not we'd know the answers. This was something the teachers didn't like, and perversely it counted against us, as well as annoying other pupils. It created even more of a barrier between 'us and them'. It was crazy – teachers would talk to us as if we were mentally backward, despite the fact that we'd already covered most of what they were trying to teach us. To be told off for doing well was just ridiculous, but somehow it happened.

Nigger, Nigger!

The teachers and children of that school plunged my sister and I to depths of degradation that I have never been subjected to since.

Mum and Dad had their own worries trying to make ends meet, and there really wasn't anyone to turn to about the bullying. One day, I was outside the school with Mum when she asked me to point out the bullies, and I was so scared I refused. If I had pointed them out, it would have taken a while, because there were plenty. There was nothing we could do, and it's hard to find words for how unhappy we were there. I simply felt despairing of everything. Everywhere I went I carried a heavy, heavy heart with me.

And then something amazing happened. Dad got a job at the Holloway Sanatorium, a psychiatric hospital at Virginia Water in Surrey, and it meant that we had to move again. No more Norfolk! The relief was immense, and only made better when I was shown around our new school, St Ann's Heath. Immediately we arrived I sussed that things were going to be different. I was shown into a class and there was a brown face there, and the brown face belonged to an *adult*! 'Is that a teacher?' I blurted, dumbstruck and excited. 'Yes,' came the reply, and I just thought, *Wow!* Suddenly, finally, I knew I was safe.

The teacher was Sri Lankan, and there were two other brown faces in the class. The other pupils were from diverse backgrounds, some from other countries, and I knew things were going to be all right. During my time at St Ann's Heath, I don't remember being called any name other than Patricia. That school was the closest to the East African experience we were going to get without jumping on a plane back there.

I loved Virginia Water right away. We moved into hospital housing again and, immediately I saw the 'Built in 1901' sign above the door, I thought, Hooray, back to civilisation! We all felt free again, and this was helped along by Dad having a job, which, at least for a while, lifted a lot of tension in the family home. Our neighbours were a lively, friendly bunch, with many Irish people making it a vibrant and fun place to be. Most of the parents worked together, so all the kids knew one another and more often than not there would be a party or social occasion to bring everyone together.

Norfolk had been a nightmare. Virginia Water felt more like a dream.

4

From Hero to Zero

When you're a child, it doesn't take much to have a dream shattered. And, as a parent, it doesn't take much to shatter a child's dream. And that's exactly what my dad did. Although he had been growing distant from me for a while, I was still clinging to the dream that I could get him to show me some love, give me some praise. If I showed him I was good, maybe he would lavish some affection on me the way he once had. Instead, not long after I turned ten, my hero started to hit me.

'You bastard child, I'll teach you, and if you want to cry I'll give you something to cry for,' he would suddenly shout, and I'd know what was coming.

But I'd hardly ever know why.

In Africa, thanks to strict teachers, I had learned what physical punishment means. You did something wrong, you were told why it was wrong and you were given a smack for it. There was no emotional display by whoever was smacking you. They were performing a function, teaching you a lesson. But, with my dad, the word 'smacking' took on a whole new meaning. It didn't feel like physical punishment, it just felt like someone losing his temper. It felt like loss of control.

It was impossible to know what would set him off, but once he started he would really lose it. We weren't allowed to swear in our house, yet when Dad flipped he'd suddenly start using every bloody swear word under the sun, and then he'd begin what he and Mum called 'smacking'. Arguments aside about what is and what isn't 'smacking', what he gave me was the full force of male anger, and it was terrifying.

And as time wore on it only got worse.

The words would come thick and fast – they were hardly sentences – it was just full-on anger accompanied by what I saw as a vicious physical assault. Dad never kicked me – his hands were his weapons. Half the time I couldn't tell if he was using his open hands or fists, but I knew that it hurt.

Mum smacked us too, though it just wasn't the same. With her, I knew where I stood – she'd punish me for swearing at her, for instance – and there just wasn't the same level of aggression and abusive language that was there with Dad. With Mum, it didn't seem so serious.

But I've never really lost my fear of Dad and to this day it still scares the shit out of me when he loses his temper.

It wasn't just me that suffered. Pru and Paula were also targeted, and, out of all of us, Paula got it the worst. We all lived in fear of one of Dad's outbursts, knowing that, whichever of us he went for, the others were probably safe for the time being. Inevitably, almost perversely, this led to a weird sense of relief if another sister was being hit. The horrible thing was that it set up a kind of competitiveness between us – it's terrible, but sometimes one would get another into trouble as a way of ensuring they wouldn't be the one that got beaten. At the same time, we would also give one another tips on how to cope. I remember one of my sisters telling me to wear extra jumpers so the blows didn't hurt so much. I wasn't convinced, but we all had our ways of dealing with it.

Crying certainly didn't stop him. If anything, it made him more angry. Trying to defend myself by putting my hands up only made Dad hit me more, and I soon realised that the best way of minimising the pain was to fall to the floor – usually in a corner – and just be passive and wait until it was over. While down on the floor I learned to go somewhere else in my head to escape the horror of what was happening. I became able to dissociate completely my mind from my body. Perhaps it sounds odd but I learned how to just *not be there*. It was the only way to deal with Dad's blind rage.

It felt like I was rising out of my body and looking down on myself as if I was someone else, as if it wasn't me that was being hurt. I knew the smacking was happening but this was a way of pretending it wasn't and, in so far as that kind of thought process can be said to 'work', going somewhere else in my head worked for me. It lessened the pain a little, but of course it didn't make me deal with it.

I couldn't believe my father was doing this to me.

During the four years that the smacking lasted, I went to

some pretty dark places in my mind. Emotionally I was all over the place. In the midst of an unpredictable domestic situation, I tried to achieve a degree of control by adopting a kind of 'diet'. Secretly, I used to have a nip of sherry – stolen from where Mum thought she had it hidden in the larder – with a digestive biscuit and a little milk, and this would often be my food for the day. I'd go as long as I could without eating, a ritual that made me feel warm and somehow safe. I felt somehow proud not to be eating, but I didn't see my habit as a diet to make me lose weight. I don't know exactly what it was all about, but I think it was just a way of escaping and at the same time having some control over an aspect of my life.

Another way of achieving a degree of control was an obsession I developed with washing my hands, tap-touching and teeth-brushing. It started when I was around 13 and went on for a year or so. I brushed my teeth obsessively, four times to the left, four times to the right, making eight times, and when I washed my hands I had to touch the taps according to a similar principle. I would touch the left tap four times and the right tap four times. My belief was that if I didn't accomplish this I would die, or that something else terrible would happen as a consequence of my failing.

This obsessive-compulsive-type habit became a real problem around dinnertime. Every night, once we had finished eating, I simply *had* to go and perform my ritual immediately. The problem was that my sisters and I were supposed to wash the dishes and my dad thought my rushing off to the bathroom was an attempt to get out of helping. This would cause terrible arguments, and of course it was nigh impossible to rationally explain my irrational compulsions to my dad. Thinking I wouldn't be able to go to the bathroom caused me terrible anxiety, but causing my dad to become angry made me panic too, and on many an occasion an argument would lead to yet more smacking. It was a real catch-22 situation I just couldn't get out of.

When you're in the middle of something bad and your emotions are all over the place, it isn't that easy to know why you're drawn to certain patterns of behaviour. *You just are.*

At the same time, I became very preoccupied with death and wrote tons of very dark, brooding poetry that, to this day, is still quite painful for me to read. Some of those poems must have been quite good, though, because I remember sending them off to Alan Freeman at BBC Radio One and to my complete surprise hearing him read one out on air. I'll never forget the moment I heard him say, 'Well, I usually read three poems from three poets on "Poet's Corner", but this time I'm going to give the whole time to a poem from a young lady called Trisha.'

As he began talking I was in the middle of putting on a dress, and somehow I managed to get the zip stuck and my arms trapped. I was desperate for Dad to hear, but I couldn't pick up the wireless with my hands to take to my parents' bedroom, so I put the handle between my teeth instead. It's comical really – my poem was being read on the radio while I edged along our corridor, trapped in a dress with the radio in my mouth. By the time I fell into the room shouting, 'My poems! My poems!' it was all over and Dad looked at me as though I was an idiot.

Those poems came from a miserable place, but they were a means of expressing all the anguish inside me, and probably stopped me from losing it altogether. I was deeply proud that my poem had been broadcast on the radio, and even more so when I received fan mail from listeners who said I'd captured their mood and helped them deal with their own pain.

But it would be decades before I really began to deal with my own pain.

During those years, I had a tendency to revert to going somewhere else in my head at difficult moments, particularly during fraught relationships with men, and this often caused a lot of friction between us. Nowadays the only positive thing about being able to detach myself is that it helps me to lift some pretty serious weights in the gym – I just block out the pain! Seriously, though, I'm still dealing with it all in therapy, and luckily my husband and kids know how to bring me back to myself whenever things look like they might be beginning to slip.

At the time, I never told anyone about what was going on at home. There was no such thing as ChildLine, no publicity telling kids that they should seek help if they find themselves in tricky situations, and I quickly sussed that if I told my friends about the smacking they wouldn't understand. They would talk about family arguments and getting the odd smack or two, but I suspected it wasn't the same for them. Perhaps I was wrong, but either way I kept my mouth shut for a long time.

I have often wondered what caused my father to behave how he did, and there are no easy answers. I've never tried to excuse his actions, but I've tried to understand them.

From Hero to Zero

Many years later, in my forties, I brought it all up with him, but our conversation didn't come to much. I told him that I didn't view his outbursts as physical punishment, but rather as him losing it. All Dad really said is that he regretted what he had done. I know that both Mum and Dad had big regrets, but I don't think they ever really thought about why they were dishing it out in the first place. I've got a few ideas, though.

For a start, there was a lot of stress between them at the time. I'm not sure quite what, but I sensed something was not well in their relationship. Massive, loud arguments would erupt between them. I remember once they were both really fighting. As they pulled each other around the bedroom, I got to the point where I thought I should call the police. I just didn't know what to do.

Also, I'm pretty sure that my mother's 'friendship' with one man caused tension in Mum and Dad's relationship. Patrick, as I'll call him for the purpose of this book, was an Irish guy, and my sisters and I *hated* him! He was always sniffing around when Dad wasn't there. A creepy, slimy smoothie with slicked-back hair, he just gave off a bad vibe. Even at that age, I knew that there was something weird about the amount of time Patrick spent hanging around with Mum. One Valentine's Day I saw him put a card through the door and I went mad and completely defaced it. Another time, Paula looked through the living-room window and saw Mum and Patrick chatting and laughing in a way that seemed far too intimate to our childish eyes.

The point is, something was definitely amiss between Mum and Dad, and I think that as kids we picked up lots of unspoken feelings from them about their relationship. They probably thought we wouldn't notice that things were bad between them, but we did. Kids are so good at picking up vibes, but they can misinterpret them and end up feeling bad for the wrong reasons. That's why I always let my kids know what's going on, be it good or bad.

Instead of being open with each other, or with us, I guess Mum and Dad did the easier thing and unwittingly took their problems out on their children. Sure, we were coming up to our pre-teens and were a bit of a handful, but there's smacking and there's *smacking*, and what we found ourselves on the end of was out of all proportion to anything we might have done wrong. All I know is there was a lot of shit going down between them, and as often as not we faced a beating from Dad when things went wrong. We bore the brunt of their unhappiness.

People pass on what they know in life, and I know that my mother suffered at the hands of the nuns who brought her up in the West Indies. You learn how to – or how not to – bring up your own kids from the way you are raised. It wasn't that my parents were rubbing their hands with glee, thinking, Let's fuck our kids up. It was just a combination of bad elements that led to what happened. At the time, they probably didn't know any better.

From conversations I've had with them in later life, I don't doubt that Mum and Dad wish they could have turned back the clock, but what happened *still happened* and, whether they regret their actions or not, it's hard to undo damage once it has been done. I was very angry with both of them for a long time, especially with my father. But through therapy I learned that being angry doesn't help you, that there are two sides to every coin, and that shit happens and not everyone knows how to deal with it. Mum and Dad struggled and, if anything, had too many kids to deal with. Kids don't come with a manual, and in some ways they fucked up, there's no doubt about that. But in other ways they were good parents.

My experience of being 'smacked' has made me vehemently against smacking to the point that, if I witness it in the street, I'm compelled to do something about it. One day, during my time in Australia, I saw a little boy suffering in a shopping centre because he kept asking his mother if he could go to the toilet and his mother repeatedly refused to let him. She kept saying that, when she had asked him earlier if he needed to go, he had said no. The kid had changed his mind, as four-year-olds tend to, but his pleas didn't wash with his mother.

'Too late. You should have gone before!' she kept shouting as she marched through the car park.

But he kept asking until suddenly the mother wheeled around, pulled back her fist and punched her angelic little boy hard in the face. I'll never forget the horrible sound as his head snapped back against a lamppost. It made me feel physically sick.

I just stopped in my tracks. The thing that really got me was that the child didn't even run away – to him, this was clearly the norm.

Stop it! Stop it! Stop it! I was thinking, and before I knew it I was screaming the words. '*Stop it! Stop it!*'

The woman turned and paced towards me, coming right up until her face was within an inch of mine. 'What do *you* want?' she hissed.

I went to speak, but instead I burst out crying. I very rarely cry, but the memories that had been brought back by what I had just witnessed overwhelmed me. After a few moments, I managed to speak through my tears. 'I just feel so sorry for you,' I sobbed. 'Jesus Christ, if this is what you're doing to this child in public, what the fuck do you do to him at home? *Who* are you? *What* are you? Why don't you just look at yourself?'

Because I had responded with tears and pity, rather than aggressive words, it completely threw her. She stood there, struck dumb, and then walked off. Whether it changed anything for the little boy, I don't know, but the incident upset me so much that I went home and wrote it out as an open letter to the woman. I faxed it to the *Sydney Morning Herald*, one of the biggest Australian newspapers. They printed it as an article, and many people responded warmly. I felt like I had at least protested in some way, perhaps made some kind of difference.

Years later, at a mental-health conference in America, a woman approached me and congratulated me on my anti-smacking article. 'I read it while studying social work,' she said.

'I think you must have the wrong person,' I replied. 'I don't know what you're talking about.'

It turned out she didn't have the wrong person after all. What had happened was that the *Sydney Morning Herald* had gone online and the anti-smacking campaign had picked up on my letter and incorporated it into their social-work course. I was surprised and very flattered. Apparently, it's still there! It makes me glad to think something good may have come from that moment of confrontation.

From Hero to Zero

Believe it or not, I hate confrontation. Conflict scares the shit out of me, which may sound weird considering the show I've ended up doing. All those raised voices from my childhood made me anxious then, and raised voices still make me panic. That panic is something I have to fight. Whether it be in a supermarket or on my show, a raised voice makes me want to either run away or put an end to the conflict. My experience of conflict definitely led me towards where I am now. I studied conflict resolution and I'm able to identify what is going on from personal experience. It's this that gives me the skills needed to help others on my show.

Often on my show, someone will tell me at length how they were smacked and it didn't do them any harm. Then they will talk for another ten minutes and most of the time it wouldn't take anyone with even the remotest awareness of psychology to work out that being smacked certainly *did* do them harm. In my view, when it's not about a few taps on the leg for a misdemeanour, but rather about a parent losing their temper with a child and reacting in the way they would with an adult aggressor, there's no way smacking isn't harmful. The messages such behaviour sends to a child cause damage that can last a lifetime. None of us should stand by and watch it happen.

Being hurt and criticised for years didn't make me feel good about myself. I usually felt I wasn't good enough, hadn't achieved enough or simply *was not enough*, and in turn I became someone who finds it easy to be critical of others, someone who's at risk of passing their shit on to their own kids. I've fought this with all my might, and I don't care if I'm in therapy till the day I die if that's what it takes to make sure I never, ever make my children feel how I was made to feel.

At one time, my father was the man I waited for at the window until he arrived home at night. By the age of 14, I was at the point where I didn't want to come home because of the man waiting for me when I got there.

But it wasn't all bad. I may have been an anxious, under-confident girl, I may have dreaded the smacking and the arguing, and I may have developed some strange ways of coping, but it wasn't all bad. There was always a haven from that misery.

And that haven lay in the world outside of our house.

5

Teenage Kicks

'You are the top five per cent of Britain's brightest women,' Miss Sames announced, 'and the fact that you are here means you will be the ruling cream of tomorrow. For years women have been oppressed, but you girls will move society on, armed with the knowledge you will gain from this school. You are the elite, and don't forget it.'

Grand words, for sure. But Miss Sames, headmistress of Sir William Perkins's School, in Chertsey, was a grand lady. She looked a little like the character actor Alastair Sim in drag and, whether or not what she told us was true, as I listened to her deep, booming voice in assembly each morning, she had me convinced she was right.

Having finished at St Ann's Heath, passing my 11-plus well enough to get into 'Willie Perks', as we called it, I found myself once again thrust into a very new world. It was a girls' grammar school and we had a uniform for summer, a uniform for winter and had to keep our hats on at all times. Many of my fellow pupils were very well to do, whereas I was used to calling lunch 'dinner' and hadn't a clue what 'supper' was. I became very posh very quickly!

I was nervous when I started, yet proud to be there, and Miss Sames took me under her wing right away, probably more worried than I was that, as one of the only dark-skinned pupils in the school's centuries-old history, I wouldn't fit in. We'd sit in her study on many occasions and, once she had prepared me some hot chocolate, she would settle down and say, 'Now, dear, what shall we talk about today? Politics, perhaps?'

I would sit there at 12 years old and blink at her with eyes like saucers, ready to absorb whatever it was Miss Sames had to tell me.

I felt like a lucky girl.

The education I received was amazing, and I found studying a wonderful escape from the turmoil of home life. The teachers really cared about bringing their subjects to life and were passionate about finding pupils' strengths and developing them. I will never forget Alison Millard, the English teacher who encouraged me with my writing. I can safely say that she was the first person who gave me unequivocal evidence that she believed in me as a person. I can't tell you how much that meant to me at the time. Sure, my mum was delighted that her 'black ambassador' was attending such an 'OK, yah' school, but to have a teacher really make me believe in myself was something else.

Along with all the other things I took away from Willie Perks, the most important one was that degree of self-confidence. And, boy, did I need it at the time. Learning to believe in myself is something that has carried me through the rest of my life. It's allowed me to walk into many a situation and appear confident, even if some of the time I've felt out of my depth. Although, when I've hit rock bottom, I seem to have forgotten those lessons telling me that I can bounce back, that I'm worth it.

Ever the leftie, Dad didn't seem to share Mum's enthusiasm for my being at such a school. The world of Willie Perks wasn't really his, and I thought he related more to the comprehensive system that my other sisters were part of. He always seemed anti-establishment, seeing the working man as just as important as the educated, and it was as though he believed that Willie Perks was going to turn me into a snob. To be honest, he was right. We were brainwashed into believing we were a cut above the rest – a belief I would later realise was very misguided – but, on the other hand, we did get a great education and a lot of self-belief from it.

Looking back, it's funny to think what a snobby little cow I was at the time. I can't help laughing when I remember trying to get Dad to park his rather cheap car round the corner on speech days because I was ashamed of it, or the times when my cheeks would burn during school plays as Mum shouted, 'Oh, Tootsie!' when I would appear on stage. Then she would laugh so loudly at the jokes that the audience would laugh at her laugh. It's terrible to be embarrassed of your parents, but most teenagers are at some point and I was no exception. Poor Mum, her unbridled enthusiasm was touching, really, but I was too much of a dreadful snob to realise it at the time.

Dad would get me back for my snootiness, though. He once walked through the school grounds and raised a leg to let out a fart because he knew my posh friends were about. He knew just how to make me squirm. Fair play to him for that. I think it was hilarious, but only now, mind you! These days I go out of my way to embarrass the crap out of my daughters. It does kids good, I say.

I threw myself into learning and did well. Whenever I succeeded, I saw an opportunity to tell my parents about it. You never know, I would think, they might be pleased. And Mum always was. There was no bigger cheerleader when I told her of my achievements, but Dad seemed at best indifferent to my success. Most of the time he'd shrug me off with something like, 'Oh, you're always talking about yourself,' and that would be it. If I was talking about myself, it was because I wanted some recognition. All I wanted was the occasional 'Well done' and I still don't understand why he could never give it to me. I can't remember any praise from him – only criticism. Why did it have to be that way? Perhaps I'll never know.

My years there were magic, and I made some great friends. Two of my best buddies were Sue and Evelyn. Sue was blonde, infuriatingly daffy, and great at Art and Welsh. Evelyn was a self-assured, dark-haired Scot, and fiercely intelligent to boot. The three of us went everywhere and discovered everything together. Each Monday morning we'd begin chatting in assembly by changing the words to hymns we were supposed to be singing. Instead of 'All Things Bright and Beautiful', we'd be singing something like 'Did you get off with that Steve?/Yes, I bloody did!' to one another, and on it went from there.

Teenage Kicks

We always had fun, and took to smoking the odd stolen cocktail cigarette behind the bike sheds (not that we inhaled, we just thought it was a bit cool) and reading the naughty bits from Ian Fleming books out loud. For 14-year-olds, it was all very innocent behaviour, and though we were interested in boys we weren't really keen on much more than holding hands and the odd snog. At that point holding hands with someone meant you were going out, or even in love!

When I was around 14, Mum was always going on about boys and sex, warning me about this and that. The funny thing was that the thises and thats she was talking about were the furthest thing from my mind, and quite obscene, I thought. 'Sex isn't a bed of roses, you know,' Mum would say. 'You can't just lie down with a man.' And I'd be thinking, Whoa, what are you going on about? Who said anything about *sex*? All I wanted to do was look cool by having a boyfriend and be seen with him and my trendy clothes.

Anyhow, the first boys I dated were as sweet and frighteningly innocent as I was in those days. First there was Bob Taylor, the local GP's son. Very lanky and thin, with blond curls, he was part of a large group of friends that hung around together. He was more of a friend than anything. At that age, if a boy fancied me I was quite flattered and I would sort of reciprocate it, and that's how Bob and I got together. We would hang out, hold hands on the way home, but, when we eventually got to snogging, that killed the dream for me. Kissing Bob was like kissing a cocker spaniel. Not, I might add, that I've ever kissed a cocker spaniel. I was probably no great shakes myself when it came to the art of the kiss, but basically I got covered in slobber when Bob and I had a go at it. It was more like a competition to see how much saliva one person could get over the other's face.

Bob was a beautiful soul, though, and, if he wasn't the best kisser in the world, he certainly had the ability to get me thinking about more spiritual matters. One evening, when I was about 14, we were walking past the Holloway Sanatorium, where Dad worked, wanting to know what time it was to make sure we wouldn't miss the last bus. I spotted an old man by a bus shelter on the other side of the road and decided to go and ask him for the time. Before crossing the road, I turned to tell Bob.

'Which old man?' he said.

I turned back to point him out, but couldn't see him. Assuming he had gone into the bus shelter, I took Bob by the hand and we crossed the road. I peered into the shelter. Nothing.

I looked both ways along the walls of the sanatorium that flanked the road. Nothing.

Nothing as far as the eye could see. There was nowhere that he could have gone. A shiver went right through me.

'Which old man?' Bob asked again.

'The old man I saw, here. There was an old man here, I swear to God, Bob. *Right here.*' I was freaking out. I'd heard all the ghost stories about the Holloway Sanatorium. 'He must be here *somewhere*,' I repeated over and over as I clung to Bob's coat.

Bob held me to him and managed to calm me a little. He didn't try to dismiss what I had seen. He didn't question my experience. And he didn't condescend. He simply talked and, for a 14-year-old, what he said was pretty good.

'There are things beyond what we know,' he said quietly, reassuringly.

'I know,' I joked, by now a little calmer, 'I watch *Star Trek*!'

But Bob was serious, and we ended up talking about the limits of human knowledge, and the fact that we think we know the truth about things but that there's a good chance we could be very wrong about many of them.

He once picked a flower, held it to me and said, 'Are we humans so egotistical and vain that we think we could ever have anything to do with the creation of something like this? There is something bigger than us and it has created this over hundreds of thousands of years.'

It was a very 'teenage' conversation, but it certainly sparked an interest in me. There was no faith in our family, and spiritual stuff hadn't played much of a part in my life until then, but Bob got me thinking about it all.

Another event that convinced me things may not be what they seem was the time when my sister Linda came down for breakfast one day and asked Mum why she had let the babysitter into her bedroom.

'What are you talking about?' Mum replied. 'What babysitter?'

'The babysitter who came into my bedroom, sat on my bed and woke me up!'

'Don't be silly, you must have been dreaming.'

But Linda insisted this was no dream. She described exactly what the babysitter was wearing, including a hat, and wouldn't let the matter go until she was told to drop it. We soon forgot all about it.

A few months later, when Dad was giving us a tour of

the spooky, abandoned old tunnels that ran underneath the sanatorium, we walked into one of the storage rooms that came off one of the tunnels. It was all a bit scary but we loved it and were soon having a good old rummage around in the storage boxes. Some of them contained bits and pieces going back centuries. Suddenly we came across records relating to the hospital staff's accommodation and set about looking for anything in them to do with our house. We found the file for 387 Stroude Road and in it was a clutch of dusty old photos. As we flicked through them, Linda reached out and grabbed a photo of a girl. 'That's the babysitter, the one Mum let sit on my bed,' she said matter-of-factly.

There, in Linda's hand, was a photo of a girl in a hat, exactly as Linda had described her that morning months ago. We all freaked, but still carried on looking through the file to try to find out more about the girl. And what we discovered only made us freak some more. At the age of 19, the girl in the hat had hanged herself in our house, probably *in Linda's room*. It was all a bit much and we reacted by screaming, 'Aaaaaarrrgghhh!' quite loudly. To his credit, Dad was a little more composed, but he didn't need much convincing that we'd had enough for the day.

The old man and the girl in the hat made me ripe for a 'there's something out there' chat. This, along with what I'd picked up in Sunday school over the years, made me interested in joining a religious group at school. It was an interest that was to last about a nanosecond. It was a very happy-clappy affair and, although I wasn't hip or ultra-cool, I soon discovered I wasn't prepared to spend my break times listening to the goody-goodies playing guitar and singing 'Jesus Wants Me for a Sunbeam'. The girls who ran the Christian group were into Cliff Richard, who I thought was a bit of a dork, and it wasn't long before I was back listening to Deep Purple with my mates. But my early experiences led to a lifelong interest in the world's faiths, spirituality and what might be.

At 14, I began getting into music in a big way. Our group of friends were forever going to gigs, sipping lager and blackcurrant and being very cheap drunks. While I was with Bob, I saw lots of bands at the Royal Holloway College. The Average White Band, Ian Dury and the Blockheads, Blackfoot Sue, Kilburn and the High Roads, Steeleye Span, Steely Dan – it was amazing the array of acts we got to listen to before they became huge. We even saw Status Quo there. The Quo were at their height then, and I loved them. Years later I got to meet Francis Rossi, their lead guitarist and vocalist. He was a guest on my show and beforehand I bounced into his dressing room blurting, 'Oh my God, I saw you at the Royal Holloway College when I was about 14.' I raved on but soon feared he was taking my enthusiasm for the past as some sort of come-on in the present. Oops!

'We must hook up after the show,' he said.

'Oh no-no-no, sweetie darling,' I joked lightly. 'Can't do kissing, sweetie, not with my make-up, not before the show...' And with that I made a swift exit, believe me!

After Bob and a few other boys, my first real 'heart-throb' boyfriend was Steve Lillywhite. Before he went on to become a hugely influential music producer, Steve was once just a teenager taking Trisha Goddard to see 10cc.

He had chubby cheeks and wore platform shoes, and we were both passionate, fiery characters who did a lot of dreaming together, often talking about how we might make it big, I as a journalist, he in music.

I don't remember anything about the 10cc gig because all we did was lie on the floor and snog. Steve was no cocker spaniel and we snogged and groped away as if life depended on it. That was all very well, but when I finally came up for air I realised that my handbag was missing. What's more, it had a week's wages from my part-time jobs in it, and life *did* depend on my earnings, because Mum and Dad didn't believe in pocket money. I wasn't a happy bunny.

Steve and I carried on seeing each other for a while, but eventually it just fizzled out. The two of us still laugh about the handbag incident to this day.

Some of the money I'd had in that bag was earned at one of our local pubs, the Wheatsheaf, in Virginia Water. I hated working there, cleaning the huge pots and pans in the kitchen. More of a laugh was the social life it afforded me and the school cruise it meant I could go on – Mum and Dad couldn't afford to help me out there. As far as I was concerned, money equalled freedom, and I have never let go of that belief.

Our clique was great fun. Boys came and went, and we got up to all sorts of fairly innocent mischief. I remember trying my first joint while listening to 'Silver Machine' by Hawkwind. I was probably going along with it so as not to look uncool, but didn't have a clue what to expect. At first nothing seemed to be happening, and then suddenly it hit me. I was stoned! I didn't exactly fall in love with

Above left: My mum, Agnes, who came over to England from Dominica. The British climate came as a bit of a shock to her – especially as she'd only brought a cardigan, not a coat!

Above and middle right: After the flat in Hackney, we moved to a caravan in Kent. The sister with a finger in her mouth is Pru and the baby in the pram is Paula.

Below left: This was taken in Norfolk shortly before we went to East Africa. *Front row, from left to right*: My cousin Amanda with her mum, my dear, late Aunty Mary; me (biting my nails as I still do!); Pru; Mum and Paula. *Back row, left to right*: My much-loved cousin, Trevor, who is now a gifted musician; my dad and his mum, my Nanna.

Below right: My parents in 1955, training to be nurses.

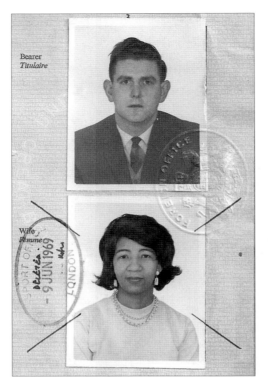

Above left: Bye bye, Brentwood – hello, East Africa. Mum and Dad's joint passport.

Above right: (*From left to right*) Paula, Pru, me and Saucy the sausage dog.

Below: Dodoma days … when I look back at family photos, I notice that I'm often standing apart from the group, and that I look darker than my three sisters.

Inset: Back then, Dad was my hero. Here, we are camping near Lake Tanganyika in the Rift Valley, East Africa.

Returning to England was a shock to the system after the freedom and adventure we'd enjoyed in Africa.

Above: I absolutely loved my time at St Ann's Heath School in Virginia Water, Surrey.

Below left: With my darling sister Linda, otherwise known as Winnie who, tragically, years later, was to take her own life.

Below right: Grammar school girl! I became posh very quickly …

Above left: Posh girls being hip! Me with the band, Eve. (*From left to right*): Maureen, Mary, me, Annie and Sue.

Above right: With Bev – we had an on/off relationship which became history when I went off in search of new adventures.

Below: Great times – the entourage in Germany in 1975. *Back row, left to right*: Me, Bev, Mike and Geoff. *Front row, left to right*: Mary, Patrick (hidden), Annie, Maureen, Sue and Monty.

Inset: My pass into the army base where we were playing.

Above left: With Nigel – our relationship was good fun at first …

Above right: Trisha Goddard, reporting for duty on the high seas. I soon found out I didn't have sea legs and was given a job based on dry land!

Below: With the girls from the hovercraft – we were a close gang and we certainly knew how to let our hair down.

Above: Tea or coffee, sir? Being a stewardess on Gulf Air gave me the crowd control training needed for my show in later life.

Below left: In the jump seat. At this point I was an 'A' grade senior stewardess in charge of the economy cabin crew.

Below right: The Gulf Air flats, which looked a bit like upmarket university halls of residence!

On one of my earliest trips to Hong Kong in my Gulf Air days. Back then, I was on the airline's 'fatties list'. We were weighed regularly, given diet sheets and warned to lose weight or face the possibility of losing our jobs.

marijuana, but I did enjoy it for many years from the age of about 15. At that stage it was very much a case of take it or leave it – if it was around, fine, if not, so what? I really enjoyed it, not as a means of coping with anything, but just because I thought it was great. I liked it more than booze, especially because there were no hangovers, but no one ever asked me to roll a joint because in all the years I smoked dope I never learned to roll a good spliff.

Outside of the house, life was pretty wonderful on the surface. School was great, and during school holidays I was hardly ever at home. I was an angsty girl, for sure, and I had my demons to deal with, but luckily I also had friends, boys who seemed to fancy me and lots of interests to distract me. I was writing passionately, getting into making films on my cine camera – I still have my letter of commendation from the BBC's 1972 'Search' Young Film Director of the Year Award – and had just joined a band. In many ways, things were looking up.

Then, days before my fifteenth birthday, I went to a party.

Mum had a West Indian friend called Edith who lived in Perivale, west London. She was having a Christmas party. The whole family were expected, but I said I would not go unless my friend Evelyn could come too. Evelyn was allowed to come, so I got in the car and off we drove.

Arriving at the party was weird. There were so many West Indians, mistletoe everywhere and loud West Indian music. I was used to being the only dark person around and it was a culture shock as I'd never seen so many West Indians in one room before. For me it was all a bit of a freak-out – I didn't get the food and didn't like the music.

Trisha – *As I Am*

I had made quite an effort getting dressed up. I had put on make-up and was wearing a long orange midi coat, a black smock top, black trousers and platforms – I always wore platforms in those days. Evelyn looked great too.

We felt grown-up. And we must have looked it too, because all these West Indian guys kept trying to grab us for a dance or a kiss under the mistletoe. I was shocked that men I didn't even know were acting that way, and Evelyn and I weren't having any of it. We looked good, but thought it was a shame about the party. It wasn't long before Evelyn said she wanted to nip out for a fag. We left the house and walked up the road to make sure nobody caught us smoking (in those days I didn't even inhale!).

A double-decker bus stopped near us and two lads got off. They had long hair – Led Zeppelin types – one blond and one dark, both good-looking. They walked towards us.

'Ooh, I like yours,' joked Evelyn, looking at the blond one.

I giggled. We got up beside them.

'Hello, darlin',' said the blond, grabbing Evelyn's arm.

'Get off,' she said, kicking out at him.

'Just saying hello, darlin'. Gotta light?'

Evelyn relaxed a little, gave him a light and began walking with the dark one, chatting away.

The blond began walking next to me, and that's when my nightmare began...

6

Attack

'What are you doing,' I said as he pushed me from the pavement into an alley. 'Get off.'

It was dark and this man was scaring me.

'Come on, give us a snog then,' he said, holding me so hard that I couldn't move.

'No! Stop it. Let go!'

'Come on, darlin', just a quick snog, it's OK.'

But it wasn't OK. I didn't want a quick snog, and I didn't want to be held against a wall. All I wanted was to get back to the pavement, which was only a couple of feet away. It might as well have been a mile – I couldn't move.

'Don't be silly, just a snog...' he said, smiling.

I struggled and protested, saying no very firmly. Half-laughing, half-scared, I let him know there would be no snog.

Then, in the blink of an eye, his face changed completely.

'Listen,' he hissed, 'don't fuck about.'

Suddenly I knew he was serious. *The situation was serious.* I was in danger, and I thought the only way to get out of it was to let him have what he wanted. So I let him kiss me.

But it isn't nearly enough for him.

Within seconds the groping begins, and I begin to scream, trying to fight his hands away from where I don't want them to be. 'Get off, get off,' I yell, but this just makes him get even nastier. I'm up against the fence and he's pushing me hard, holding me, trying to prise my legs apart, tearing at my clothes and saying, 'Come on. Come on, *Janie*!' His voice is calm, scarily calm, and flat.

Janie. Who the fuck is *Janie*?

'I'm not Janie,' I shout, as he tries to hold my knees apart with his leg. 'I'm not Janie!'

But what I'm saying makes no difference. He gets his arm across my throat. *Jesus, this is serious, what the fuck's he going to do? He's choking me. This man is going to do something awful...*

I kick him and the arm comes away for a few seconds, long enough for me to scream louder than I've ever screamed before.

'Help me, help me, *help me!*'

Nobody hears, there's nobody to help. I am alone.

'Come on, Janie, don't be fucking silly. *Come on*, Janie.'

Already I'm tired. I don't know what to do. I'm at the mercy of a maniac. Then there's a noise, a bang, and he loosens his grip on me for a moment, but still holds on to my coat. *Two couples have come out into their back gardens. They must have heard me!*

Attack

'Help me!' I scream.

They do nothing but stare uncertainly at me and the maniac.

'Come on, Janie,' he says. 'Don't be silly.'

One couple carry on staring for a second or two, then turn around and walk towards their back door. As they open it, I see their television and recognise the sound of Val Doonican singing a carol for some Christmas special. They've left me, I think. *They've just gone and fucking left me!*

Before he has a full grip on me again, I struggle free and run. Boy, do I run. I didn't know I could run this fast, didn't know *anyone* could run this fast. But I'm running blind down an alley behind gardens in a place I don't know. *Where am I going?* I get to a corner, stop for a second and then he's on me before I have time to blink.

He's got me up against a wall again. I'm gasping for breath and he's ripping at my top so he can get at me. I've given up on words, now I'm simply screaming.

Suddenly there's another voice.

'What's going on here then?' it says.

The maniac stops to look. There's an old man at the end of the alley, staring at us.

'Oh, Janie,' the maniac says loudly, light-heartedly, 'look what you've gone and done. You've got this old man to come out. Why don't you stop being silly?'

The old man keeps on staring. *This is my chance.*

'I'm not Janie,' I shout desperately. 'I'm not Janie! My name is Patricia Goddard and I live at 387 Stroude Road, Virginia Water. My name's not Janie...!'

All the while the maniac is saying, 'Come on, Janie.'

But his words don't fool the old man. 'You let go of her,' he begins to shout. 'You let go of her, you bastard.'

The maniac lets go, rushes up to the man and knocks him down with a vicious punch, and I begin to run again. This time I find myself running out of the alley into the street.

I run and I run. My top's all torn, my trouser zip's ripped, my arm hurts badly, but I run through the pain, on and on, never looking back, not knowing where the hell I am. All I'm looking for is a house with a light on. All I want is anyone else, anyone apart from this nasty bastard who is somewhere behind me.

Suddenly I find what I'm so desperate for – the house I run towards is bright with electric light. It's the promised land. Thank God, I think, as I see the light.

As soon as I feel I'm safe, only seconds from the house, I trip over. I fall to the ground, winding myself as I tumble. Before I have a chance to get up, the blond is there to yank me up from the pavement and drag me back into a nightmare I thought I had escaped.

We're down yet another alleyway. Now I'm really lost.

'Right, no messing around now,' he hisses. He's angry, he wants to get his way and he's unbuttoning his trousers, saying, 'Touch me, touch *it*!'

'No,' I repeat over and over as I look up at the stars. I begin to remove myself, going to another place in my head, and I start to pray as I feel him pull my hand towards him. 'Our Father, Who art in Heaven,' I say out loud, shaking feverishly as I feel the disgusting hardness of his penis start to rub against me.

'Shut up and touch me,' he hisses, thrusting *it* towards me.

Attack

I don't have any idea what I'm supposed to do to make him happy, to make him stop. *I've never touched a penis before.*

As he tries to get me to touch him, he begins to touch me. He gropes my breasts – nobody has touched my breasts like this before – and it hurts. He pulls my pants aside and shoves his fingers inside me roughly. It feels so wrong, *it hurts so much.*

'Dear Lord, I am in your hands,' I say, praying as hard as I can, filled with a sudden, desperate faith.

He's getting nastier, telling me to shut up and calling me names, and keeps pushing, trying to get my hand on to his repulsive thing. But I keep resisting, keep praying.

And then he stops.

Is it over? Has God answered my prayers?

'I didn't think I'd have to do this,' he says, reaching into his pocket, 'but you've asked for it.' And as he takes his hand from his pocket I see what he is holding.

He has a knife. There is a knife in his hands. I'm going to die. Oh, God, don't let him kill me, please.

He starts to bring the knife to my face, and begins to speak. But as he does so I hear someone else begin to shout.

'Pat... Pat... *Paaat!*'

It's Evelyn. Evelyn is calling me, and I'm screaming back to her.

'*Evelyn!*' I shout. 'Evelyn, help me, help me, I'm over here.'

And Evelyn appears, running towards me, running to save her friend. With her is the dark guy, who runs up shouting, 'Leave her alone, mate, leave her alone, let go of her *now.*'

He tells Evelyn to run for help, which she does, and we need help because the maniac seems to be pointing the knife at the dark guy. 'Piss off, Paul,' he threatens. 'I don't want to have to go for you too. Just fuck off and leave us alone!'

But Paul doesn't move a muscle. He stands his ground and keeps telling the maniac to let go. But he won't.

All of a sudden there is a great commotion. It must be the help that Evelyn went for. It's the sound of men. They rush towards us, several men from a party around the corner, and they mean business. But before they get to us the maniac panics and runs. He runs in the way that I had been running only minutes ago. *He is gone*, I realise, *he is gone and he is never coming back*. And then I am crumpling into Evelyn's arms, shocked and breathless.

I was an absolute mess. My trousers were ripped open, the top of my smock ripped away and my bra torn apart at the back.

'I'll look after her,' Evelyn assured the men who were standing around us, and, as they went back to their party, Evelyn and Paul helped me to my feet. I was wide-eyed and in shock, my breathing fast and shallow, and the tears just kept coming. The shock of it was almost too much, but I knew I was safe as we walked slowly back to the road and the party, where my parents and sisters were still dancing away.

It turned out that Paul, the dark guy, had only met my attacker on the bus. They weren't mates and only knew each other vaguely, but had struck up a conversation as the blond had just got out of prison and was keen to talk about it. Presumably he wasn't too worried about going back, judging by the terrible things he'd just done to me. I felt I'd somehow invited the attack or deserved it. Paul felt terrible, but Evelyn thanked him, said goodbye and we returned to the party.

We sat upstairs, where everyone had left their coats, and stayed put for the rest of the evening. I smoked and inhaled for the first time – hardly surprising considering what had just happened. As I smoked, I just sat and shivered, silently, numbly, until it was eventually time to leave.

I never told Mum and Dad. My first sexual experience had been at the hands of a monster, but I didn't want to tell anyone. Or, if I wanted to tell someone, I didn't know who. I was devastated, hurt, confused and somehow thought what had happened was my fault. My thinking was that I had been stupid enough to walk out of the party in an unfamiliar place, that maybe my little bit of eyeliner and clothes made me look too 'tarty' for my age. I thought that I had invited it – I felt guilty for having fancied the guy at first sight. (I'll never get Evelyn's 'Ooh, I like yours' joke out of my head. To think that I'd actually liked the look of that monster makes me sick.) I thought I'd asked for it because I let him kiss me to get it over with. *Why had I been so stupid?*

It was 1972. Phone helplines didn't yet exist and I didn't know how to report a sexual assault. Even if I had, the shame of it all would probably have stopped me. Things were different in those days, and people were much more ready to blame a woman when assaults took place. Things are different now, thank God, but there's still a lot of work to be done to reinforce the fact that a woman always has the right to say no, and that being assaulted is *never* a woman's fault. I have drummed this into my girls, and they know exactly what to do should they ever end up in a bad situation. They also know that they can tell me anything and I will never judge them.

But my experience became a dirty secret that played itself out in my dreams again and again for a very long time.

What happened affected me badly. For about a year afterwards, I tried to control how I felt by controlling what I ate. According to my diary, I positively tried *not* to eat, and I have no doubt this was linked partly to the trauma of that night and partly to my unhappiness at home. Understandably, I also became wary of men and sex. I wasn't mistrustful of the boys in our Virginia Water clique, but from then on I looked at the other men in the world differently.

In my young mind, the attack set up an association between violence and sex. I felt that sex was something that men do to women whether women want it or not. Women might not always feel good about it, but men do what they want. That was my 'version' of sex. I saw women as voiceless when it came to sex. Choice was not a part of it. In addition to this, I also thought men could hit you when they wanted without your having to understand why.

I was angry for a long time, and it took several relationships before I was at ease with sex. I was able to have sex, but not able to see it as much more than a man doing something to a woman. It was for the pleasure of the man. Sex and love didn't really go together in my mind for a long while.

Attack

A year after that night I lost my virginity, on my sixteenth birthday. There was no violence, there were no threats and I didn't say no. But I felt very little about it, except that I was cheap and it was a let-down, and I can't help but think that my experience of discovering sex could have been very different had that terrible man not interfered so callously, so inhumanely, with my innocence.

Being attacked is not something I would wish on anyone, but, amid all the negative emotions that came out of that event, there was a positive.

I was wiser to the world and the potential for bad things to happen. It made me more cynical, more wary and more determined than ever to look after myself. From then on, I resolved not to take any shit from anyone.

And 'anyone' now included my father.

Life at home was business as usual, which meant Dad was still up for 'smacking' us whenever he felt like it. But, after the incident at the party, his bursts of aggression took on a whole new meaning for me. Just the thought of him hitting me made me start to panic.

I was 15 and he was still hitting me occasionally. I didn't know how much longer I could take it.

One day I could tell it was about to begin. Dad was shouting, his voice full of menace and anger, and his face took on that cold look that made me feel I was nothing to him. I moved towards the corner I always went to. I was caught, as usual, and I thought I knew what was coming.

Then, before he snapped, something snapped in me.

I stood in that corner and turned to face him in all his fury. 'Go on, hit me,' I challenged him, filled with anger and exasperation. 'Fucking hit me, Dad, go on!' I screamed, the adrenalin coursing through my veins. *'Fucking do it!'*

He stopped in his tracks. Suddenly the man who had been hitting us for years was standing before me, frozen to the spot, speechless. I'd tried tears, curling up and going limp before, but it only made him hit me more. Now I was telling him to hit me, he couldn't. I was as stunned as he was.

And do you know what happened? Nothing.

Dad stood there, staring, unmoving, and then turned on his heel and walked away from me! I don't know what emotion my outburst must have provoked in Dad, or what sudden realisation he might have had, and I never asked him. But I do know that he never hit me again.

A door in my heart started closing. The smacking was finished, and so was something else. I could no longer emotionally trust my father at all. One moment he could have me laughing at his John Cleese-like, boyish antics and the next I'd look into those once warm eyes and see a look of cold anger that hardly seemed to recognise me. He no longer got physical, but any sense of emotional safety my father had ever given me was now gone for ever.

7

School of Life

The smacking was over, but it didn't mean I wanted to start spending more time at home. I had better things to do. It was 1973, and Evelyn, Sue and I had just got Saturday jobs at Woolworths.

Aside from extra money and lots of free sweets (plus a few aching teeth), Woolworths provided us with a new friend, Maureen. And what made Maureen cool was that she was in a band. Even better, she wanted me to join it, and she asked one day if I would be interested in playing keyboards.

Was I interested? Hell, yeah. I'd played the piano since I was five! Off we went on the bus to Slough and the rest is history. Not quite musical history, but Trisha history nonetheless.

We called ourselves Eve. It wasn't the hippest band in the world – we played covers, and only a few originals –

but I absolutely loved it. There was Maureen singing and playing guitar, my best friend Sue on drums, Mary on bass and me on keyboards – four posh girls having a go at being hip, and a big fat manager called Geoff, who was married to Mary and quite a lot older than us. Geoff was a salesman by day and thought he was a Simon Cowell type by night. To be fair, he was good at selling the band, especially because at first there wasn't much to sell – we were abominable.

But we worked hard. I always gave my all to everything, and the band was no exception. If the band was a turd to begin with, we certainly managed to polish it! Soon enough we were gigging virtually every Friday and Saturday night, mainly in pubs and working men's clubs. We slogged our guts out rehearsing and performing, but it was enormous fun.

I'll never forget seeing Queen before they became international rock gods. I got chatting to Brian May about equipment and what he thought about the venue. Freddie Mercury was in the background, and pretty shy, so I didn't get to meet him. It was just so casual talking to Brian, and whenever I see him on TV now I just think, Cor, I met him!

It wasn't long before we started earning decent money, and I'll never forget the time I saw one of my dad's payslips and realised I'd earned as much as he had in the same two-week period. It was a great feeling for a 16-year-old. It gave me a sense of freedom I'd never felt before, and marked the beginning of a transitional period in my life. I was still doing well at school, and passed my O-levels with flying colours, but home life was becoming increasingly unbearable. Also, I'd started sixth-form at Willie Perks and it just wasn't as enjoyable as the lower forms had been. We were suddenly treated as adults, with no uniform and less educational structure, which completely threw me. I found school life boring, thanks to having to concentrate solely on A-level subjects. I wasn't happy.

And then it dawned on me that there was no need to be unhappy, so I quit school.

It wasn't like I had nothing to fall back on. The band was doing well, I had money in my pocket and I wanted to have some fun. I don't really remember Mum and Dad's reaction, because at that point I don't think I cared what they thought. I just remember thinking I was destined for something other than A-levels.

I was dead keen on music, but my ambition to be involved in film still burned in me. This led to my getting a job in London as a junior at Morris Angel and Sons, one of the biggest film and theatre costumiers around. Even though I ended up spending most of my wages commuting between Virginia Water and London, I didn't care because it was so exciting to be involved in the industry, and I was completely in love with all the clothes. There were rails and rails of costumes, some a hundred years old, and it was my job to research what outfits would be appropriate for whichever film, play or show required our services. Being in the heart of London was a real buzz, too. Previously I'd only been there on theatre trips with the school, but now I had the chance to really get to know the guts of Soho and it was incredibly new and exciting to me. I felt a growing sense of independence – I was in control, a master of my own destiny.

Trisha *- As I Am*

Apart from being skint, the only problem I had was one of my bosses, a real evil dandy, who dressed a bit like Austin Powers and regularly reduced me to tears with his bitching. He was a proper queen and I was still pretty shy, but I persevered anyway and kept the band up at the same time. We rehearsed hard and were gigging regularly with our all-girl act. Then one day we received an offer to go on a tour of Europe for a good amount of money. It didn't take me long to make my mind up and throw in the towel in London. A new adventure beckoned and I was raring to go.

Touring was great, and Eve ended up doing two tours in 1975. We played US army bases in Germany and it was pretty 'rock'n'roll', I suppose. We played most nights, we boozed, we partied and we earned pretty good money for those days. We also spent it as quickly as we earned it – one day I'd be loaded and the next I'd be broke. Touring toughened me up, and dealing with my fair share of slimebags and crooks in the music world taught me to live by the law of the jungle, always going for the jugular before someone went for mine.

One of the highlights was getting to support James Brown on a Frankfurt army base. My God, that man was incredible. I remember standing at the side of the stage watching him perform, and I've never seen so much energy (and sweat!) pouring out of one man. He was dressed in a purple cape and hot pants, and didn't stop moving for a second. The drummer was pretty keen too – he was so forceful they had to chain his kit to the floor. In rehearsals he was very demanding of his band – not one mistake escaped him – and his professionalism was a real inspiration.

School of Life

Looking back, I thought I was something pretty special at the time, but there were always incidents that brought me back down to earth. It's hard to forget one particular night in Germany.

It was after a gig at a military base and I was perched on a bar stool in a black satin, plunge-to-the-waist, halter-neck number, convinced I was Miss Gorgeous. There I was, surrounded by a load of female-starved American soldiers, and lapping up their attention. I thought I was a proper class act as I sipped my cocktail, playing it nice and cool while my suitors all searched for pick-up lines. How lovely, I thought, to be surrounded by a load of hunky men hanging on to my witty, sparkling words!

The only problem was a rather insignificant and ugly-looking black guy who kept ruining my act by tapping me on the shoulder and saying, 'Pssst, sister.'

At first I ignored him graciously, but, after one tap on the shoulder too many, I lost my cool a bit and decided to send him on his way by telling him to fuck off.

At this point he lost his composure too. 'OK, sister, I'll fuck off,' he said, 'but I was only trying to tell you that your tit's hanging out!'

I looked down and, sure enough, resting on the bar was one ample brown breast. I was mortified, and thought I was about to wet myself. With all the dignity I could muster (not much), I tucked my breast back into my top and ran into the toilets while everyone laughed. So much for my class act – it hadn't been my words that had so transfixed these guys! My ego certainly took a bit of a bruising, but it didn't do me any harm. I probably needed to be brought back to reality. Needless to say, having given a whole new meaning to the phrase 'making a tit out of oneself', I didn't resume my place at the bar.

Strutting our stuff on stage around Europe was great, but eventually the cracks started to show and we began bitching ourselves to bits. Eve split up and I joined another band called Montana. This time I was the only girl. After rehearsing in Colchester for a few weeks, it was back on the road in West Germany and then Holland. But a bout of bronchial pneumonia brought on by too many fags eventually forced me back to England, where I quit smoking and also quit the band. It was time to move on again, so I did what every self-respecting middle-class dropout musician did in the 1970s – I moved to London and into a squat just off the Portobello Road.

I was 18 and had been seeing a guy called Bev for quite a while. Bev was a guitarist, originally in a band called Fizzer (another act managed by Geoff), but he left them to join us in Montana as we went around Europe. More than anything else, he was a good friend and, although he'd cheated on me and I'd cheated on him, we were still 'together' and took a room in this crazy squat, and we stayed there for what turned out to be one of the maddest, happiest periods of my life.

There couldn't have been more of a contrast between my old life in Virginia Water and where we lived in Notting Hill. Our flatmate, Tim, was an unpredictable character. One minute he'd be as nice as pie, going out of his way to help and paying compliments to people, and the next he'd be ranting and raging, screaming and calling you – his words, not mine – a 'fucking c**t'.

We were all broke and as a way of surviving we had a

hilarious time writing to food manufacturers with petty – and entirely fictional – complaints in the hope they would send us freebies. Writing a polite letter to a yoghurt producer complaining that the cherries were missing from their cherry yoghurt resulted in vouchers for more yoghurt than we could eat in a year being sent to us.

The neighbours were certainly interesting. Upstairs from our flat there were two gay guys – real queens – who were constantly arguing and bitching at each other. Furniture and other household goods would regularly come hurtling out of their windows and shatter on the street below. If you heard nothing smash on the road for a couple of days, you almost wondered if something was wrong.

There were always kids playing in the street, and we got to know them because they were lippy, confident and friendly. Oh, and they were outside most of the time because their mothers were prostitutes. As a result, the houses were out of bounds for the kids during 'office hours'. It was quite a shock the first time one of those kids said to me, 'Oh, I'd better run up and tell Mum her two o'clock customer is here,' but we just came to accept it all as normal.

The women themselves looked great, and when they came downstairs for a fag they would pat me on the head with an 'All right, darlin', did you hear those two queens having a fight?' If they noticed the cops coming down the road, they would bang on drainpipes to warn the ones upstairs, while the kids would spill on to the street to slow the coppers down.

To an 18-year-old girl who had attended a posh school and been brainwashed into an 'us and them' way of

69

thinking, squatting was a real education. I was living among characters completely out of my usual sphere – prostitutes, drug addicts, people who would fight in the street and two hours later be sharing a joke – and yet there was a real community atmosphere. I got a warmer feeling from hanging around Notting Hill than I ever got from being a jumped-up snob and looking down on others, and it was during this period that I learned what a mistake it is to judge others by who or what they are. It taught me to weigh up an individual on their merits rather than on their class or how they look, and it was a valuable lesson that prepared me for so much in later life, not least the *Trisha* show! Put simply, by the time I left Notting Hill, very little could shock me.

That period was a kind of escapism for me, and I had never been happier. Bev and I got all left-wing and community-oriented, wearing second-hand clothes, smoking dope and witnessing the dawning of the punk era. It was a sort of freedom from reality that was great while it lasted, but eventually I began to feel a little guilty about bumming around, getting pissed and watching protest marches. I'd been conditioned to achieve things and be productive, and decided it was time to get a job and move on.

Things were very on/off with Bev, and the whole situation was really doing my head in. After a couple of shop jobs and a lonely Christmas being broke in a tiny bedsit in Lewisham, south London, I eventually made Bev, and London, history. It really was time to move on. Again!

I was sitting on the number 12 bus one day when I spotted an article in the newspaper. It was about a wonderful new form of transport, the hovercraft. Part of the piece focused on the stewardesses and mentioned that British Rail's Seaspeed hovercraft service was recruiting for jobs based in Dover. Right, I thought, I'll have that!

I got off the bus, found the nearest phonebox and called up to book an interview, telling them I could speak French, which would be a real bonus in a job that involved crossing the Channel. Before I knew it I'd got the job and was driving to Dover in my first car, my tatty, beloved red Mini Countryman. I was off to sea, and couldn't wait.

8

From One Extreme to the Hover

As the hovercraft sped out of the harbour, I discovered something about myself that put me at a distinct disadvantage as regards working on a hovercraft. I was the worst sea traveller in the world. Nowadays I get called the Queen of Chat, but working on hovercraft turned me into the Queen of Sickbags. No matter whether I ate, drank, starved myself or took pills, all my efforts were in vain – every time I stepped aboard, I was as sick as a parrot. I was a joke!

The ground staff thought it was hilarious but, after three weeks of hell, luckily my bosses decided some of us should be seagoing 'purserettes' and some of us land-based. Hurrah! That's when I got a job on solid ground. It was good to have a settled stomach and, having hung up my sickbags for good, I soon settled into life in Dover. I moved into a damp little house with two other purserettes, and we bonded straight away.

Our sense of camaraderie grew when we received a porn mag in the post one morning – the previous tenant had evidently forgotten to cancel his subscription. Reading it, we discovered that a man in the local area had advertised in the Contacts section. We answered the ad and arranged to meet him. It was a little mean, because all we did was agree a meeting place in Dover before hiding in a shop doorway and giggling as we watched this grubby little guy walking up and down, waiting for his 'date'. Every time a woman went near him, he went to talk to her and made a real prat of himself.

Aside from our wonderfully immature, girly antics, our social life was great. A big gang of us spent a lot of time in the pub and having picnics, playing tennis and going clubbing, and there was rarely a dull moment.

I must have been one of the only black people around. I'll never forget the day I was walking along the street in my uniform and an old white man walked into a lamppost as he stared at me. I guess I looked like a bit of an alien to the people of Dover.

Certainly, I experienced a fair amount of racism during my time there, mostly in the form of jokes, even from the friends I hung out with. It was nothing unusual to hear the odd nigger joke or to be called 'Brownie' to my face. These were the days when Bernard Manning was at his peak and there were programmes like *Love Thy Neighbour* and *The Black And White Minstrel Show* on the telly, and you just learned to live with it. It's a different world now.

I must say it makes me laugh to see the extent to which people are sensitive about race these days. Young people might go mad about a 'racist' incident on *Big Brother*, but that's nothing compared with what black people had to deal with years ago. Then, the best way of dealing with that sort of comment was just to laugh it off or jokingly tell people to get lost. More to the point, it was sometimes a good laugh to give people as good as I got. I'd often be down the pub and, if someone picked on my colour, I'd pick on their weight or whatever it was about them I could take the piss out of. It was a kind of tit-for-tat trade in insults. Not very politically correct, but that's how it was. In my experience, humour often wins people around far more quickly than a fight.

Overall, life was pretty good and I was glad to be away from London. There was just one problem. I was putting on a lot of weight.

I just got bigger and bigger. I had an exciting new life, but perhaps I was going through some sort of depression without really being aware of it, because when I wasn't at work or socialising I was at home, watching TV on the couch and eating for England. I'd down a meal that would be enough for an entire family and I remember being able to eat a whole gateau for pudding! I'd cut a slice, telling myself that was all I was going to have. Having made short work of the first slice, I'd think, Just a little more won't hurt. Before I knew it I would have eaten half a cake, then be worried what my flatmates would think if they found a half-eaten cake in the fridge, so I would polish the lot off to cover my tracks. It was a form of denial, and behaviour similar to that of an alcoholic trying to hide their drinking. I would fold up the cake boxes really small and hide them at the bottom of the rubbish bin in the hope that nobody would notice.

The weight soon stacked on until eventually I had to ask for a new uniform at work, and that was pretty damn embarrassing. At that point I realised I had a problem. I was a good size 18 and took myself off to the doctor. 'I just can't stop eating,' I said, expecting to be put on some sort of diet.

But the doctor didn't put me on a diet. She gave me a sewing set!

'I want you to start making a quilt,' she said, handing me a quilting template and half a dozen squares of coloured fabric. 'And you're not to use a sewing machine. You must make it by hand.'

What? I thought. She refused to explain the logic of her sewing cure, but I followed the doctor's orders, and from then on sewed however many squares she'd told me to sew before I saw her again. It certainly kept me busy while I watched TV, and there wasn't any time to be scoffing slices of gateau.

By the third time I saw the doctor, I had half a quilt with me. 'Let's get you on the scales,' she said. I was nervous, but did as she said and, to my surprise and relief, I'd lost a stone in a month. I was over the moon, and the doc was pleased too. 'There,' she said, 'I worked out why you were eating and when you were eating.' Basically, the doctor thought that I was eating out of boredom. And I realised she was right.

That doctor was a clever woman. She sussed the reason I was putting on weight, and never mentioned the word 'diet', one which I think can often make people want to reach for the biscuit tin. People become fat and eat the wrong things for a variety of reasons, including boredom, unhappiness and, in particular, frustration. It might sound odd but I think a lot of aggressive people become fat. Check out how many road-ragers are really fat, it's amazing. My theory is that because fat people have trouble moving around with ease they get frustrated – and I used to be fat, so I'm speaking from experience here. But once they get into a car they are suddenly free to move and they're thinking, No motherfucker's gonna get in my way!

Road rage aside, though, often fat people are crap at saying no to anyone or anything. Lack of assertiveness often shows up on the scales.

I think the majority of obese people are using food as an emotional crutch. I certainly did, and I can't blame lack of education. I'd done domestic science and I knew what was shit, but it didn't stop me from eating it. I let myself get bored without realising it, and started diving into the cake. Who would have thought that sewing a quilt could have snapped me out of it? But it did. Eventually I had a complete quilt, though to my horror the doctor told me to give it away.

'I've worked for months on that,' I protested.

'That quilt represents your weight,' she replied, 'and you've got to let go of it for ever.'

So I did, and I've never been as big again. You won't find a half-eaten gateau on my coffee table. These days you'll find me running round the park. Not that my weight hasn't gone up and down over the years, or that it's been easy to keep it off. I've always been an up-and-down person, but right now I'm at a weight I'm at ease with. But I have to work to keep it that way. I don't want to sound rude, but I'm sick of people who aren't happy with their weight saying, 'Oh, Trisha, you're so lucky to be that size.' The last time someone did that, I replied cheekily, 'Well, I'm off to the park for an hour, so why don't you come and be lucky with me?' It is nice to be complimented on the way I look, but, believe me, ladies, luck has nothing to do with it.

While I was working at Seaspeed, there were always men around, and I had a fair amount of fun with them, but my first proper boyfriend there was a guy called Nigel Armstrong. Nigel was a really sweet guy and much brighter than most people I knew. He was so clever, in fact, that I wondered why he was working as a ticket collector on a hovercraft. It turned out he was trying to make it as a freelance photojournalist and needed some extra cash.

At first our relationship was nothing heavy. We just hung out together and I had a good time smoking dope, doing *The Times* crossword and laughing a lot. Nigel also shared my interest in cars, and we'd bomb around in my Ford Capri having a fine old time. (I'd managed to kill my Mini because I never put any oil in it – no one ever told me to!) When my mate Michele and I had to move out of our flat, Nigel was very keen for me to move in with him, and it seemed like a reasonable idea. Why not? I thought.

As soon as I moved in, our relationship changed.

Nigel started acting differently. I have always been obsessed with going to work come hell or high water, but one morning I woke up and my throat and eyes were burning. I had the killer cold from hell, and I was so dizzy I could hardly stand up. I told Nigel I couldn't go to work, but for some reason he wasn't having any of it.

From One Extreme to the Hover

'You're going!' he said.

He couldn't seem to accept that I was sick. It turned into the most horrendous row, until he stormed out of the house, leaving me at home. That argument made it dawn on me that there was something not right about our relationship.

At some point, things had changed and there was no going back. It was a case of 'Bang, you're out' and, although I carried on living with him for a while, it was because I was preparing myself for another change.

Life at sea had been awful; life on the ground had been brilliant. But what, I wondered, might life in the air be like? It wouldn't be too long before I would find out.

9

Down But Not Out

It was at a party that I met the man who became my first love, or at least what I then thought was my first love. I have not used his real name (I'll call him Adrian) and I can't be specific about when or where these events took place.

At the party, he and I were introduced and I immediately warmed to his sense of humour and good looks. He had real charisma and a bluntness that appealed to me hugely. We had a good laugh, and the next day he offered to drive me to pick up a bed I'd bought second-hand. It wasn't the most romantic date in the world, but our relationship started there.

We had a drink when we got back to my flat and he said something I'll never forget: 'I'm not gay, me. I can fuck all night.' I nearly passed out with shock. As chat-up lines go, it was pretty direct – but at least he wasn't lying.

We started dating, and the relationship became pretty intense very quickly. We went away together, smoked dope and generally had a great time. But things started happening with Adrian that, looking back, should have made me get out of the relationship right away.

Adrian revealed he had a dark side that he could not control.

We were at another party. I'd just come out of the loo and had bumped into a (male) friend of mine. As we chatted away, someone came up to take a photo of us. My friend put his arm over my shoulder and we both smiled. And that's when it all kicked off.

All of a sudden, Adrian was squaring up to my mate, screaming like a madman, 'Get your hands off my woman.' He was out of control with jealous rage, and it took several other guys to pull him back and try to calm him down.

'For God's sake,' I said to Adrian, 'this guy is my *friend*; he's not trying anything funny!'

'I thought he was touching you,' he replied a little sheepishly.

All I knew was that Adrian had acted abominably and made a right prat of himself. I turned and went into another room, hoping I'd find something that better resembled a party.

Two minutes later, a girl came up to me, saying, 'Bloody hell, what a terrible fight. That Adrian, he's *awful*.'

I thought she was talking about what had just happened, but it turned out that, after I had left the room, Adrian had followed my friend into another room and beaten the shit out of him – I hadn't heard the commotion from where I was because the music was so loud. I was furious, and stormed back into the room to witness Adrian being dragged away from my poor friend.

Adrian was shouting his head off and a few people were telling him to get out. Realising the party was over for him, he looked at me and said, 'Come on, you, we're leaving.'

'I'm not leaving,' I said. 'This is your problem. You started a fight, so you can leave. But I'm staying here.'

Adrian's response to this was to drag me out of the door and on to the stairwell.

'Let me go!' I shouted, trying to pull myself free. 'I'm staying here!'

Adrian certainly let me go and before I knew it I was in a heap at the bottom of the first flight of stairs. I was completely shocked. I looked up at him as he walked calmly down the stairs towards where I lay.

'You *bastard*,' I yelled. I made such a racket that people began to come out of the party to see what was happening.

'It's nothing,' Adrian said to the onlookers. 'She tripped and fell, that's all.'

'No I didn't,' I shouted. 'It was his fault!'

Adrian pulled me further down the stairs, and people went back inside. We argued all the way back to the flat, with him insisting I fell, which I thought was a bit rich when it had felt like a push to me. The argument continued inside, and he just got more wound up until he totally lost it and began punching the panes of glass in my front door. One by one they smashed and soon enough he cut his hand. Then he started crying, and as he blubbed he said he was sorry. 'I've got in so deep with you,' he cried. 'You mean so much to me and when I saw that guy touching you I just lost it. I won't do it again, I promise.'

Trisha – *As I Am*

Like a fool, I believed him. Instead of realising that I was dealing with someone with serious issues, I took pity on Adrian. Poor man, I remember thinking, he's besotted with me. I even managed to convince myself that I had tripped down the stairs. The thing about violent men is that they are often very persuasive. Adrian was so convincing about how passionate his feelings were, I ended up reasoning that he wouldn't have done that to me on purpose. Talk about self-deception.

As for the broken glass, Adrian fed me a few lines to the effect that he thought I was going to lock him out so he smashed the panes because he didn't want to be locked out of my life. I believed this, too. Looking back, it's easy to see he was talking a load of crap, but then I was very keen on Adrian and naïve enough to swallow his story.

So, being young, I forgave Adrian for what he had done, and we carried on as normal. There was only one problem. Adrian was a violent man. He had been a violent man when we met and he'd shown his violent side very quickly. The other problem was that, for some reason, I kept on putting up with it. But in those days, no one really talked about domestic violence.

One night we were at a restaurant with some friends. There was a disco and I was bopping away. Suddenly – these things always happened suddenly – Adrian had come up to me and was in my face screaming, 'What are you staring at him for?'

'Who?' I said, utterly baffled.

No sooner had I said the words than Adrian was pushing and shoving a guy who was dancing near me.

Down But Not Out

'Come on, fucking come on then,' he was shouting at the guy, whose mates soon gathered around.

'Adrian, what's going on?' I said, frightened of what might be about to happen.

But Adrian wasn't listening. He was already way beyond reason, and had a look of utter rage in his eyes.

'Don't you touch my woman!' he yelled at the bloke, and with that I knew everything was about to go very wrong.

I tried to intervene by stepping in front of Adrian, but instead of listening to what I had to say he threw a punch. Whether it was meant for me or the other guy, who knows, but the next thing I knew I was on the floor.

I must have been hit pretty hard because I passed out for a few seconds. I came to and was helped up by several people who were concerned as to whether I was OK or not. I didn't even really know what had happened, but Adrian wasn't so worried – he was too busy fighting like a mad dog. There was nothing I could do but walk away, and a couple of girls helped me to the car, where I sat and nursed a split lip until Adrian came outside and we left, another night ruined.

I'm sad to say that nights like this became all too familiar. Adrian would calm down, maybe cry, beg forgiveness or blame me, and we'd move on.

But Adrian's violent behaviour didn't always involve other men. On many occasions it involved only me.

One night we were out in his car when an argument about something trivial started. As the row escalated, Adrian began steering with one hand while using the other to hit me again and again in the stomach. 'You fucking bitch, you stupid c**t!' he spat.

'Let me out!' I screamed. 'Stop the car, Adrian, I'm getting out!'

'You're not getting out. You'll get raped,' he retorted.

I was willing to take my chances. Luckily for me, Adrian had slowed down to a crawl as he was hitting me. I couldn't take it any more. Desperate to escape, I held my breath, opened the door and, putting one foot to the road, jumped and rolled out of the car, grazing my arm as I landed on the tarmac. Compared with the pain I'd been on the receiving end of until now, it was nothing.

Adrian drove on a little and stopped the car, but he didn't get out.

There were no houses around and it was pitch-dark. All I could see were the brake lights on Adrian's car. All I could hear was the sound of Adrian's car purring as the engine ticked over. I was terrified of being left in the darkness and I was terrified of getting back into the car.

I was helpless.

After a few moments, Adrian reversed back along the road and wound down the window. 'Fucking get back in the car,' he said. 'I'm not going to hit you.'

I didn't have much choice. I got back in the car, and we drove home. Adrian didn't hit me again. He seemed to calm down and I was relieved.

We arrived back at home. As we walked away from the car, Adrian grabbed me by my collar and shoved me up against the pebbledash wall near the entrance to the flat. He began screaming at me, having a go at me again, and all I could do was cry as he shook me and the stones in the wall tore into my back.

My arm was a mess. My back was a mess. My clothes

were a mess. *I* was a mess. But somehow, after Adrian's tears and self-loathing, I forgave him in the end.

At work, my colleagues saw the state I was in and asked what had happened. I made excuses for the scratches all over me, saying I'd fallen down the stairs. I doubt what I said really convinced them, but what I said was enough to put an end to their questions. They had no choice but to at least pretend to believe me.

An incident sticks in my mind when we were staying with Adrian's parents. One night, I was in the bathroom. I've always been religious about moisturising myself from head to toe after every bath and shower and, one night, Adrian came into the bathroom at the very moment I was rubbing cream into my boobs. 'What the bloody hell are you doing?' he demanded. I started to explain that I was applying some moisturiser but Adrian didn't seem interested and walked off. Fine, I thought and, frankly I was glad not to have to explain myself any further.

That night as we lay in bed, Adrian brought up what he had seen in the bathroom. 'You were masturbating,' he said, accusingly. 'I don't want you masturbating. You're only to have sex with *me.*'

'I wasn't masturbating, I was applying ...'

'I don't want your excuses. From now on, you don't masturbate, OK?'

There was an angry edge to his voice. Somehow, Adrian had got it into my head that I had been touching myself, and the thought of my doing that had provoked a jealous reaction. I his paranoid, inner world, that meant I was potentially thinking about someone else.

He was in the same kind of rage he would get into with other men in bars. I could tell he was building up to hitting me.

'If you hit me, I'll scream,' I warned him. As we were staying with his parents, it was pretty obvious he wouldn't risk them hearing what a monster their son could be.

Adrian responded to this by putting his hand over my mouth and hitting me hard three times in the side, just to show me he could do whatever he wanted. They were hard blows, and I began crying from the pain. I was as miserable as can be. It was all so wrong. By this stage, Adrian had stopped grovelling after he was violent towards me. Gone were the days of tears and excuses – the violence had become a given in our relationship. Life with Adrian had always been fiery, yet there had always been good times that somehow balanced out the bad. But that balance was shifting, and increasingly things were becoming just terrible.

I began to wonder what had become of me. Why was the woman who, at 15, had been assaulted and afterwards resolved never to take any more shit from anyone, allowing the man who was supposed to love her to beat her up whenever he felt like it? Why didn't she stick up for herself or just get out? Good questions, but I wouldn't come up with answers for quite some time. I might have been questioning myself at the time, but for some reason I stuck by him, even as the violence intensified and the good times fell right away.

I started living in fear of what Adrian would do to me next.

Towards the end of our relationship, I did try to fight

back. I was in the kitchen, cooking dinner. I can't remember why, but Adrian decided to go for me. He struck me a few times and left me crying by the stove.

Suddenly, amid my tears, I was gripped with anger. I seized a knife from the counter and rushed into the next room. Holding out the knife, I stormed right up to Adrian. 'I'll show you what it's like to be scared,' I roared, pointing the knife at him. 'I'll show you. I'm sick of what you're doing to me. I've had enough!'

Adrian didn't move.

For a second I thought he was scared, but he wasn't. He simply stared at me disdainfully, as if daring me to do something terrible.

'I'm sick of it!' I shouted again, but as I said it an awful feeling of defeat consumed me. Adrian didn't look a bit scared; he just gave me a look that said, 'You're pathetic.' I knew I wasn't going to stab him, and so did he. I didn't even want to stab him. I just wanted him to stop what he was doing and this was my one desperate effort to make him stop. I stood there, frozen for a few moments, wondering what to do next.

There was nothing I could do but return to the kitchen and lay the knife back down. My outburst had achieved nothing, and I felt trapped and humiliated. A minute or so later Adrian came into the kitchen and fists started flying again. My attempt to stop him had been a real triumph – not! Weirdly, I can almost laugh about it now. It just seems so crazy that I ever allowed myself to remain in such a terrible situation. But I was a different person then.

My other attempts to stop Adrian were equally fruitless.

A number of times I threatened to call the police, but he just laughed.

I had to deal with this.

There were two events that finally made me see the light and leave him. The first step towards getting Adrian out of my life was a conversation with Mum that happened when I was on a brief visit to my parents' place. Adrian was still laying into me, and I was starting to get really down about everything. I didn't say anything, but Mum noticed something was up. 'What's the matter, Tootsie?' she asked as we drank our tea. 'You're not your usual self. What's happening?'

Mum and Dad had met Adrian and found him completely charming, so I think it came as a bit of a shock to Mum when, after quite a pause, I came out with it.

'He hits me,' I said plainly. I looked at her, wondering what she would say. I'd admitted it to someone, and just saying it was a relief of sorts. I began to whimper.

Mum went mad. 'Get out of that relationship!' she shouted. 'Get out *now*! Leave that bastard. I didn't bring you up to put up with that sort of treatment.'

She was totally sympathetic and at the same time utterly forceful about how I was an idiot if I didn't get away from Adrian. She was telling me what I already knew, of course, but it was hearing somebody say it that made me realise I really had to do something. But I didn't have it in me to walk out on Adrian right away. I don't know why, but perhaps a part of me still believed his violent behaviour would stop. I went back to him, but it wasn't long before the event that sealed the relationship's doom would happen.

Down But Not Out

I was in bed at home trying to get some sleep before an early start but I couldn't sleep because Adrian had some mates over and they were drinking and laughing in the next room. There was loud music playing too, and I didn't stand a chance of nodding off. I lay there, tossing and turning despairingly, and eventually came out in my nightie and politely asked them to keep it down a bit.

Adrian looked at me with fury in his eyes. 'Fuck off,' he shouted.

His mates went quiet with embarrassment.

There wasn't much I could say to that, so I went back to bed. I lay there a while longer listening to the racket, which seemed to grow louder every minute. In my head, I weighed up whether it was worth making more of a fuss. I was scared of Adrian when we were on our own, and often held my tongue so as not to get hit, but I knew he wouldn't go for me in front of his mates. Fuck it, I thought, I'll ask them to be quiet again, and that's just what I did.

Big mistake! But a mistake I'm glad I made.

'Right, you fucking bitch,' said Adrian as I entered the room. With that, he stood up and rushed at me, fists flying. His mates jumped up and tried to hold him back. Even though some of them were massive guys, Adrian was so fired up he managed to break loose and get me into the bedroom. He was laying into me and literally frothing at the mouth. His mates eventually managed to pull him off and wrestled him to the floor, screaming, 'Adrian, mate, what are you doing?'

Adrian was writhing around and hollering all sorts of obscenities – it was obvious he was determined to beat the shit out of me at any cost. Looking at this out-of-control monster made me utterly petrified. I had no idea what to do.

Then a voice said, 'Get out, Trisha, get out!' It was one of Adrian's mates. I took his advice and grabbed my car keys, slid the window open and jumped out. The video player followed because Adrian had managed to push his mates off and throw it through the window after me. Luckily, it smashed into the ground and not me.

Still wearing my nightie, I ran to my car and drove to a friend's place. I banged on the door, a weeping wreck. I told her everything and she was wonderful about it all. She made me hot chocolate and showed me to the spare room.

Mum's words echoed through my head, and this time I knew it was time to really listen to them. Things had gone too far. They had gone too far a long time ago. Things had to change before one of us did serious damage to the other.

The next day some friends came with me to get my belongings while Adrian was out. I moved somewhere else and never set foot in our place again.

I next spoke to Adrian a few weeks later. He pleaded to be allowed to come to where I was staying. Two very large male friends of mine lived opposite and stood vigil, watching everything through their window, while we talked just in case he went for me. But I knew he wouldn't. After all, he was trying to get me to come back, and hitting someone is not a great tactic.

All the usual apologies fell from his mouth, but now they were falling on deaf ears. He was in full flow, telling me for the millionth time how he would change, when I cut him short. 'I'm not coming back,' I said, 'so save your breath. You're not going to do this to me any more. It's over, Adrian. That's it, so you might as well leave.'

He began to cry, and begged some more, but I wasn't having any of it. 'Get out!' I said.

And he did.

When I look back at my relationship with Adrian, I'm still amazed I stayed with him so long, but there were reasons why I was with him. There were good times, some of which I've mentioned, and he was good-looking, funny and articulate. He had a good side and a dark side, and towards the end the dark side won out. It was as if his demons got worse and worse until he was so out of control that he was ready to beat me up in public. But, leaving aside Adrian's charm, I think there was something in me that associated love with aggression, a part of me that thought it was OK. And there's only one place that part of me came out of – my childhood.

A lot of women who end up victims of domestic violence were hit, scared or intimidated by their fathers but got on tolerably well with them and still loved them despite the episodes of violence. When this happens, a strange association between love and violence can develop in the child's mind. It is a confusing feeling but I think that, from the way my dad treated me, I somehow 'learned', or saw in my head, that someone who cared for you could also hit you for your own good. When I was a child, I was made to feel I deserved what I got in some way, and ended up subconsciously accepting that violence was a part of 'love'.

Through therapy, I've been lucky enough to discover that, during my relationship with Adrian, I was subconsciously continuing a pattern. Even though Adrian would give me a good thrashing, there was always a part of me that somehow blamed me, not him. *There was a part of me that felt I deserved it.* That's why it took me so long to get out.

It is amazing what a grip someone's childhood has on them – hitting a child can affect them for such a long time and play a part in dictating how they conduct their relationships as adults. I'm not saying it is entirely my dad's fault that I put up with Adrian hitting me, but I don't doubt that the 'smacking' that became the norm during my childhood made it much easier for him to get away with what he did for so long. By the time he began hitting me, I'd already been accustomed to such behaviour in the past. If Adrian had tried it with someone who hadn't been beaten as a child, the shock may have been greater and they would have seen the violence as far more unacceptable than I did and got out right away.

Now, of course, I believe that no woman ever deserves to be beaten by her man, and, if I could speak to every victim of domestic violence in the same way that my mother spoke to me, I would. The best I can do is help women on my show, and tell them in front of a supportive audience that they deserve better. Much better.

From experience, I can say it is never worth believing the lies and excuses and going back to a violent man. I went home to one every night for several years, and in the long run I'm wiser for it, but I wish I'd been wiser at the time and got out sooner.

I only saw Adrian one more time, about two years later. He tracked me down and got in touch, suggesting we meet. Thinking it had been a while, and remembering that, despite everything, we had actually been very good mates, I agreed. Although a bit wary, I was quite looking forward to seeing him, and knew I had moved on from him completely by having a good few words with myself and a few violence-free flings here and there!

It was an odd feeling seeing him again. Even though he was the same size, he appeared smaller, a diminished figure in some way. He seemed very uptight and angsty, and I quickly realised that he only wanted to see me to feed me some sob story about how he was broke. I listened, but didn't really know what he expected me to do about his problems. Then he started trying to get into a 'whatever happened to us?' conversation. Oh-oh, I thought, and tried to nip that in the bud – getting back together with Adrian was about as appealing as a plane crash. I let him know that our relationship would never get going again.

The next thing I knew he had lost his rag. He had grabbed my jacket and was holding me threateningly against the wall.

When I had been together with him, Adrian only had to make a sudden movement to make my heart leap into my mouth. My adrenalin would surge and I'd feel sick. Now, two years on, I didn't even react. I was cold. The balance of power had shifted. He was down on his luck and I was on the up again.

Calmly, I looked him in the eye. 'You better let go of me,' I said icily. 'I *will* scream, I *will* call the police and they *will* come.'

He began to look unsure of himself. He didn't let go of me, but he didn't seem to know what to do.

'If you're going to do anything to me, you'd better finish the job off, because if you don't I'll make sure the next time you see me is from behind bars.'

No doubt shocked by the cold conviction in my voice, Adrian released me and backed away. He began to cry really hard, his shoulders heaving up and down. 'It's all gone so wrong for me,' he whimpered. 'I've fucked everything up and got no money. I've got nothing.'

I was as cold as ice. Coolly, I took my purse from my bag, opened it and pulled out a £5 note. 'Here's some fucking money,' I said, throwing the fiver on to the bed. 'Goodbye, Adrian, you will never see me again.'

He went to speak, but it was too late. I was already closing the door behind me.

10

Arabian Heights

Once I'm bored of something, I let it go. I've never been the kind of person to remain in something for the hell of it. Living in Dover had been fun, but it had its limits, and after two years I knew I was bored. I decided to change my situation and started applying to airlines to become an air hostess. I wanted to see the world and I wanted to get paid to do it. I was interviewed by British Airways, who were offering six-month contracts, but as I came out of the interview someone tapped me on the shoulder and said, 'If you want to fly for longer than six months, Gulf Air are recruiting.'

I walked across the corridor and looked at their poster. On it was a picture of a stewardess in a red-veil-type hat. I loved hats and I was sold. I knocked on the door and said, 'Hi, my name's Trisha Goddard, and I'd like to work for you.'

Little did I know at the time, but it was the most important knock on a door I would ever make.

It was 1980 and I was heading to the Middle East, to Bahrain, a place that, only weeks earlier, I could not have pointed out on a map. Now I was boarding the plane with a sense that I was about to begin a great adventure. The moment we took off, England felt like ancient history.

I didn't know much, but I knew the Middle East was a war zone and, while I was incredibly excited to be on my way there, a tiny part of me thought, Oh, Trisha, what have you got yourself into now? But my anxiety was short-lived, and the moment I arrived I loved everything about my new world.

All the new recruits were put up in the posh Gulf Hotel, and we had a ball right from the start. There were girls from all over the world from every social class, but the combination of a crew room for us to hang out in and plenty of booze meant that we all got on like a house on fire. Oh, and the training was interesting too.

It was a fantastic education. We learned an incredible amount, from how to prepare meals of scrambled eggs for two hundred people to how to chuck those same two hundred people out of a smoke-filled plane should the occasion arise. It was a very steep learning curve. All of us trainees loved it because we had all gone for the job for the same reason – we were hungry for new experiences, all desperate for that feeling of 'where will I go tomorrow?' Training to be a hostess meant that feeling was just around the corner.

We were moved into the Gulf Air, or 'Pepsi', flats – they were on the site of a former Pepsi factory – large blocks of grand, marble-floored apartments, a bit like upmarket university halls of residence. I shared with one girl who was a really heavy drinker, and another girl, Sally. Many a time we'd return home to find this girl splayed out on the floor, passed out drunk. It was amazing she managed to hold down her job. She really was all over the place most of the time. Not that we didn't put away our fair share of drinks. Unsurprisingly, the British girls were the worst. We really knew how to have a good time, and when we weren't training we used to drink like nothing on earth. The partying didn't stop once the training was over and we began working for real – we just had to make sure we stopped drinking at least 12 hours before a flight.

Being around Arab men for the first time was an eye-opener. I'll never forget the first night we all went out to a disco. I was sitting with the girls, sipping my drink, when an Arab guy came up to me and said, 'You! Dance!'

Being ordered to dance was a lovely chat-up line, but I declined with a polite 'No, thank you.'

But he wasn't easily deterred, and seemed to think repeating himself might work. 'You! Dance!'

This time I ignored him and he went away.

Five minutes later, he was back, but there was a new twist to his approach – before telling me to dance, he threw a bundle of money on to the table. And it was quite a substantial bundle at that.

'Excuse *me*!' I shouted. 'How *dare* you?' I was shocked that this man seriously thought he could pay me to perform for him. What a bloody cheek, I thought, and some of the girls shared my disgust. However, some of them didn't. 'If you won't dance, I will,' said one girl when the guy came back offering *jewellery*!

And with that, up she got and smooched with the Arab.

That night split the girls into two camps – those who would sell themselves, and those who wouldn't. It wasn't like they became prostitutes, but some girls were prepared to go along with what the men wanted in exchange for all manner of gifts. It was the 1980s and the oil industry was booming, so the Arabs who courted us had a lot of cash and were eager to lavish it on Western women. There were plenty of girls without scruples who were happy to sell out to their sugar daddies.

The funny thing was how easily you could spot a girl who had become a bit on the side for some wealthy businessman or sheikh. Nine times out of ten she would be wearing a diamond ring and, bizarrely, driving a Honda Civic. It was crazy, all these Hondas with consecutive number plates lined up in the airport car park. Don't ask me why they all got Hondas, but they must have been readily available. Inevitably, some blonde bimbo would come up to me on a flight and say, 'Mohammed and I just got engaged!'

'Oh, honey, that's great,' I'd laugh. 'But I think you'll find he's probably engaged to a couple of girls on this crew and a few on the last too!'

Then she'd notice a girl or two wearing the same diamond ring and the penny would drop. I couldn't help but find it amusing.

Being black meant I was able to get on well with a lot of the Arabs – they wanted stereotypically white, blonde Westerners hanging off their arms (and driving their

Hondas). Because I spoke a bit of Arabic and didn't flutter my eyelashes at them, we were able to just have a laugh, which suited me fine. Overall, I liked the Arab people. The majority of them had a real dignity about them that I found truly admirable. But within any group of people you get good and bad, and the Honda-buying men were certainly the exception rather than the rule in Arab society. It was just that the guys with money and power happened to be the ones Westerners were more likely to have contact with.

Once the training was over, being up in the air was wonderful from the word go. Dealing with passengers on a plane is the best lesson in crowd control you could ever have. It certainly prepared me for the future – coping with a noisy audience or troublesome guests on my show is nothing compared with some of the situations I came up against at two thousand feet. And, guess what, the Brits were the worst when it came to bad behaviour. I hadn't been on the job long before this rough-as-guts lout shouted, 'Excuse me, darlin', I can't do my seatbelt up.'

As I went to help him, it quickly became apparent it wasn't just his seatbelt he was having trouble with. His trousers were also undone, and his penis was hanging out of them. I gasped and ran along the aisle to my favourite steward, Ray 'Lily' Bishop, a towering, reed-thin, blond Aussie bloke who was as camp as Butlins and bore some resemblance to Kenneth Williams. Lily had seen it all before and knew exactly what to do. I'll never forget watching him take a hot towel, mince down the aisle to the lout's seat and dump the towel on to his penis as he passed by the seat. 'That should keep you warm, sir,' he said over his shoulder. I was in hysterics. 'That's what you do,' Lily said to me, 'or tell them I'll do their seatbelts up with my teeth!'

Inevitably, I had a fair amount of racist comments aimed at me, but at that stage it was like water off a duck's back. Whenever a passenger got lippy, I'd just make a rude quip and happily saunter off. It was hard to take incidents of drunken bigotry seriously. I just viewed those who picked on me for my colour as ghastly little people, and that was that.

One of the most obnoxious passengers I had the misfortune of dealing with on a flight was a well-known comedian. He was sitting with his mate in first class and near them was an Arab man in traditional dress. It wasn't long before he began talking very loudly about 'ragheads' and making all manner of disgustingly racist jokes. I had to serve him and listen to his pathetic comments and it really got to me that these two oiks were acting so offensively while an extremely gracious Arab gentleman sat by with no option but to listen to a tirade of insults. By then, I was a senior stewardess, and knew all the ground staff, so I was very tempted to get him to say something very offensive to me so I could have him arrested when we landed, but I held my tongue. Ever since then, I've hated him – the very sight of him makes me feel sick. In my opinion, he's a small-minded, sexist bigot. Perhaps he's changed a bit since then, but I'll never forget his behaviour on that flight.

In contrast to the Brits, Indian economy-class passengers weren't offensive, just sweet and hilarious. Most of them were labourers being moved between countries, and they hadn't seen, let alone flown on, planes before. They had obviously been told by people who had only flown in planes without pressurised cabins that it was a good idea to stuff their ears with cotton wool, because whenever we had big groups of Indians on board they'd all be asking for it. We'd always run out and were often left with no choice but to cut up tampons from the first-aid kit and hand them out. It was very hard to keep a straight face while doing the safety demonstration and looking down the aisle at a load of passengers with bits of tampon string hanging out of their ears. Poor things, they were so polite, but everything was just so new to them.

A lot of them had never seen a knife and fork or a Western meal before, and they would do things that seemed pretty peculiar to me, such as putting the little packets of butter in their tea. It was also fairly common for them not to know where to do what in the plane's toilets. This aspect of their behaviour wasn't so endearing, especially when it was Muggins who had to clean up the hand basins after they'd used them, let's say, unconventionally. But, through no fault of their own, they weren't familiar with our ways, and I felt no animosity whatsoever towards them.

I loved the travelling, not least the fact that we got to stay in some of the best hotels in the world, which was pure luxury. Seeing how 'the other half' lived made me want to live that way and I decided pretty quickly that the Good Lord did not intend for me to be poor. I made a pact with myself that I would always be able to look after myself, and decided financial security was something I simply had to have. I was earning great money with Gulf Air and I saved every penny I could. I was eventually able to buy a mews cottage in Surbiton, not far from where I'd lived with my parents, which I rented out. It felt like a real achievement. I was laying the foundations of my future while having the time of my life and living for the moment as I travelled the world, working hard and partying hard.

Then, in 1982, something happened that made me question how safe I was in the air.

'Ladies and gentlemen, we're having a few problems with the undercarriage,' said the captain over the intercom.

Everyone on the plane sighed, and I cursed because I'd just cooked the first-class passengers' breakfasts and now I couldn't serve them.

There'd been a noise. A loud grinding sound that I'd never heard before. That must be what the captain is talking about, I thought.

We landed at Bombay airport – where we'd just taken off from – and after a short while I spoke to the chief engineer who had just been working on the plane. 'All sorted out?' I asked. I'll never forget his reply.

'Yes, madam, everything is tickety-boo,' the engineer said in his strong Indian accent.

As I closed the door to the plane, he gave me a beaming smile and put both thumbs up. Thank God, I thought, as the plane took off. Now I can get breakfast going.

But within seconds the grinding noise was back. For God's sake, I thought, we're going to have to land again, and the eggs have turned green and solid!

And then it happened – BANG!

The plane jolted and, even though I was strapped into my jumpseat, I was still thrown half off it. A few passengers screamed. 'Oh my God,' I said to myself.

Something is very wrong, I know it. An engineer dashes

out of the flight deck, strides into the economy-class cabin and looks out of a window. Then, his face ashen, his eyes full of dread, he marches back to the flight deck.

Seconds later, 'bing-bong, bing-bong' chimes through the cabin. My training floods back – two 'bing-bongs' means 'Captain to all crew'. Shit, I think, moving quickly to my station. Taking a deep breath, I grab the phone and wait for the captain to address the crew.

Then I hear the words I never dared dream I would hear.

'We're going to have to do an emergency landing,' says the captain. 'Part of the right-hand-side undercarriage has sheared off and we've lost a section of the wing. Begin 15-minute minimum-time emergency preparation.'

Oh, God, this is it! Emergency landing. Put on the Urdu emergency landing tape, I think. Hardly any of our passengers speak English.

The emergency landing tape is for the passengers to hear, but the Urdu tape is not working, nor is the Hindi, so we must go down the aisle literally miming to everyone what to do, row by row. *And we've only got 15 minutes.* It's the sickest game of charades I've ever played, but there's no laughter; I'm just tense and brutal.

'Take off your glasses, remove any jewellery and false teeth, take off your shoes, and put your heads down and wait until we shout, "Brace!"' is the message we tersely struggle to 'show' them. I feel like I'm in a dream; I'm just going through the motions of a drill I know backwards. I am not thinking. I'm like a robot. *This cannot be real.*

We've stowed the trolleys, we've briefed the passengers and I'm strapped into my seat tighter than ever. People are starting to panic. There's nervous murmuring from some, others are praying out loud. I hear everything from 'Allah Akbar' to 'Hail Mary, Mother of God'.

I don't need this. If only they'd shut up!

The plane banks, we're dumping fuel, and I look out of the window thinking that whatever is there will be the last thing I see. On the ground below are some vans with red crosses on. It takes a few moments for me to realise that the vans are for us. Great, I think. In all those American movies, there's foam on the runway and the latest fire-fighting trucks and medical equipment. Here I am about to crash-land in Bombay and all I can see is a load of little ambulances waiting. *We're all going to die.*

I try to appear calm, but inside I'm a mess. I'm going mad. I want to get up and run and scream. *I don't want to go like this, but what good will running and screaming do? There's nothing you can do. Whatever you do, Trisha, you are going to hit the ground.*

I look out of the window and force myself to calm down, try to think straight. I can see India's green fields spread out below us. *Remember this if this is the last thing you are going to see. Focus on the green, be calm, there's nothing you can do so try to be at peace, for this is it. Please, God, just don't let the people I love find out about what happened to me in a horrible way…*

We begin our final descent. The damaged part of the undercarriage is on the right, so I know it's the right side of the plane that's going to collapse when we touch down, and that's the side of the aircraft I'm seated on. My eyes are closed, my teeth clenched.

'*Brace!*' says the captain over the PA, and the crew and I start yelling the word to the passengers.

Arabian Heights

Here we go.

We land and it all feels normal for a second, then BANG! The right-hand side of the plane hits the ground and in an instant, through the nearest windows, I can see huge flames. But the captain manages to steer the plane off the runway. We plough on into the Indian soil, and all we can see are flames and dust.

For a moment there is silence. Then a cacophony of human screams and crashing, groaning metal fills the air as the plane careers and skids onwards into the dust. It's the chaos before death, I think.

And then it stops. For a second I wonder if I am dead.

The plane has ground to a halt, and the dust has killed the flames. There's nothing but dust and an eerie silence.

Am I alive?

Yes, you are alive. Now start your evacuation drill. Check the door, Trisha. You're at work, remember!

As soon as I realised I was still on planet earth, I pushed a bar trolley off me and jumped into action. We couldn't evacuate through my door, so I looked across at my senior, Stella, who was calmly and confidently going through her drill. First, she checked to see if outside looked clear, and second she opened her door and deployed her slide. I was thinking out loud, my adrenalin was pumping like crazy, and before I knew it I was crossing my arms and jumping down the slide.

I was in shock, and later got on the coach back to the hotel like a zombie. I sat down and stared ahead. The whole crew did the same. Once at the hotel, the captain of the plane ordered, 'Everyone to the bar!'

The crew gathered and he ordered brandies for

everyone, including the Filipino stewardess who said she
didn't drink. I made an exception to my no-spirits policy
and necked a few brandies very quickly. It was the only
time we ever drank in uniform and, boy, did we need it!
We didn't really talk, but just drank through our shock.

The amazing thing is that we were given just the requisite
minimum of 12 hours' rest before we were back in the air
again. Getting back on a plane 12 hours after having crash-
landed has to be one of the most horrible feelings I've ever
had. My polite stewardess act went out of the window, and
on that flight I was like Satan. If anyone made a fuss, I just
shouted at them, then I'd go back to the crew area and just
shake. Mind you, the whole crew was like that. It's funny
how shock makes you behave.

The guy I was seeing at the time picked me up after the
flight, and it was only when I got in the car that I really
fell apart. He comforted me, drove me home and helped
me calm down.

The crash didn't put me off flying, but I developed a
habit I have to this day of not relaxing on a flight until I
hear the undercarriage come up safely. Many of my fellow
crew members on that trip left the airline over the coming
year, but basically I still adored flying with Gulf Air and
now had a whole new appreciation of how well we were
trained. Even though I would end up staying with the
airline for three more years, I was starting to think about
how I might move on in my life, despite the fact that, at
26, I had been promoted to senior stewardess.

Because of my interest in journalism I ended up getting
in with a crowd of journos from the *Gulf Daily News*.
They were a passionate bunch and, the more I hung out

with them, the more my life of constant partying with the Gulf Air crowd came to seem a little dull. After all, there's only so much drinking a girl can do. Living at Gulf Air's flats eventually started to drive me a bit mad because my flatmate's drinking meant that she would often be ranting and raving and I was getting fed up with dealing with it. When you've been on a 12-hour flight packed with drunken passengers the last thing you need is to go home to a piss-head. I liked her, but enough was eventually enough and I was keen to leave.

I moved into an Arab village on the Bahraini island of Muharraq. I loved being in the thick of a truly Bahraini atmosphere and I still had the option to dip in and out of airline life, which was ideal.

Thus far, I'd absolutely loved the job, and adored the travelling and writing bits of journalism, but it wasn't enough. I was hungry for more, so during my spare time I began doing journalism and television courses in the UK. I loved them, and a friend helped me get work experience whenever I was available. Very quickly I was bitten by the bug of the TV studio. On one course I'd been taught by BBC TV journalist Kate Adie and I remember her telling me she thought I had what it takes to carve a career in the medium. It was such a buzz being in a creative environment, and the contrast between TV work and my vacuous time flying and partying was stark. I was ready to embrace any opportunity, and planned to apply to join a trainee scheme at the BBC. Little did I know who would board my plane next ...

11

Three Proposals and a One-Way Ticket

Never go out with a passenger you meet on a plane. This was my cardinal rule, and, no matter how many Hondas or diamond rings I was offered, I stuck to my rule for nearly five years of flying. And then, early in 1985, I found myself not sticking to my rule. That is to say, I completely and utterly broke it. But I wasn't being offered a Honda or a diamond ring, I was being offered a radical change in life, and a move to the other side of the world.

It all began as follows. I was on a flight from Bombay to Bahrain via Dubai as a senior stewardess, which meant it was my job to deal with the tricky passengers. On this occasion, I found myself doing just that before the plane had even left the ground in Dubai. First class was overbooked and a number of first-class passengers were kicking up a real stink because they'd been shoved into economy. The man kicking up the biggest stink of all was a distinguished-looking but very pompous Australian gentleman. Wearing a cravat and making lots of loud noises, he wasn't an easy man to deal with, but I did my best and eventually he piped down for the rest of the flight.

Once back in Bahrain, I changed out of my uniform in the loos and checked in as a passenger on the next flight to London. I was heading for my final interviews with the BBC and couldn't wait. I boarded the plane and moved towards the one free seat left in economy. As I approached, I noticed a very familiar face in the seat next to mine – it was the pompous Aussie from the previous flight to Bahrain.

Shit, I thought, just my bloody luck! I hoped he wouldn't recognise me.

'Hello again, what are you doing on this flight, young lady?' he enquired as I sat down.

Oh well, I thought, so much for going unnoticed. I explained I was trying to get into the BBC, and he responded with interest, introducing himself as Robert Nestdale, as if I might recognise the name. I didn't, but he wasted no time in telling me he was the leader of the Australian Young Liberals (the equivalent of Britain's Conservative Party) on a trip as part of something for UNICEF.

Despite his being a lot older than me, his slightly peculiar, haughty way of speaking (very posh and patronising) and the way he dressed (a blazer and tie, a handkerchief in his top pocket), he turned out to be very interesting, and we had rather a lot in common in terms of our interest in the Middle East. I was used to hanging out with flight attendants and hard-boozing scruffy journos, so this guy was a bit of a contrast, but we got on very well. Besides, he looked a bit like a dark Robert Palmer, and I *loved* Robert Palmer.

At the end of the flight, Robert gave me his card – I didn't give him anything but my name – and I went home to Mum and Dad. The BBC interviews went very well, and it wasn't until I was back in Bahrain a week or so later that Mum called to tell me a Robert Nestdale had called them up to ask after me. Robert had obviously managed to track me down from my name, and Mum told me she'd given him my PO box number in Bahrain.

Then the letters started pouring in.

I wasn't quite sure why Robert was writing to me, but the letters were interesting and pleasant enough. He would let me know what he was up to, and I would do the same. He talked a lot about his charity work, and also did a fair amount of namedropping about the high-powered politicians and journalists he knew, including the legendary Ron Saw, who wrote for the *Bulletin*, a magazine in Australia. To someone who was interested in getting ahead in journalism, what Robert had to say was very intriguing, and I was pretty impressed by it all. Still, I was a little bemused about why a 40-year-old Australian politician kept writing to a wannabe trainee journo in Bahrain.

Robert kept writing that I was welcome to come and visit him any time, and I wrote back saying if I was in Australia I would surely love to. Then there was a bit of a gearshift and the letters became a little more emotional. He started writing that he couldn't stop thinking about me, and paying me all sorts of compliments. Repeatedly he urged me to come to Australia and listed all the people in politics and journalism he would love to introduce me to.

It was weird. I was having a long-distance semi-relationship with someone I barely knew. Eventually I thought, Sod it, why not take a trip to Australia? I had other friends who lived there, and I needed a break. So off I went.

I was a little nervous about the prospect of meeting Robert again, but he was very charming and courteous from the moment I turned up in Sydney. On the first night he took me to a glittering do at a theatre, and immediately we walked in I was, like, *Wow!* Suddenly I was in a world I'd never had access to before – it was a proper red-carpet and flashbulbs job. Robert escorted me around the room and I was introduced to a Who's Who of Aussie politicians and journalists.

Robert was a very confident man, and he breezily introduced me to the then Prime Minister Bob Hawke, among others. I met filmmakers from the ABC (Australian Broadcasting Corporation, the country's BBC), including David and Sue Flatman, who would later become great friends. I was totally out of my comfort zone, yet I didn't feel uncomfortable. It was simply thrilling, and I felt inspired to be around such people. At 27, I was being seduced by a very glamorous and unfamiliar world.

The rest of the week was a whirlwind of dinners and events, and we even went hot-air balloon racing, which made a change from being on an aeroplane. I stayed at Robert's house, an amazing little place in Paddington, a trendy area of Sydney. We slept in separate rooms, and each morning I woke up thinking, It's a bit surreal, all this, but I'm having a ball, so who cares!

When I had time off from Gulf Air, I would travel as much as I could, in this instance to Thailand.

This picture of Robert Nestdale was taken a few years before I met him. Although our marriage was a disaster, it would be years before I discovered the true extent of the dark secrets he was keeping from me.

© Newspix

Presenting *Play School* was a bit of a contrast to the news reporting I'd been doing, but I adored it. The picture above shows me on the set in 1997, singing with Big Ted and Little Ted.

I was the first black television presenter in Australia – and it caused quite a stir, as you can see from these press cuttings. I was thrilled when Michael Parkinson wrote this column in support of me.

CASANOVAS PUT PAID TO CRITICS

By ANGIE KELLY

HER critics were out in force before she'd even taken her first bow.

But Trisha Goddard, the ABC's newest 7.30 Report anchorwoman, silenced them in the best way possible — winning ratings and even a few hearts.

A few rotten tomatoes are still being hurled, but now it's mostly gifts from love-struck viewers that Trisha, 29, and unmarried, receives.

"They're all sincere proposal letters and they're usually four or five pages long," said Trisha.

"I never laugh at them and I reply to every one thanking the writers for their compliments.

Suitors

"I've had so many letters but it's very hard to reply because you're dealing with people's emotions."

Together with declarations of love, Trisha, who took over the 7.30 Report from Jane Singleton on February 1, said her hopeful suitors send cards, photos, je-welly and poetry.

Trisha wins battle for ratings — and viewers' hearts

Trisha in the street, bestowing on her a star status she has not yet learned to cope with.

"When I hear whispers and see people staring I sometimes just want to run away," she said.

"It's so weird when people talk to me in the supermarket — I'm not used to it yet."

But the warm reception from viewers is a pleasant change after being the target of a large body of critics.

And the ratings clearly show that viewers do not share the

tory over commercial rivals on two nights in this week's TV timeslot battle.

"I'm pleasantly surprised and quietly optimistic about the ratings," she said.

"But it's not just thanks to me. The whole team works hard."

Danger

Trisha goes on the road as a reporter for the first time in tonight's program and hopes the role will become a regular part of her new job.

"I think it's a danger to be locked away and out of touch with what's happening," she said.

"I have always made it clear that I didn't just want to present the show, I want to do re-search as much as

WINNER: Trisha Goddard has won the minds — and hearts — of v

Parky DOWN UNDER

Toughing it out in black and white

Australia's latest television star is a woman, a Pom, and black. This has not been allowed to happen without some comment.

Giving a prestigious current affairs job to a Sheila from Surrey is one thing but the fact the girl is black has posed new questions for a country whose idea of black involvement in the media has hitherto been confined to watching the Bill Cosby Show.

Trish Goddard's television debut was given the same slightly awed scrutiny that she might have expected had she been a visitor from another planet.

Those demented souls who ring radio stations envisaged Miss Goddard as a kind of black Pol Pot who would lead the heathen hordes across the continent destroying all that white Australia stands for like Vegemite factories, koala parks and breweries.

They found a sympathetic ear with those equally demented creatures who tout for their calls.

After Miss Goddard has said that the publicity prevented her shopping at her local supermarket without being recognised, one phone-in host said: "If she went at night and didn't open her mouth she'd be invisible."

This jibe is only worth repeating because it set

the level for the general tone of the debate.

However, Miss Goddard is toughing it out.

The ratings show that in spite of, or perhaps because of, the publicity Miss Goddard is not the sort of person you switch off.

Moreover, apart from being attractive and bright Trish Goddard is also a gutsy lady.

Fighter

She told them straight that if the public didn't like her then that was her business. She'd go home and get a job on Channel Four.

The Aussies approve of this kind of talk.

They love a battler, black or white.

In this infuriating yet lovable country Miss Goddard might soon make the leap from being an alien to becoming a Dinki-Di Aussie.

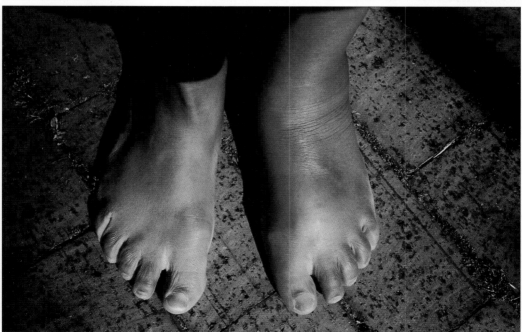

Above: My beloved VW convertible. I designed this car from scratch and even had the roof taken off! This photo was taken on a trip Mark and I made in 1987, up to the Byron Bay area of New South Wales, in the days before we had kids.

Below: Ouch. It's true that Australia has more dangerous creatures than any other country and this goes to show it! My foot swelled up like a ballon after I was bitten by a Redback spider.

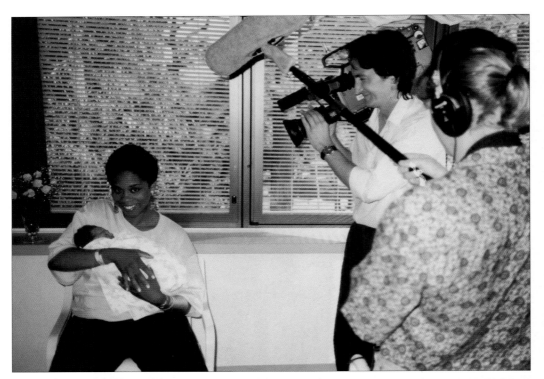

Above: This is me just two – yes, two! – hours after I gave birth to Billie. I was filmed in hospital to open the *7.30 Report* show I should have been presenting.

Below: Playing happy families with Mark – how things were to change. I was still breastfeeding at this time and was about a size 18.

After Mark and I split up, it was just me and my girls – until I met the man who would become the love of my life …

On Sydney's Palm Beach in the early days of meeting Peter. Behind the dark glasses, I was still fragile but getting stronger all the time.

Three Proposals and a One-Way Ticket

Then I awoke one day to find Robert sitting at the end of my bed. He didn't say anything, but just looked at me like a man possessed. I know it sounds awful but my first thought was, Oh, this must be the end of the free lunch – time to cough up, Trisha! Oh well, I thought, I suppose I'd better close my eyes and think of England.

Robert moved towards me for a kiss. If my first-ever kiss with Bob Taylor had been like kissing a cocker spaniel, with Robert it was like kissing a salivating walrus. When Robert was all dressed up in his politician's suits, he looked pretty distinguished and handsome, but unfortunately the same could not be said for what he looked like naked. When Robert's wobbly bits were out, he looked a bit like a lump of baking dough – the contrast between him and some of the other, more athletic guys I'd been out with was pretty difficult to get over. His skin was pallid and squidgy, and had that blue-grey tone that smacks of poor circulation. Let's just say it wasn't much of a turn-on, but I remember thinking, Oh, I could get him fit. I was still obsessed with exercise and saw Robert's poor physical state as a challenge. How naïve I was to think I'd be able to change him.

I let Robert carry on 'making love' to me, even though I didn't anticipate the earth was about to move. I was right not to expect much. The only thing that moved was a very clumsy Robert, who appeared to have the sexual maturity of your average 12-year-old boy. He barely knew how to put what where, and when he managed to get going he seemed to think it was necessary to make all manner of noises to show that he was having a good time. It was all very Austin Powers but, luckily, before he'd grunted too many 'oohs', 'aahs' and 'Oh yeah, babys', it was all over. He seemed happy enough, and afterwards we just got on with the day. It seemed that I'd acquired a lover of sorts, though exactly where we stood with each other was a little unclear.

The press cleared up that issue for us. It was a ten-day trip, and before I'd got back on the plane home there were already articles appearing in papers about Robert Nestdale's new love interest. According to the *Bulletin*, Robert and I were besotted with each other. In a funny way, I did like Robert quite a bit, but looking back I do wonder if it was his world I liked more. Either way, I got on the plane back to Bahrain just a little confused about what I wanted.

It had been an amazing trip, and returning to Bahrain was a bit of a downer, to put it mildly. My job started to seem repetitive and boring, and lots of my colleagues were moving on to other airlines or other careers. In short, things just weren't the same any more, and I was beginning to become impatient to leave. I was waiting for the BBC to let me know if I'd made the trainee scheme, and I wasn't quite sure what the whole episode with Robert had meant, or how I felt about him.

Robert appeared to have no such doubts. Within days of my being back in the Gulf, the letters were pouring in again. Robert didn't mess around when it came to declaring his undying love for me – he missed me, he was desperate to see me, he wanted me back in his arms at the very first opportunity. And on it went. It was very flattering, and looking back I can see how easy it was for me to fall in love with the idea of such a romance. I was in love with the idea of being in love.

Three Proposals and a One-Way Ticket

But, before I could deal with Robert's lovesickness, I had to deal with an illness of my own. Quite suddenly, I fell victim to one of the most painful experiences I've ever had – an impacted wisdom tooth. It was so serious that I was flown home to England for an operation. I reacted terribly to the anaesthetic, and had an insane fever. I couldn't eat or sleep and just sat upright on my parents' couch, whimpering and drinking water through a straw. I had two black eyes from the trauma of the operation and must have looked a real sight for a week.

The funny thing was, one day towards the end of the week I received three phone calls from three guys asking me to marry them. Word must have got around that I had been flown back to the UK because I was critically ill – which I wasn't, of course – and my suitors must have thought they needed to make a gesture before I died or something.

The first caller was Adrian, which was a shock. He seemed to think I might want to commit to a life of violence with him. Let's just say it was a short phone call. What a joke!

The second caller was David, an Aussie journo I'd been seeing for a while. A wonderful man, I liked him a lot and travelled with him to Africa retracing my childhood haunts, but he was a bit of a wet lettuce in a rainstorm, and I didn't really fancy moving to the country and surviving on two meagre journalists' salaries. My response was ultimately thanks but no thanks, though I tried to do it as politely as possible. I think I hurt David, and I feel bad for that. He was a sweet, sweet man.

The third caller was Robert, and you already know

about him. Robert's charm, his letters, his Interflora flowers, his contacts, his comfortable lifestyle and the sheer romance of the idea of marrying and moving to another country made him the front-runner.

I mulled it all over as I lay there with a straw in my mouth, looking like death. I was glad the proposals had come over the phone and not in person – the way I looked it would have taken a madman to get down on bended knee at my bedside. I remember Mum saying, 'Remember this day – three men wanting to marry you!' and her chuckling over and over again.

A lot of my friends were getting married, I was 27 and I remember thinking, Well, it's about time I got married too. To have been thinking like that sounds strange, I know, but I was a pretty strange person at the time. Looking back, I hardly recognise the Trisha I was then. But there it is, I felt like it was about time I got hitched, so I sounded my parents out about it.

'This guy Robert wants to marry me,' I said to them as I lay propped up on the couch.

'Don't be stupid, you hardly know him!' said Mum.

'It could work out very well,' said Dad, 'and you could grow to love each other very much.'

Dad's response was the one I wanted to hear. I started to seriously consider my options.

A few days later, the BBC asked me when I could start. I'd got the traineeship. I was over the moon. The dream of my lifetime had just come true – I was going to be a journalist for the BBC.

Then they told me the starting salary.

Ten thousand pounds a year was the offer. I was

shocked. I was one of 12 candidates chosen from over seven thousand and they were offering me for a year what I was earning every couple of months as an air hostess.

Some might say it's daft to turn down a prestigious traineeship because of the money, but at the time I wasn't so interested in what some might say. On the spur of the moment, I thought, Sorry, BBC, I'm off to seek my fame and fortune in Australia.

I managed to convince myself I was falling for Robert, and my dad's words about growing to love someone stuck in my ears.

With hindsight, I can say Robert and Australia offered me a way out of my situation, and a way of getting ahead. I wanted to jump and Robert was my parachute, but if anyone had put it that way at the time I would have fiercely denied it.

I didn't say yes to marriage straight away, but I bought a ticket for Australia.

And this time it was a one-way ticket.

12

The Politician's Wife

I'd done it. I'd finally said goodbye to Gulf Air and was ready to start a new life with Robert. I moved into his house in October 1985 and was thrust into a new world of political meetings, cocktail parties and posh dinners. I spent the first few weeks accompanying Robert everywhere. I was having a ball, but it soon became apparent that marriage was something he wanted really badly, for he kept on mentioning it.

His proposal was slightly bizarre. We were sitting in a hotel foyer, chatting before a function in Parliament House, Canberra. Then, mid-conversation, Robert went very quiet and tears started streaming down his cheeks. I asked him what was wrong.

'I don't want to lose you,' he said.

I didn't think I'd given him any reason to worry about losing me, and wondered what he was talking about. It was a bit disturbing watching this haughty creature crying in front of me and not really understanding why.

It was then that he produced a ring. 'This is for you.'

I accepted it but, as I slipped it on to my finger, I felt strange. I certainly wasn't in love, and I wasn't so sure he was either. I cared for Robert, and he had certainly made me feel cared for too, but looking back I realise I agreed to marry him because I was in love with the idea of being engaged. I also realised that Robert might take me to places I wouldn't otherwise have been able to go so easily and he might introduce me to people I would not ordinarily have met. There's no denying that my behaviour was a little mercenary but Robert's motives for marrying me were suspect too, as I would later discover.

It was October and we agreed to marry in December.

After eight weeks of wondering if I'd done the right thing, the wedding day had arrived and I was running late for the service. I kept getting the car to drive me around the block near the church. I was having serious doubts and wondering how I could run away. My head was spinning. I tried to tell myself I could grow to love Robert, that my jitters were just last-minute worries that would go away after it was all over. But what was I getting myself into? I kept thinking. I tried to convince myself it was all a good idea, but at the same time I wanted to escape.

The problem was, I had nowhere to go.

I knew a few people in Australia but didn't want to dump myself upon them. As for going back to England, I'd passed up the BBC traineeship and I could not face the prospect of returning to Mum with egg on my face. If I could have come up with an escape plan, I would have taken it, but I couldn't think of anything viable.

After the car had gone around the block several times, I just said to myself, 'Trisha, you're gonna have to get on with it, for God's sake!' I told the driver I was ready to go in.

As I walked down the aisle of the Wayside Chapel in Kings Cross, Sydney, my head was filled with doubt. Let's just say I had a feeling this wasn't going to be the happiest day of my life. I arrived at Robert's side and smiled. I felt ridiculous, but I went through with it all. As I said, 'I do,' I thought, What have you done, you silly cow?

We were married by the late Reverend Ted Noffs and, along with a few ex-Gulf Air Aussie pals of mine, the congregation was a real A-list of politicians and society types – famous Aussies such as Philip Ruddock, Michael Photios, John Dowd and Ron Saw were in attendance, along with many others, but none of it mattered to me. All the way through the service, I just felt hollow and angry with myself for not listening to my mother when she told me I barely knew Robert and that I was daft for agreeing to marry him. I walked out of the church as the wife of a man I barely knew. My heart had sunk, but I knew it was me who'd got myself into this predicament. I resolved to make things work. I kept in mind my dad's advice, and tried to silence the memory of my mother's words.

None of my family had been able to make it over from England. I was surrounded by loads of strangers and it was a pretty lonely day. We had a bit of a 'do' at Robert's house, a very modest, joyless reception. Once everyone had left, Robert said something that unsettled me, to put it mildly. 'I'm off to Canberra in the morning,' he casually dropped in.

I was expecting to be going on some sort of honeymoon, if not spending the next day together at least. I told Robert I thought it strange that he hadn't mentioned the Canberra trip earlier. 'Oh, come now, darling,' he replied dismissively, 'you didn't just expect me to lounge around with you, did you?'

I was gobsmacked. Robert's words were enough to tell me that things had already changed – the ring was on my finger and there was no need for pretence or charm any more. He didn't invite me along with him, something he certainly would have done before we got married. Robert had got what he wanted – a token wife – and that was that as far as he was concerned. But, much to his dismay, Robert would soon realise he'd picked the wrong person for the job. Whether I'd been a bit daft marrying him or not, I definitely wasn't going to be anyone's 'token'.

We didn't consummate the marriage that night and when I awoke in the morning Robert had left for Canberra.

From that day on, all pretence was dropped and Robert revealed his true nature. He was a control freak, and it was his controlling nature that would eventually drive me mad.

Robert lived like a bachelor, but would call on me when he needed me to attend a function or go on business that required him to be seen with a partner. I could cope with that, but what I couldn't stand was the way he would not let me wear what I wanted to. Whatever I chose to wear, nine times out of ten he would tell me to take it off. I had a collection of beautiful and exotic clothes from India, but Robert hated them all. Whenever I wore them he would simply say, 'Oh, sweetheart, yuk!' or, 'No, no, no, you can't wear that.' If I protested he would simply answer, 'I have spoken and that is it, now get changed.'

Often Robert would call up and say something like, 'Darling, we've got this cocktail party at six o'clock.' He'd drop that on me and when I'd ask about the dress code the reply would be: 'Oh, don't worry about that, my secretary's coming over with something for you to wear.'

If I didn't do as he said there would be a massive row that consisted of me shouting and him being cool and calm – the consummate politician. The rows were so intellectually exhausting that I would often end up giving in to him just to get him off my back.

When he got his way, Robert would always parade me around whichever occasion we were attending and in his loud, pompous manner declare to everyone how 'super' and 'divine' I looked. I would feel like a right gooseberry. If I stood my ground and wore my own clothes, I would often receive compliments from others. When this happened in earshot of Robert, he would simply glance at me, shudder disdainfully and walk off. He had a knack of putting people down and embarrassing them in front of others, and he started trying to do this to me with alarming regularity.

But by then I was my own person, and I wasn't going to be told what to do.

Sure, I'd give in to Robert sometimes, but only to make things easier. It wasn't easy to control me, and Robert knew it. He even joked about it on many occasions, saying, 'You're a challenge, darling, but I'll break you.'

It seems he was pretty dedicated to his cause, because he soon progressed to new methods of control – he began to 'accidentally' lock me in the house.

The downstairs windows were double-padlocked for security, so all Robert had to do was double-lock the door from the outside to ensure I was stuck inside until he fancied coming home. I remember calling his office and saying, 'You've gone to work and bloody locked me in!' to which he replied, 'Oh, darling, so sorry. But never mind, I'll be home at four, darling, so I'll let you out then,' as if locking me up was perfectly acceptable. When he got home, he insisted it was a mistake. If it was a mistake, it was a mistake he would make many, many times.

Being frequently stuck in the house and not being able to wear what I wanted when I went out without Robert kicking up a caustically worded stink soon made me realise I'd made a bit of a boo-boo getting married. I wasn't allowed to put anything up in the house either, pictures and so on, so it wasn't like I could do a bit of home improvement while locked up.

Our sex life was pretty diabolical too. When we did try, Robert either couldn't get it up, or would suddenly 'lose interest' during sex. It wasn't long before we stopped doing it altogether, which was actually a relief. Within three months, we were in separate beds.

Even though I refused to be a good little wife, I was useful to Robert, especially within UNICEF and diplomatic circles. My being black, and able to speak French, German and a bit of Arabic and Swahili, made

Robert look very good when we met international delegates. I was a talking point and got him lots of press.

Robert was obsessed with image, and I made him look good. But our private relationship was totally shambolic.

Thankfully, there was something that saved me – work.

Whether it was because he genuinely cared, or because he just wanted me out of the way – having not managed to tame me despite all his efforts – Robert eventually delivered on his promise to help my career and introduced me to Peter and Claire Wilkinson. Peter was a top TV journalist for Nine Network's *A Current Affair* and his wife Claire was in PR.

'So you want to be in TV?' asked Peter.

Silly question – I was *desperate* to get into TV. Peter gave me all sorts of advice, and before I knew it Claire had taken me on to work with her on a PR exercise called Campaign for World Vision. I was thrown in right at the deep end and I absolutely loved it from the start. We were making a TV programme with lots of celebs in it. Within days I was talking to Torvill & Dean, Pat Cash, Peter Garrett from the band Midnight Oil (all of whom were at the height of their fame then) and writing parts for them to read in the charity documentary. I was so pleased to be doing something I liked after having had my brain on pause while I was at Gulf Air. Claire and Peter became great friends of mine, and I'll never be able to thank them enough for giving me my first break in the media. In fact, I look upon my darling Claire as my surrogate sister.

After a while, Claire decided to close down the company and move on. Luckily, I got another job right away. I went to work for Jan Murray, whom I'd met through John Brown, then Minister of Tourism. Jan ran a PR company that dealt with huge campaigns, and I was in the right place at the right time. I worked alongside Sue Pieters-Hawke, the daughter of the then Prime Minister Bob Hawke, and we really hit it off. We worked like dogs, and I loved every minute of it. There were insane amounts of cash around in the mid-1980s, and one of the best things about the job was that I could come up with mad-sounding PR schemes and be taken seriously. The money that people would spend on promoting something was unbelievable.

The opening of the Gold Coast International Hotel was one such lavish affair. I was put in charge of organising helicopters to fly over the hotel in formation while an orchestra played 'The Ride of the Valkyries' to guests before they partied in the grand ballrooms, each of which was lavishly themed. The funniest part of it all was smuggling guests Jason Donovan and Kylie Minogue between rooms because nobody knew that they were seeing each other at the time. We made sure they could have a good time together, and nobody suspected a thing.

Another time we did PR for an event at which Joe Cocker was playing. He'd just written 'You Can Leave Your Hat On' and for this number he wanted a stripper who could lap dance around on stage with him. I'll never forget driving around Kings Cross and approaching likely candidates to ask them if they would come to the Sydney Entertainment Centre. Eventually we found a willing candidate and got her on stage just in the nick of time. Joe gave me a signed photo by way of thanks and I only have to look at it to be transported right back to the beginning of my career.

Those initial months of work were fantastic. I got a real kick out of work and knew that I was on the up. I was determined to keep on rising and was soon calling TV channels to let them know I was ready and willing for anything they could offer me. I screen-tested for MTV, but nothing came of it. The executive producer angrily told me he had been ordered to veto me because Australia wasn't ready for a black TV presenter.

Then I got my first break in TV, on Channel Ten's *Off The Dish*. My job was to present a fitness workout for kids – not quite what I'd had in mind when doing my journalism courses, but still it was the foot in the door that I was so desperate for. Life at work was great. Great because I loved it, and because it kept me away from Robert.

Life with Robert was shit. There's simply no other word for it.

When I was around him, he showed no interest in my work, and disapproved of the people I was mixing with. Jan, Claire and my other friends were pretty entrepreneurial and free-thinking, whereas Robert was just to the right of Genghis Khan, so it was hardly surprising they found him a bit of a 'quaint oddball'. Whenever I made friends with anyone, he would go to extraordinary lengths to find evidence that they weren't 'suitable'. I just thought he was a stuffy control freak, and completely ignored his mutterings and put-downs about my mates. Let him do what he wants, I thought. Besides, my friends just put up with Robert for my sake, so it didn't really matter.

But it wasn't long before I discovered how much of an interest in controlling me Robert was really taking. To my horror I discovered that he had people inadvertently spying on me. And not just any old people. Robert's 'spies' were my friends.

I had a group of mates – Stella, Guy, Nicki and Noel – that I'd regularly meet for coffee or to go to the gym. We'd catch up, bitch about things and have a right laugh together, and I'd often let off steam about Robert. One day I'd been mouthing off to them about what a boring old fogey Robert was before saying goodbye.

Later that night Robert and I were talking when he dropped into the conversation, 'Well, since you think I'm such an old fogey...' It was strange hearing my words quoted back to me, but I assumed it was merely a coincidence – perhaps Robert thought he was an old fogey too and was just guessing my feelings, I told myself.

The trouble was that this kind of thing started to happen to the point that it was uncanny. I started getting paranoid, but didn't mention to my friends what was going on because it sounded a bit mad. After all, none of them knew Robert very well and Noel had never met him, so it seemed impossible that Robert could know what I'd been saying to them.

Then, one night after I'd been at the gym with Noel, everything became horribly clear. For a few days Noel had been troubled when he was with me, and had led me to believe it was because something awful was about to happen in a showdown between him and his father. Then, a few days after the 'dreaded meeting' had supposedly occurred, we were drinking wine at his place and I was asking what had happened. After a few drinks, Noel confessed that his troubled state had nothing do to with his dad.

'Well, what is it then?' I asked. 'You've been stressing out for days. You had this meeting with your dad and you haven't said a word about what happened.'

'You're going to hate me,' he said, 'but it's Robert.'

'My Robert?'

'Yes. He phoned me.'

'What?' I said, shocked. 'How come? He doesn't have your number. What did he want?'

'He wanted to do a deal. He took me to the Hilton for dinner and said he wanted me to sleep with you so that he wouldn't have to have sex with you any more. He thought he might lose you if you don't have a sex life. He told me what turns you on, what you like to do in bed, you know...'

I was utterly shocked. For a start, Noel was openly gay and for a few seconds my head was just spinning as I tried to work out what the fuck was going on. It was madness. Suddenly I became angry that one of my closest friends had been talking to Robert about me behind my back. Noel knew about all my troubles with Robert, and it felt like betrayal. I could tell he was in a mess about it, but I was livid with him for having agreed to meet Robert in the first place. Noel told me that he knew Robert had been in touch with Guy and Stella too.

I went mad, and lost it with Noel. My reaction wasn't helped by the wine I'd drunk, and I really let loose on him, calling him a fucking traitor, among other things. I probably went a bit over the top. After all, Noel had felt bad and confessed all to me, and that had to count for something. I knew how persuasive and controlling Robert was, and, while I was pissed off with Noel, it was Robert who was to blame. I stormed out of Noel's flat and marched home. Noel followed me down the street, apologising and begging me to calm down, but I shrugged him off.

Robert was in bed when I got back to the house.

'You fucking bastard!' I screamed, bursting into his bedroom and turning the light on. 'I thought I was going mad, but I wasn't going mad – you've been calling my friends up and finding out about me. What the fuck do you want from me, you arsehole?'

Robert jumped out of bed and moved towards me, repeatedly telling me to calm down. I had no intention of calming down. His patronising instructions only made me grow even angrier.

'Are you out of your mind?' I yelled.

'Calm down, dear, don't get hysterical. You're not well.'

I was hysterical, and for good bloody reason! From the moment I'd married him, my husband had been trying to control every aspect of my life – from what I wore, to what I said, to the company I kept – and now he was using my mates to find out what I was saying and doing when I wasn't with him.

Robert came closer and grabbed my wrists.

'Don't you fucking touch me!' I shouted, pulling myself free.

'You're being hysterical, dear,' he said calmly, dismissively, like a parent to a child. 'I'll call the doctor and he can come and give you a shot to calm you down.'

'*Injections!* I don't need fucking injections. I'm fucking

angry! Don't you get it? You've betrayed me and you've made my friends betray me. You went along to Noel and discussed me and my sex life like I'm a kept animal! *How dare you...!*'

Robert kept coming towards me, steadily and slowly, shaking his head as if I'd got it all wrong. He looked at me as if I were mad.

'Keep away,' I said, 'leave me alone and go back to bed. Just leave me alone!'

I went downstairs to the kitchen and tried to regain my cool, but I couldn't. To make things worse, Robert followed me. I told him to stay the fuck away from me, but he wouldn't listen. He kept approaching me slowly, creepily. He knew how to get inside my head, and he was purposely doing just that by behaving like this. I think he got some kind of sadistic kick out of it. He just kept his politician's lecture going. 'It's time to calm down now, dear...' And so it went on.

All I wanted was for him to go away. Anything he said just added fuel to my fire – I needed to be left alone. But he wouldn't stop. I was totally hemmed in, trapped and claustrophobic. I didn't know what to do. Since my days with Adrian, situations like this made me panic.

So that's when I grabbed the knife.

'*Get back!*' I screamed. The moment I had the kitchen knife in my hand, I felt strange, as if I'd got myself into something I hadn't intended to. I certainly had no intention of using it. It was just a desperate measure, a demonstration. It was drama.

Robert totally misread what I was doing. He started talking to me in clichés, like I was some kind of murderous idiot. 'Just put the knife down, you don't need to do this, this isn't the answer...' he said as he came closer.

All I wanted was for Robert to go away.

'You're not the most stable of people, Trisha, we know that, don't we?' He was utterly demeaning. 'I can get a doctor for you; we can take you to a hospital and get you the help you need.'

I was going crazy. His patronising words were rattling around my head and all the time I knew I had a right to be angry. Robert was denying me that right, he was talking to me as if I didn't exist, as if my mind was not my own. 'Now, now, Trisha, calm down, dear...'

Robert was getting closer, and the panic in me kept rising. I kept telling him to stay back, and for a second I felt it was within my power to stab him. As I stood there, frozen, knife in hand, trying to control my wild thoughts, he suddenly launched himself towards me, catching me off-gaurd.

I'll never forget the sound of spattering across the ceiling. It was the same as the sound of wet paint being flicked on to a surface. But it wasn't paint, it was blood.

My blood.

The cold realisation of what I'd done came a few seconds later. As Robert had thrown himself at me, I had simply panicked. In a moment of madness, of total despair at an impossible situation, I had turned the knife on myself. I'd plunged it hard into my wrist. It had gone deep, deep enough to sever an artery and spray blood on the ceiling.

In a split second, I went freezing cold. I dropped the knife and clamped my right hand over my left wrist to try and stop the blood pouring out. I made for the telephone across the hall, but didn't get there. I collapsed on the floor.

Robert was panicking, shouting hysterically, 'Oh my God' over and over again.

'Shut up and call 999 *now!*' I told him. Then, bizarrely, I started doing first aid on myself, telling Robert to help me keep my left arm raised. He was shaking non-stop while he mutely did as he was told.

Robert called an ambulance and told them what had happened. Then, just before he hung up, he added, 'I'd appreciate it if you didn't use the siren. We don't need people to know about this.'

I could hardly believe my ears. Staggeringly, Robert gave more of a shit about his image than whether I lived or died.

When the ambulance turned up, Robert fussed around, not over me but urging the stretcher-bearers to hurry up. 'We don't want people seeing this,' he kept saying.

'I think it's a bit too serious to be worrying about that!' said the paramedic, who looked completely thrown by Robert's brazen display of selfishness. 'Is he your husband?' he asked me as he turned away from Robert and lifted me into the ambulance.

'You can fucking call him that if you like,' I replied as the ambulance door closed.

Robert remained on the street. Now I was on my way to Accident and Emergency, he was finally ready to leave me alone.

The pain was like nothing else. I arrived at the hospital but they couldn't give me anything to lessen the agony until the alcohol was out of my system. I had cut through a load of nerve endings in my wrist and I was wailing like an animal, howling the place down at times and at others just whimpering and shivering.

After a few hours, Posh Boy waltzed in wearing his cravat and navy blazer, and introduced himself to everybody. Robert was all charm and show, but when he got around to me he simply said, 'Keep it down, darling, keep it down.' He didn't seem to care a bit about the state I was in. I was just a bit of an embarrassment to him. I remember looking at him then and for the first time in our relationship I thought, I truly hate you and you will never know how much. I had a sense of utter loathing for this man, and I knew that what had happened was his fault. Worse still, I was hating myself for thinking I could make myself love him. A couple of nurses noticed the distress Robert was causing me and eventually asked him to leave.

I find it hard to describe the thinking behind what I had done to myself, but I know it was a moment of desperation that resulted from a culmination of non-stop manipulative shit from Robert that had gone on for months and months. He had pushed me to the point of madness, and in a moment of hysteria I had struck out. Scary though it is to admit, I believe if I hadn't turned the blade on myself I'd have ended up in prison for manslaughter. I didn't want to die, but I didn't want to carry on living the way I was. Although I was on the 'suicide ward' I knew that mine had not been an attempt to kill myself. Rather, it was a destructive means of escaping a horribly suffocating situation and losing my temper with Robert – but mostly with myself. I was mentally in a bad place, but I had not wanted to die. I had wanted to escape.

Luckily, I had an amazing surgeon to operate on my wrist and reconnect the nerves; even so, another doctor casually informed me that I would never regain use of my left hand. I felt totally winded – it didn't seem possible that this is what my actions had led to. It was devastating news, but I resolved there and then to somehow prove them wrong. I simply wouldn't accept what I was being told. Bollocks to what the doctor said, I was going to use my hand again come hell or high water.

I spent most of my time in hospital as high as a kite on pethidine, an incredibly powerful painkiller. I would highly recommend it to anyone with their hand hanging off – I was off my face on the stuff. I remember my friend Stella coming to visit me while I was on the pethidine drip. I felt like I was floating somewhere at the top of the ward and I said to her, 'Ooh, Stella, you're a long way down there.' It was great. Not so brilliant was the fact that pethidine was highly addictive. By the time they released me I was totally dependent on it.

Peter and Claire Wilkinson had told me not to go back to Robert, but all of my belongings were there, and after his first visit to the hospital Robert had returned and turned the charm back on with me and every other patient on my ward. To my surprise, he was very supportive and kept saying how he wanted to make things work between us once I got home. Part of me thought that he had realised where he'd gone wrong and wanted to patch things up. I thought he might change a bit and give the control-freakery a rest, so I went back to him. Hah!

Trisha – *As I Am*

My left arm was in a massive plaster cast. I was in severe pain and felt helpless. On my first day back at home, Robert offered to cook. All I could keep down was soup so I asked for pumpkin soup. 'You sit down and stay there, and I'll go and make you your soup,' he said.

He came back with the soup and set it down on the coffee table in front of me. 'There you go, darling, eat it all up.'

I sniffed the soup and it sure didn't smell like pumpkin. It smelt like oxtail. My vegetarianism was always something that Robert tried to change about me. Ever since we'd got together, he had regularly placed meat in front of me and told me to forget my silly principles and eat it. Now he was doing the same thing again on my first day out of hospital. If I hadn't been such a mess at the time I would have laughed at the audacity of the man. 'This is oxtail, Robert,' I said in disbelief. 'You know I don't eat meat.'

'Oh, well, now you're home again, we can forget about all that nonsense. Be a good girl and eat it up.'

How stupid I had been to think Robert might have rethought his ways. The man had no empathy at all. I was living with a narcissistic maniac. Oh, God, I thought, I can't stay here. *Robert's going to drive me mad...*

I was disabled and addicted to pethidine tablets. Robert hid these and used them as a way of controlling me – I had to do as I was told to get the pills I needed from him – and I soon realised that he had me completely in his power. Robert was finally winning his struggle for control. It was then that I really did start to feel suicidal.

I had to do something. I had to escape.

The Politician's Wife

Salvation came when my dear friend Sue Flatman convinced Robert that I needed to go to a retreat so I could detox from the pethidine. Even Robert could see how bad my dependency on the drug had become, so he let me go off to an ashram at Mangrove Mountain, 90 minutes' drive north of Sydney. Noel came with me (I'd forgiven him for his betrayal by then) and we spent ten days there.

But it was no spa, more like a boot camp. I had to get up at 4am, take freezing showers and work my arse off on the land before doing yoga and meditation to try to deal with the pain of withdrawal from pethidine. And, boy, was it painful, both physically and mentally. I'd be screaming down the walls at times, and when I was asleep the vivid nightmares were horrendous, but with Noel's help I got through it and returned to Sydney a recovered pethidine junkie.

I went back to Robert's place, but was very wary of him. I knew I had to deal with my farce of a marriage, but first I wanted my hand to heal and to get back to work. I wasn't having any of the doctors' pessimism about it. I underwent huge amounts of physio. It was a pain in the arse, and the wrist, but after a year of hard work I had recovered nearly full use of my hand. The only thing that did not fully return is my sense of touch, and now I have only 60 per cent feeling in my left hand. It doesn't prove much of a problem but I have to be careful with hot water or fire in case I burn myself without knowing it. Also, I've been unable to enjoy my passion for playing the piano like I used to.

I was very disturbed by everything that had happened,

139

and I felt so alone. In truth, I was pretty fucked up, and things had been made worse by being with Robert. It was he who suggested I go and see a psychiatrist, although ironically I felt that if it hadn't been for him I wouldn't have needed one. I was sceptical but agreed to go. Little did I know that Robert would come with me. I had so much to get off my chest, but with him in the room I was unable to talk honestly about everything that was getting me down, and it was completely pointless. He kept chiming in with his theories on my 'behaviour'.

I considered going back on my own, but the knowledge that Robert knew the shrink I was seeing set alarm bells ringing. If he can get to my friends, I thought, what would stop him persuading a shrink to give him some inside information? Visiting a psychiatrist should offer someone a completely safe retreat from the world, but, if Robert had knowledge of what I wanted to tell the psychiatrist, it would have given him the power to turn my life into even more of a living hell with any number of mind games. The prospect of that didn't appeal, to say the least.

Robert's antics had pushed me to a point of anxiety where the only people I could completely trust were strangers. It was this that made me step into a counsellor's office in the red-light area of Kings Cross one afternoon as I was walking home from the gym. I saw the sign and thought, Why not?

Right away, a woman was available to see me. She had long dark hair and was incredibly nice. She sat me down and told me to tell her everything from the start. Because I was talking to a complete stranger, I was able to let it all out – most of it anyway. By that stage, I was so paranoid that a part of me felt that what I was saying would somehow get back to Robert. But by the third session I was completely relaxed, and I was starting to feel a lot clearer in my head. We'd been talking about whether or not the marriage could be saved, and the woman helped me untangle my messy feelings and examine them clearly. It was all going fine until I produced a photo of Robert. Immediately the woman saw Robert's face in the photograph, she froze.

'Get out!' she said, interrupting whatever I was saying.

'What?' I said, confused.

'Get out of that marriage. Leave. Do you have somewhere you can go to?'

I was baffled. 'But two seconds ago you were talking to me about saving my marriage, about getting my needs met,' I stammered.

'Forget all that,' she said. 'Take my advice and leave him right away. I'm not at liberty to tell you why I know you should leave, but, believe me, I know.'

The counsellor spoke with such conviction, such honesty, that I couldn't ignore her. I kept asking her what she knew, but all my pleas were in vain. She was duty-bound not to tell me. All she could say was: 'Leave him.' To say I was intrigued is the understatement of the century. What could be *so* bad about Robert, I wondered, that a randomly chosen counsellor would urge me to leave him immediately? It would be some years before I got an idea.

I walked out of her office knowing exactly what I had to do.

The next day, three months after I had slashed my wrist,

I rang a removal man, then stuffed all of my belongings into plastic bags. When Robert came home that night in November 1986, he was greeted by a removal man and yours truly glued to the old chap's side as we lugged black bin liners into his van. The truly farcical thing is that Robert was so scared of his image being tarnished that he pretended he knew I was moving out and jovially chatted with the perplexed removal man. He even made out he was helping me. 'Here, darling, don't forget this one,' he chirruped, holding out one of my carrier bags.

Robert didn't even have a clue where I was going. And that's the way I wanted it.

I jumped into the van and shut the door. Me, my plaster cast and plastic bags were all on the road.

13

News Beginnings

SBS, the so-called 'ethnic diversity' Australian public TV channel, was looking for a new reporter on its *Nine O'Clock* news and current affairs programme, and it was the night before the deadline for applications. Jan Murray and I had just been working on a PR project with popular SBS newsreader George Donikian, who told me about the vacancy. 'Just do it!' he said. 'You've got what it takes, I know it.'

I had four hours to get my shit together and put my CV in, and I didn't waste a minute. At 11.50pm, my mate's car screeched to a halt outside SBS. Out I jumped and through the letterbox went the envelope containing what I hoped was my ticket to the future. Nothing ventured, nothing gained, I thought.

I was called to an interview and screen-tested, sent away, then called back again. I can't say I wasn't nervous as I waited in the newsroom at the desk of *Nine O'Clock*'s Executive Producer, Neil Bowes.

'I think you've got what it takes to be very good,' he enthused as he sat opposite me, 'and I'm impressed.'

I was waiting for a 'but'. If there was going to be one, I expected it would be 'but you're black'. I'd already heard it several times in other interviews for on-air TV jobs.

'You've got something,' he continued, 'you've really got something. You're gonna surprise a lot of people in this industry!'

You're quite mad, I thought, but, if that's what you think, then I'm not going to try to convince you otherwise.

'Does this mean I've got the job?' I asked.

'Of course it does, Trisha, welcome to SBS!'

Up until then, apart from the kids' TV show *Off The Dish*, the only other TV work I'd done was unpaid work experience on Channel Nine's *Midday Show* with Ray Martin. But this time I really was in at the deep end. I was to be a current affairs reporter on a channel that engaged with politics and current affairs on a local, national and global level, and I needed to know my stuff. I had only been in Australia a year, and I had learned a lot about the machinations of Australian politics from Robert, but there were big gaps in my knowledge of the country's history and culture. Ever mindful of my mum's advice – 'You've got to work twice as hard to be half as good' – I threw myself into reading anything I could get my hands on that might help me in my job.

As SBS was an ethnic channel, I got to cover a wide variety of issues in my stories: domestic violence against Filipino brides, Aboriginal deaths in custody, the building of Sydney's Darling Harbour, mental illness – the list goes on. I also learned how to work researching and producing, and one of my early jobs was to work with presenter Christina Katsoukas when she interviewed Archbishop Desmond Tutu talking about Nelson Mandela.

I was really driven and determined to get ahead and succeed. I worked obsessively on my stories, researching every angle and always working with the cameraman to make sure I had the right video footage to accompany a report. Many reporters would just hand their material over to an editor and leave it there, but I was a bit of a control freak and always sat with the editors (sometimes into the early hours of the morning) to achieve a finished product that I was happy with. My obsessive traits resulted not just from a desire for perfection but also from a huge fear of criticism – I had to make sure there were no cracks in my work, otherwise I would be open to negative comments from others.

It's odd to think I might not have done so well if the seeds of self-doubt had not been sown when I was young. After the constant criticism from my father during childhood, I was always terrified of disapproval, and it was this that spurred me on to go the extra mile at work. I had to make sure that what I did was approved of, and I was really addicted to hard graft and learning anything and everything from anyone I could. Looking back on the initial stories I filmed and edited, I am proud of them. Without wanting to blow my own trumpet, they were pretty damn good for a beginner!

Even though I was working crazy hours, I was full of energy and had an insatiable appetite for more TV experience. After a few months, I was asked to do my second audition to be a presenter on the ABC's children's show *Play School*. During the audition, I had to jump up like a jack-in-the-box with presenter Philip Quast. As I sprang up, my braids swung wildly like a cat-o'-nine tails, whipping Philip across the face! I think it was my looking at the camera, smacking my plaits and saying, 'Naughty hair!' that got me the part.

Play School was something of a contrast to news and current affairs reporting, but I adored it. The team had a huge commitment to children's education and entertainment and from a technical point of view I learned a huge amount about working with multiple cameras on live (or 'as live', meaning 'taped in one go') TV. 'Multicam' was a very hard thing to get to grips with, but once I'd mastered it I was set up for life – without my *Play School* experience there's no way I would be able to feel so at ease on my show today.

I stayed with *Play School* for 12 years. One of the reasons I kept going for so long was the amount of racism in Australia. If I'm on TV twice a day in front of four-year-old kids, I always thought, then there's a good chance they will grow up thinking black people are no big deal. It was highly likely that I'd be the only black face a lot of kids would get to see and, if I couldn't crack bigotry in older generations, I was sure going to do my bit to make sure the up-and-coming generation got it right.

My life was work, and very little else. At SBS we started at 7am and would normally finish around midnight or 1am. There was such a buzz in the newsroom that the time simply flew by, and as a result I'd finish work absolutely full of adrenalin. I'd be absolutely knackered but unable to

A new chapter of my life, with happiness and stability at last. It took a while for my girls to feel settled around Peter but the birthday party he organised for Billie certainly helped to win her over!

Peter and I got married in Cortina, Italy. This time, I got married for all the right reasons.

Opportunity knocks! Malcolm Allsop from Anglia TV was as good as his word – he took me to England and made me a star. Here is one of the early publicity shots from *Trisha*.

All change! One minute I was in Australia, the next I was back in England. *Above left*: The snow was a great surprise for the girls. Here they are, trudging to school in Norwich. *Above right*: Being back in England meant I could see more of my mum and that my parents could spend more time with their grandchildren.

Below left: Peter and I in Cannes. Madi took us by surprise by jumping out, wielding a camera and pretending to be a paparazzo. *Below right*: And here's Madi's reaction to being snapped by Peter, the other 'paparazzo' in the family.

Above: My great friend, Claire, who I look upon as a surrogate sister. It was Claire and her husband, Peter, who gave me my first break in television.

Below left: With our great friends from Australia, Madison (*left*) and Kevin (*right*). More recently, Peter arranged for them to be surprise guests at my fiftieth birthday party – and what a welcome surprise it was!

Below right: My personal trainer, Darrell, was like a brother to me. Tragically, he died after he hit his head while trying to get out of a moving car.

Above: King and queen of daytime TV? With Jerry Springer in New Orleans in 1999.

Below: With the brilliantly talented Whoopi Goldberg.

I'm addicted to exercise and running is my passion. When people say that I'm lucky to have the figure I now have, I tell them that they can have the same luck if they come on a twelve-mile run with me!

20:35:02   16-03-2005 20:36:54   31.1   16-03-20

Above: The press liked the story of how I saved a woman from choking using the Heimlich manoeuvre – and the CCTV footage was soon in the hands of the world's picture libraries! I knew my first aid training would come in useful … © *Rex Features*

Below: This is quite a recent photo, taken when Peter and I went on a trip to Dubai. We flew with none other than Gulf Air but the uniform had changed a bit since my day!

wind down. This was a real problem since I had to be up again in a few hours. Luckily, there was an answer – dope!

Up until SBS my dope smoking had always been a social, take-it-or-leave-it thing. Now it became something of a necessity. I'd feel slightly guilty about it but it got to the stage where I'd have a spliff just to knock myself out. And I wasn't the only one – loads of us in TV were at it. Once the work was over, booze and dope were the order of the day. I wasn't so into drinking because of the hangovers on those early mornings, but I did have a bit of a love affair with dope. After a joint or two at bedtime, I could still function well the next day. Mind you, we weren't smoking the crazy shit people smoke now. It's never healthy smoking weed, but the chemically enhanced skunk that kids mess about with these days is worlds away from what we smoked. I rarely bought my own dope, as one or other of my mates would always be happy to share some.

Another mate from this time was Scott, a brilliant tape editor that I had a bit of a crush on, and we worked closely together. It was through him that I ended up meeting the man with whom I would spend the next six years of my life, Mark Greive.

Mark was a tape editor too, and the first time we ever noticed each other was at an industry bash called the Jump Cutter's Ball. I was wearing a very low-cut, tutu-like dress – I could get away with that kind of thing in those days – and had my braids up in a high ponytail. Mark was sitting at the SBS table, with a girl hanging on each arm, and snogging each of them in turn. Whenever he took a break from doing that, his glazed eyes were focused exclusively on my tits – it was as if they were the only part of me that existed. Hardly a class act, I must admit, and I can't say I fell for him that night, but in the weeks that followed we started hanging out together.

It's a little sad to say it but one of the things that drew me to Mark was that he usually had dope on him. Mark liked getting stoned, and I was more than happy to join him. Also, Mark was quite good-looking then, and we did have a real laugh together. I was so focused on work that I wasn't interested in much more than going on dates, mucking around and getting stoned. We slept together on and off, and I saw Mark as a mate I was sort of going out with, but nothing serious.

The only reason our relationship went to another level was that we found ourselves having to move out of our respective flats at the same time – I'd been living with a friend of a friend since leaving Robert – and ended up getting a place together. I was very reluctant at first, but Mark was very keen and kept on about what a great idea it would be. In the end I just thought, Fuck it, what does it matter? Work was so busy that it was an easy option to move in with him.

We took a run-down shack of a cottage with a garden in Cammeray, on the North Shore of Sydney's Harbour. With the help of a few friends, we redecorated the place and turned it into a home. I was able to get to work easily and my new living situation suited me just fine. Unfortunately, the same could not be said for my new living partner. Within a few days of our moving in, it was crisis time for Mark.

'You're never here,' he began one night. 'You're at work all the time and I'm in this place on my own.'

As an editor, Mark had set shifts, whereas I was still working very long, unpredictable hours. He was right, I *was* out a lot, but I didn't remember telling him I would be around all the time. There was no way I was going to slow down at work just because I'd found a place with someone. God knows what he expected me to say, but I gave it to him straight. 'My career comes first, Mark, and I've never pretended otherwise!'

'Well, I'm not sure if I like that,' he snapped at me.

'Well, if you don't fucking like it you might as well move out now because there is absolutely no way I'm gonna do anything like cut back. I love my job, I'm learning and I'm going to work all the hours I can get. After Robert, there's no way I'm giving up this dream for any man!' I meant every word of it.

Mark's reaction was to give me an ultimatum. 'Well, which comes first, me or the job?' he said dramatically. 'If it's the job, then I'm outta here!'

'Bye then!' I said.

If Mark thought I was going to cut back my pursuit of a career and turn into the ideal girlfriend, he was having a laugh. I thought I'd already made myself pretty clear, but it seemed I had to really spell it out.

'If you're going to live with me, you'd better understand my terms,' I told him. 'My career comes first, and if you can't live with that you can piss off out of it. I'll give you three days to decide what you want to do. If you decide to stay, don't ever bring it up again.'

God, I was a mercenary cow back then! I was deadly serious about what I'd said. If Mark had said, 'Stick it up your jacksie!' I would have been sad but not devastated. I just knew what I wanted and wasn't prepared to compromise, especially with what I saw at the time as a fling. I was unashamedly ambitious, determined and ruthlessly driven. I'm not sure how healthy my obsession with work was, but that's the way things were and nobody was going to get in my way. Besides, after my experience with Robert and his controlling ways, even a whiff of that kind of behaviour in Mark was enough to make me want to run. I went on the offensive as a means of protecting myself. In the end, Mark agreed to do things my way, but I think he hoped I'd get the work bug out of my system as time went on.

Time did go on, and I carried on working as hard as ever. When I wasn't in the newsroom or on the road reporting Mark and I had a good time and became really good friends. We shared ideas about work, smoked dope, had friends round. When I did have time off, we'd take off in the car together for a couple of stoned weeks of adventure up to Byron Bay. I cared a lot about Mark but, looking back, I wouldn't say I was in love with him. In fact, I don't think I would have been able to be in love with anyone at that time – I was just too wrapped up in my career to spend much time thinking seriously about my personal life.

Perhaps if I'd taken the time to really think about what I was doing with him a bit more, I would have realised that Mark was a good-time boy and should not have been much more to me than a mate. But I didn't think about it and our relationship just bounced along.

Little did I know that the most of the hard work, both personally and professionally, was still to come.

14

Presenter, Me?

I've never done anything in my life for the sake of fame. I don't court it and being recognised in the street still makes me nervous. As far as I'm concerned, fame gets me a good table in a restaurant every few months, and that's about it. Aside from that, I'm only interested in what I'm doing, not how well known it makes me – fame is a by-product of what I do, not an end in itself. My work at SBS and on *Play School* made me a familiar face in Australia, for sure, but it didn't prepare me one bit for the media circus that would centre on me at the end of 1987. It's funny to think that ultimately it all stemmed from five casually spoken words: 'OK, I'll try for it.'

'It' was a chance to work on *The 7.30 Report*, a current affairs programme on the ABC that was similar to Britain's *Newsnight*. A great executive producer called Alan Hall from SBS's news and current affairs department had told me that his mate, who was the executive producer on *The 7.30 Report*, had seen me reporting and presenting for SBS and been impressed. His mate's name was Phil, and Phil was looking for new blood. He wanted to know if I'd be interested in trying out.

God, was I interested! I loved *The 7.30 Report* for its in-depth coverage of mainstream – not just ethnic – events and I knew moving to the ABC would be the next step up for me. Alan said the work could be reporting or presenting – he wasn't sure quite what position they were looking to fill. I was dead keen and said, 'OK, I'll try for it' to hide my excitement.

The next thing I knew I was over at the *7.30* offices getting a right grilling about the issues of the day, why I thought I was cut out to work for them and so on. A couple of days later I heard I'd been short-listed. *Wow!* I thought. But short-listed for what? They hadn't mentioned a specific post, but I imagined it was to be one of the reporters on the show.

And then it all went a bit quiet.

Often, when I'd filmed a story and was at the editing stage, I would go into the office looking like a right old scruffbag to make sure that I didn't suddenly get picked to be sent out on a last-minute story. If I was a mess, there was no way anyone would be sending me down to report outside Parliament House, or anywhere else for that matter. It was in this scruffy state that I picked up the phone when the secretary to David Hill, then managing director of the ABC, called. 'Is this Trisha Goddard?' she asked.

I'm sure you can guess my reply.

Presenter, Me?

'Welcome aboard!' she said. 'We'd like you to come over right away so we can make an announcement.'

Yes! I thought, I've got the job, whatever it is – I was so over the moon I forgot to make sure I'd got it right. 'Thank you,' I said excitedly. 'I'll be over right away.'

And as I put the phone down I realised what a mess I looked.

There was no time to go home and change into something appropriate. I scanned the office until my eyes fell on Christine, a Kiwi girl who worked on the newsdesk. Five minutes later I was wearing her dress. Next stop was Lexy Hamilton-Smith, whose belt I was soon tightening around my waist. I had an outfit, but it was something I wouldn't normally be caught dead in – little puffy sleeves on a Laura Ashley-type frock – but beggars can't be choosers, and before I had time to think I was in a cab to the ABC.

I arrived in minutes and before I knew it I was standing there in my dress, bewildered by what was happening. David Hill, the ABC's MD, and Phil were asking me if I had any skeletons in my closet. They looked excited, and seemed nervous. I assured them I had nothing to hide and they looked at each other and smiled. 'I think she's ready,' they said, and then David turned to his secretary. 'You can let them in now,' he beamed.

Ready for what? I thought. Let *who* in? What's going on? Before my head had too much of a chance to spin, the room had filled up with journalists. There was an expectant atmosphere, but I was in more suspense than anyone. I didn't have a clue what was happening. Then David stood to speak and it all became clear.

'Ladies and gentleman of the press,' he announced, 'let me present to you the new presenter of *The 7.30 Report*...'

If this was news to the entire Australian press, it was certainly news to yours truly. It took a couple of seconds for David's words to sink in. *Presenter? Me? What? Why? Shit! I thought I was going to be a journo!* But my thoughts were cut short as a journo-packed room turned into a sea of raised arms and rapid-fire questions.

'How does it feel to be the country's first black TV presenter?' came the first.

I looked down at my skin. 'Black, me? Oh yes, I am!'

'What do you mean?' the journalist said. 'How does it feel?'

'Well, when I filled in the job application it didn't ask my colour – I didn't apply for the job of first black TV presenter! I just applied like anyone else.'

Another question flew at me: 'Miss Goddard, don't you think the first black TV presenter in this country should be Aboriginal?'

'Yeah, I do actually,' I replied, 'but I didn't choose me for the job!'

'So why are you here?'

'I don't know...'

And suddenly that was it. The press filed out and I went back to SBS. (And yes, I took the dress and belt off ASAP. It still makes me laugh when I look at the newspaper cuttings of me wearing that girly outfit.) My return was met with stunned congratulations from everyone. Someone pointed out that I should probably hand my notice in, so I went down the corridor to do just that. SBS offered me my own show with more money, which was shocking and touching and made me feel quite guilty, but, though I loved SBS, I knew the ABC would be the right move. What I didn't know was what awaited me the next morning.

Once the story of Australia's first black 'anchorwoman' broke, the media went nuts. Suddenly I realised what I had let myself in for. Every journalist in the country seemed to want a piece of me – they were banging on my door, calling me on the phone, writing pieces for all the papers. Radio DJs were holding phone-ins about me. Such instant publicity was pretty overwhelming, but there was an aspect to it that made it downright exhausting and offensive – it was almost entirely focused on my colour.

To visit Australia and to live in Australia are very different things. When I had arrived to move in with Robert, one of the things that struck me most about many Aussies was their overt racism. I was pointed at and talked about on buses, hassled by the police, turned away by cab drivers and experienced countless instances of rude prejudice. I'm sure all nations have their racists, but Australia seemed full of them to me. One very good reason for this could be one of the things I love about Australians – they don't muck about when expressing themselves, they tell you things as they are. Unfortunately, this means they don't always hold their tongues when it comes to their feelings on race and colour.

After getting the job on *The 7.30 Report*, I learned that a large part of the Australian media were as happy to mouth off about my colour as your average white Aussie in the street would be. Some of the reporting was overtly racist. I'll never forget radio presenter Ron Casey saying,

'We shouldn't have blacks… she should go back to where she came from.' I just had to stop listening to the radio after that.

I kept being asked to explain why I had agreed to be a black presenter on *The 7.30 Report* when I'd only been in the country two years. Didn't I think that the first black presenter should be Aboriginal? All I could do was throw my own question back at them: how could *they* explain the lack of Aboriginal candidates for interview? I think I said this on *Midday* and the audience applauded. I wasn't being smug or conceited, I just couldn't think for the life of me what I was supposed to say. I'd applied for the job because I wanted to work on *The 7.30 Report*, and, if there were many things about myself that I *could* change, I sure couldn't change the fact that I was black, or for that matter a Pommie.

I was being truly bombarded by the press, and I hadn't even begun to present the show. It probably says something about our relationship that I can't really remember Mark's reaction to it all. He was always in the background, just cruising along, whereas I barely had enough time to think. We soon moved from the cottage into a duplex flat and, while Mark probably thought, Shit, there goes my dream that Trisha will calm down on the work front, he was very good in that he drove me around and, as far as was possible, helped me stay away from the glare of the media. I'll never forget Mark driving me to the gym as I lay flat in the back of his car. Normally I drove in my lilac VW convertible bug, but that was no longer an option. Once, I arrived at the gym only to realise that I had been followed all the way there by a couple of reporters. While I was working out, one followed me from one piece of equipment to the next as he interviewed me. It was mayhem. At one point, early on, someone even took the trouble to spray 'KKK' on our front door, which was charming of them.

As for the job itself, initially I was flying by the seat of my pants. I was introduced to a talented and dedicated team of hardcore mainly male journos and, in an intense and frenetic atmosphere of testosterone, swearing and breaking news, I had to sit down every evening and anchor a live current affairs show in front of a nation that seemed to be slagging me off. I was aware of the gaps in my experience, and once again put into practice my 'got to work twice as hard to be half as good' ethos. I worked like a dog – even more so than at SBS! The pressure of the job was immense, but I rose to the challenge and had to adapt myself.

The dope smoking was cut back, but only a bit. Although I carried on puffing away, there was no way I could afford to have anything but a completely clear head in order to deal with my responsibilities. Every morning we had a very early newspaper conference and I had to be as sharp as a knife if I had a hope of knowing my stuff for the evening show. Many of the guys on my team were hard-living, shit-kicking Aussies, but there was no mucking about when it came to work. It always came first. To this day, I still obsessively read at least four newspapers a day – more at the weekend.

A lot of the press got nastier and nastier and I got more and more distracted from the fact that I was in a great, challenging new job. And then, one day, one Michael

Parkinson came to my rescue. Michael used to visit Australia to do *Parkinson* with Aussie celebs, so was very well known and respected. What calmed things down was a piece he wrote in the UK's *Daily Mirror*. In it, he drew attention to what was being said about my appointment and how disgusted he was that Australia and its press were living in the dark ages. The story started to spread to America and the Middle East and the more liberal Aussies began to realise that they looked like a bunch of hicks. In short, the Australian media started to tone it down and the sections of the press who'd supported me really started to make me feel I wasn't entirely a lost cause.

Whether the Australian public loved me or hated me, they certainly wanted to see me. Some of the press had tried to whip the nation into a frenzy, so immediately I appeared on TV everybody switched on the ABC so they could have a look at this 'black TV presenter' and see what all the fuss was about. Obviously, I was determined to prove myself and win people over, but I can't say I wasn't nervous at first. My predecessors had all been very confrontational interviewers who used aggressive Jeremy Paxman-like tactics to get what they wanted. That just wasn't my style, and I became known for a slightly softer, yet (sometimes) just as effective, approach. I used charm and a bit of humour to get the people I was interviewing to relax and speak and, though I say it myself, it often worked.

Others must have agreed too, because once the media madness had died – I think eventually everyone realised that, rather than making a racial statement, I was just another Sheila on the telly trying to do her job – the ratings kept on going up until they had doubled. And, accordingly, so did my salary. The initial deal saw me only being paid the same as any of the other reporters on the show. My brilliant lawyer, Richard Cobden, got the ABC to agree to double my salary the next year – but only if I rated well. It wasn't long before 'the nigger', as some members of the public referred to me in messages left on our show's phone-in number, was one of the top earners at the ABC. I certainly couldn't complain about my situation, I adored my job and every day was a different challenge.

And then one day the phone rang. It was my mum.

15

Tragedy

I'll never forget Mum's words. 'Oh, Tootsie, Linda's been burned...'

'What do you mean, "burned"?'

Mum had the weary, hesitant tone of voice of someone who doesn't know how to break news. It was as if she didn't want to drag me into the hell she'd been thrust into.

'There's been an accident,' she continued. 'Your sister's got first- and third-degree burns... she's in a medically induced coma... we were hoping she'd be all right but...'

'When did this happen?' I interrupted.

'About two weeks ago,' said Mum.

'What?' I shouted, shocked and angered. 'Why didn't you tell me?'

'Tootsie, we thought she might get better... There's no time now. They say she's got septicaemia – we don't know if she'll last... the next 12 hours are crucial.'

Trisha – As I Am

I was in a state. Twelve hours! My baby sister! The flight home would take 28 hours. I rang my boss, David Hill, in a state of utter panic. I told him I had to get back to the UK and he was great. Immediately, the ABC arranged a return ticket to London for me. I would leave the next morning.

Two weeks and no one had told me. Now maybe Linda had only 12 hours to live and I was only just boarding a plane from Australia. I was terrified. I didn't know if I would get to see my sister again and I was an absolute mess.

I was crying on the plane. The panic came in waves and it was simply a case of getting through each hour. I couldn't even let myself think about what had happened, about the situation I would walk into when I arrived home. I tried to rise out of myself and limit myself to just breathing in and out, in and out.

Sitting back in the noise of economy class and being recognised by people was only making things worse. A man asked me for my autograph, but I was in no state to focus well enough to give it. It was obvious I was in distress, but when I politely declined to sign my name it didn't go down well, for the man skulked off muttering, 'Who does she think she is?' to himself. Unbelievable! Seconds later, I was crying and a Qantas steward came and held me. *She might be dead by now*, I kept thinking. Try as I might, I couldn't expel that thought out of my mind. It was almost too much to bear.

Halfway through the flight, I was asked if I'd like to come up to first class. The invitation came from a guy named Geoffrey Robertson, an international lawyer and husband of the successful London-based Australian writer

Tragedy

Kathy Lette. I'd met him a couple of times through Robert, and somehow he had discovered I was on the plane. He strode down the aisle to find me and asked if I'd like to sit with him. We sat together for the rest of the flight, and he listened to everything I had to say and really looked after me, even though he didn't really know me from Adam. He had no reason to do what he did, he just did it anyway. Sometimes the kindness of strangers is truly remarkable, and I will never forget Geoffrey for easing the pain of that terrible flight.

After what seemed like an age, the plane touched down at Heathrow. I scrambled through Customs and ran to a phone box to dial home. Linda was still alive! There was hope, and filled with that hope I rushed to meet Mum and Dad. That's when I found out the truth about why my sister was on the verge of losing her life.

What had happened was no accident. Earlier that day, and apparently against medical advice, Dad had collected a clearly distressed Linda from a psychiatric hospital. Once home, Linda had left the house and got into Mum's tarpaulin-covered Fiat. She had a petrol can and a bottle of brandy with her. Once inside the car, she must have drunk some brandy. Then we think she lit a match, opened the petrol can and dropped the match into it. Instantaneously the flames engulfed the car. Need I say more?

Seconds later, my dad came out to look for Linda and heard a *whoomph* from under the tarpaulin. Running to the car, he found a car full of smoke and his daughter on fire. He dragged her out, burning himself in the process, and a neighbour turned a hosepipe on her. The ambulance arrived and just before they took her away Linda apparently looked at Dad. 'Dad, Dad, I'm so sorry, Dad,' she cried.

These words would haunt my father for a very long time. Perhaps they still haunt him today.

The hospital was shockingly filthy. I walked along the grubby corridors, past the waiting rooms stuffed with overflowing ashtrays, through the swinging doors and into intensive care. I'd spent two days trying not to imagine what I would find when I arrived at Linda's bed, and now I was faced with a scene that was worse than my worst nightmares. The shock was heart-stopping. My parents had had some time to get used to Linda's condition, but I just reeled at the scene I walked into.

Parts of my little sister were burned to the bone. There was so much burned flesh, but Linda's face was still recognisable. She was in a drug-induced coma – if she had been conscious, she could not have withstood the pain from the burns. She was covered in tubes, her body surrounded by machines that hummed, buzzed, beeped and flashed mysteriously as they kept her alive. I could barely speak, and when I did there was no response at all.

Words cannot describe the pain of finding a loved one in such a state. The shock, the fear, the guilt, the anger, the sadness and the horror are unbearable. There is nothing to console you, nothing to ease the inner desolation of watching a body you love struggling to survive.

But this was not the first time Linda had been in hospital. It wasn't the first time she had struggled to survive. For years, since the age of 19, Linda had been fighting another gruelling battle – not with her body, but with her mind. That she was fighting this battle was pretty much a family secret. Linda's struggle was with a mental illness and the prejudice and misunderstanding that surround it. My sister suffered from schizophrenia, and as I sat beside her bed in the intensive-care unit I knew that it was her suffering that had led to what I was looking at.

Thanks to ridiculous stereotypes and wholly inaccurate definitions that have been passed from generation to generation, many people have a grossly distorted view of what schizophrenia is. Some people think of it as meaning a 'split personality', a Jekyll-and-Hyde type of insanity where the sufferer thinks they are one person one minute and someone completely different the next. Others think it signifies a dangerously unhinged individual who at any moment might wield a knife and run amok in society. These inaccurate stereotypes have led to the label 'schizophrenic' being used in jokes, in the playground, in the office and even in the press to create a cartoon-like, insulting image of someone with a serious condition.

This ignorance I detest. The idea of the 'schizophrenic' is nothing but a cruel myth that only stigmatises and marginalises those who do suffer from this complex, painful illness. It may come as a surprise to you that one in a hundred people suffer from schizophrenia. My sister was one of them.

In truth, 'Schizophrenia' is a broad medical term used to refer to an illness characterised by an impaired ability to process reality. Perhaps I should explain that a bit. There's no such thing as a 'normal' person, but it is fair to say that many of us experience the world in a similar way. We look around and see similar things – we have shared perceptions, and we get those perceptions from looking, smelling, touching, hearing and tasting. Those shared perceptions, along with the shared values we have, are called 'reality', and most of us get on with reality one way or another, even though we may have widely different thoughts and opinions about what's going on in the world. In our minds, we also have private thoughts, ideas and imagination, and our inner world is unique to each of us. We know our minds are private and not part of the reality we all share – no one can get into our heads unless we invite them to. As a result, we can usually tell the difference between what is going on in the world and what is going on in our heads.

For a person suffering from schizophrenia, the ability to distinguish his or her own intense thoughts, ideas and imaginings from reality is impaired to one degree or another. They may start having difficulty 'thinking straight' to the point that sequences of logical thought become impossible. As a result of such jumbled thoughts, the person's speech may be confused and make little sense to others. A person may experience hallucinations, possibly hearing voices that seem real, even though no one else can hear them, or seeing or smelling things that are not there. Some sufferers experience delusions – beliefs or experiences that others don't share. They may believe, for instance, that other people can control their minds or that they are being followed or persecuted by someone when there is no evidence to anyone else that this is what is really going on. And you know what, these symptoms can suddenly emerge in any 'normal' person's head, especially if they smoke dope or take cocaine.

Tragedy

While it may be difficult for the people around the sufferer to accept and deal with, it's ten times worse for the sufferer to cope with. Imagine reality crumbling around you and *not knowing why*. Many of the symptoms I've described can be really frightening and distressing for the person experiencing them. Hearing voices, seeing things, feeling confused and not understanding your own confusion – all of these things can lead a person to become very quiet, very withdrawn, or alternatively might make them move around constantly in an effort to escape the confusion of it all. An isolating experience in itself. The saddest thing of all is that the strange behaviour sufferers may exhibit can result in friends and even loved ones regarding them as strange and essentially ignoring them. Then, once left alone, the sufferer can feel even more isolated and descend into depression, which makes a bad situation worse.

There are many theories about what causes the onset of the illness, but nobody knows for sure, and each case is different. Much research is being carried out about the brain chemistry involved in schizophrenia, and several studies have shown strongly that stressful life events may trigger it in people with an underlying genetic predisposition. Childhood sexual or physical abuse, homelessness, poverty, losing a loved one, or so-called 'recreational' drug use – all have been identified by sufferers as the cause of their problem.

Linda was diagnosed as having schizophrenia at 19. She was troubled, she was hearing voices that confused and scared her. The voices told her bad, confusing things, sometimes suggesting to her that the Devil would get her.

And the voices wouldn't go away. She ended up being taken into a psychiatric hospital. The diagnosis didn't take long – Linda was probably viewed as a fairly 'classic case' – she was given medication, kept in hospital for a while and then sent home with her prescription. Things are a little different now, but in those days there weren't many options for medication – the 'neuroleptic' drugs Linda took kept the voices at bay, but she was taking some heavy shit and, like most people who have to take it, she hated the side effects.

More to the point, Linda didn't like the fact that she was on medication, full stop, and she wasn't offered any decent long-term talking therapy to help her out either – that's not really something that happened back then. A pattern emerged – Linda would go through periods of taking her medication, feeling 'well' and then coming off the pills because she felt better and desperately wanted to think she'd be OK as herself. But then there'd be another breakdown, the voices would return and poor Linda would be back in the psychiatric unit again.

As this cycle continued, Linda's life was effectively put on hold. She became more and more dependent on Mum and Dad, and, even though she was often stable, she wasn't in a position to go out and take the world by the balls career-wise. She ended up at home a lot, knowing her three sisters had all moved on to make their way in life, and understandably this made her angry with her situation, and herself, so alongside the schizophrenia she could well have been suffering from a degree of depression too. Unfortunately, in those days, good social and psychiatric support was just not there to help people like

Tragedy

Linda and she fell by the wayside, ending up in a 'revolving door' situation with the mental-health services. She was in one month, out the next, maybe in a 'halfway house' for a bit, then back again soon enough, and so it went on.

I knew Linda had schizophrenia and always kept checks on how she was over the years, but back then I didn't have the same understanding as I do now. I didn't think it meant 'split personality' or 'raving loon', and I knew what a funny, smart, sensitive girl she was, what a talented actress she had been and how kind she was to others. As far as I was concerned, she had a problem for which she needed to take pills and when she didn't take them she'd end up in hospital, her head full of voices, rocking to and fro. But until I got that phone call, until I was sitting by that bed next to my dear sister, I must be honest and say I had never fully realised the extent of Linda's distress. Over the years, I felt I'd been coping more with supporting my parents and listening to the seemingly endless saga of my poor mother's distress about her sick daughter.

And for years I kept what I did know of Linda's illness to myself. My parents gave the impression that they wanted to keep Linda's problems as quiet as possible and this was something I unquestioningly picked up from them. I didn't even tell my friends. You just didn't talk about things like that in those days. Somehow, my sister's condition became a dirty secret, something to be ashamed of, and I am ashamed to say I kept my mouth shut about it for a long time.

After that initial visit, I left the hospital and went home, stunned, distraught, confused. How had it come to this?

How had I not known things had got so bad? What made my sister make such an attempt on her own life? Was there any chance she would survive and, if she did make it through, what kind of a hellish life would she have afterwards? I had no answers, only questions.

At home, things were just awful. When a family member tries to kill him- or herself, the rest of the family implode. It's a grief that doesn't bring people together. Instead, it sends each individual member into their own personal hell. My father, who had always been the man with the stiff upper lip, began to fall apart with guilt. He would cry, blame himself, tell himself that he should have seen it coming. Not long before Linda did this, one of his patients who also suffered from schizophrenia had set themselves on fire in a field, and I think he felt he should have learned from that loss and protected Linda more.

Also, Dad had recently got Linda out of hospital. He'd thought she was well enough to come home, and now he couldn't handle what had happened so soon after her return. Somehow, he felt he had made a gross error of judgement, and he couldn't forgive himself. He got to the point where he was saying that he didn't know if he wanted to live. I had never seen my father such an emotional wreck before, and it was a shock. I remember putting my arms around this man with whom I had so many issues – it was a bit like hugging an ironing board. I didn't know what to do to help him out of his guilt and sadness about Linda.

Mum, on the other hand, took on the role of the strong one, which was surprising. Given her normal, loud, emotionally full-on self, I would have expected her to wear her heart on her sleeve a little more openly. In fact, I would have expected her to be screaming the roof down! But instead she went into nurse mode and became a bit of a rock. She held it together, even though, inside, she was going through a mother's ultimate nightmare. Her boast was that, during all of this, she never shed a tear. That freaked me out.

In the first few days, it was just a case of getting through the hours and the minutes. Conversations, when we had them, seemed to revolve around whether or not Linda would make it through the next 24 hours. It was exhausting. My parents were clinging to every hope, and Mum always seemed optimistic. Looking at the state Linda was in I could only see their positivity as wishful thinking and little else. I was being torn apart by two things. On the one hand, I had an overwhelming desire to be able to talk to my sister again and for things to be OK, *for her to survive*. On the other, I was racked with guilt because, deep down, for Linda's sake, *I didn't want her to live*.

Linda had a big hang-up about her looks – she always felt that she was the least pretty of us sisters. I had similar feelings about myself, but the difference was that I had confidence in other ways and this made up for what I thought was lacking in my looks. Linda didn't have that confidence and had struggled with dyslexia, which also was not really recognised and treated in those days. Her looks were dear to her and she was always trying to make the best of herself. I knew that, were she to survive, she would find herself covered in horrendous scars and skin grafts, she would discover an ear missing, plus some of her toes and fingers amputated due to the extent of the burning, she might not be able to walk, and she would still have all those voices trapped in her head. I simply didn't think the Linda I knew would be able to live like that. But as the days wore on I kept these thoughts to myself while I watched the minutes tick by at home or at the hospital.

I couldn't sleep. I couldn't eat. I could hardly think. My parents and sisters were a mess – we were all in a terrible way, but we tried to keep our strength up. My parents, sisters and I would take it in turns to sit for hours next to Linda, gently stroking her hair, and we'd talk about our childhood and laugh together about East Africa and some of the holidays we'd had as kids. A couple of times, a hint of a smile appeared on Linda's face, and just that was enough to let us know that we were doing something to ease her pain. In a way, it eased our pain too. We were getting through.

At one point it became clear that Linda was in some sort of extra discomfort – her body was writhing a little, there was something going on. It turned out to be period pains. Christ, I remember thinking, We never get any let-up, us women! Once we knew what was happening, Paula and I sang 'Sometimes It's Hard To Be A Woman' at the top of our voices and fell about laughing – we really went through the gamut of emotions by that bedside. We sang tons of songs, and when I contacted Richard Branson (who I'd met when I launched Virgin for him in Sydney) about what was happening he took the trouble to get some bands into his studios to record Linda's favourite songs and sent a tape over for us to play to her. Richard was incredibly kind, and during that period he invited me to get-togethers at his place – something that really helped to distract me a little and give me something of a let-up.

But nothing changed for Linda. She just hung in there, day by day, and there was no improvement in her physical state. One day a Canadian intensive-care nurse who had been around from the start spoke to me over Linda's bed. He was obviously aware of the private agony each of us was going through, and at some point in the conversation he said, 'You know, we do have a grief counsellor here.'

Despite the mess he was in, Dad refused point-blank to go to the counsellor. Mum felt he might benefit from it, and tried to encourage him. 'No way,' he said, and that was that. I'm not sure whether Mum went, but I went along to her office. It couldn't hurt, I thought.

In my mind, what I was going through was pretty horrific, and I was sceptical about how some counsellor was going to change anything. As I sat there in front of her, my arms and legs crossed, she must have cottoned on to something, because it wasn't long before she said, 'What's that look on your face?'

'What do you know about grief?' I said defensively, angrily. I will never forget her response.

'I'll tell you what I know,' she replied calmly. 'I was a single child, and so was my husband. Our parents had died and all we had left was each other. We had a child and she grew up and had a baby. One day my husband was getting ready for work when he fell down, clutching his heart. An hour later, he was on a life-support machine following a massive heart attack. I called my daughter and

I could hardly speak – my daughter, her husband and their baby immediately piled into their car to come and support me. On the drive up here from the West Country, they had a massive car crash not far from the hospital where my husband was. My daughter was killed outright, her husband went into one intensive care ward and the baby went into another. I didn't know what to do, or who to turn to – I had to race from one ward to the other. Within 48 hours, I had lost my entire family. For a long time I didn't want to live, but I didn't give up and trained to be a grief counsellor. That's what I know about grief.'

Let's just say, by the time she had finished speaking my arms were no longer folded. The knowledge of this woman's devastating loss, and the fact that she was now using her experiences to relate to others, was astounding, admirable and humbling. It didn't make my pain go away, but her story and the conversation that followed taught me something. 'Strong' is a bit of a naff word, but from that woman I learned to be strong both inwardly and outwardly – and, boy, did I need strength then! – and I also learned that you can use the hell you've been through to help others.

The other person who gave me real strength during that time was my aunty Mary, the aunt we'd stayed with when we came back from East Africa all those years back. This time she came to stay with us. Unlike Mum and Dad, Aunty Mary was a deeply religious woman. During my time with Robert, I had become very interested in the Baha'i Faith through our involvement with UNICEF. The Baha'i Faith emphasises the spiritual unity of mankind and the equality of men and women.

Humanity is seen as a bird – the male is one wing, the female is the other wing, and unless they work together in perfect strength and synergy the bird won't fly. Baha'i sees most of the world's religions as equally valid – the basic beliefs of Christianity, Islam, Judaism and Buddhism are seen as different versions of the same God. To me, these were beautiful principles, and I still live by them now. If I had to pin myself to a religion, it would be the Baha'i Faith.

During this agonising period with Linda, I had turned to God more than ever, but as the only one in the family with any faith I had no one to share my spiritual thoughts with until Aunty Mary arrived. Although a Christian, she was happy to talk to me about my faith and how it could help Linda and I. Mary didn't judge me and she didn't try to tell me I should be a Christian. Despite our different faiths, we could talk openly and spiritually, and that's what made the difference.

As a hard-headed journo, I was always pro-euthanasia, but the more Mary and I talked about Linda's situation, the more I started to question my belief that it's a good thing to turn off the switch. We talked about the potentially terrible effects such an act can have on the family who agree to it – they have to carry on living, in some cases not knowing what might have been if the switch had been left on, and that uncertainty can bring about doubt and guilt which can last a lifetime. Before talking with Mary, I'd been thinking, Why the hell don't we flick these machines off? What's the point in all this fucking suffering? I'd wanted to release Linda and I'd wanted to release us. But our talks made me think that what was happening was a process we were perhaps meant to be going through, a process that was in some ways essential to dealing with what might be yet to come. We discussed so many things and I don't know what I would have done without good old Aunty Mary.

After six weeks, Linda was showing no signs of improving. It was the same thing day in, day out. Mum and Dad were still talking with desperate yet understandable optimism. They still thought she was going to pull through. By the end of that week, I had begun to realise that she was not going to live. Deep down, I knew it. The ABC were on the phone every day, wondering when I was going to come back. They were incredibly supportive but were having to deal with all sorts of speculation in the Australian press – the question everybody wanted to know the answer to was: 'Have they got rid of the black presenter?'

After discussing it with Aunty Mary, I decided, whatever was going to happen, it was time to leave my sister. There was nothing more I could do.

The last time I ever saw Linda, I was at her bedside. I pulled up a chair, stroked her hair and spoke to Winnie, as we all used to call her. 'Winnie,' I began, 'I have to go back to Australia. I want you to know that I don't blame you for what you did, I'm not angry with you. I know you are still here with us, and I know why. We've all of us had to make a journey. If you had died straight away, the family would have destroyed itself, but we've made this journey and I want you to know how much I value you still being here. I understand why you're here and I don't blame you for anything that has happened.

Tragedy

'Remember you used to call me your hero, Winnie? Well, let me tell you, you're my hero. Everything you've gone through with your mental illness, now I understand what it's driven you to, and you know what, fuck that! No one should have to go through what you've been through, and I promise you I'm going to do everything I can to try to make sure they don't have to.'

I paused. 'Can you hear me, Winnie?' I asked, searching for any sign. 'Can you hear me?'

Her eyes moved. Her eyelids remained closed, but there was a twitch that I knew was Winnie saying, 'Yes, I can hear you.'

I smiled and felt a warmth inside me. I was elated, filled with love for this wonderful woman and at the same time I was unspeakably, heartbreakingly sad. I sat there a while longer, stroking her delicate hair before I spoke again.

'I love you, Winnie,' I said in her ear. If only she could have realised how much I loved her.

I knew she had heard me, and at the same time I knew it was time to leave. There was only one thing left to say.

Slowly I rose, and said the word.

'Goodbye.'

Three days later, the phone rang at six in the morning. I was back in Australia. I jumped from our bed.

'She's gone, Tootsie,' said Mum. 'They tried to give her a tracheotomy and it was too much. Her heart gave out.'

There was nothing to add. We'd been through so much. I told Mum to call the others and said I would speak to her later. We said goodbye.

It was as if I'd been punched in the stomach. As I put the

phone back down, I fell on to all fours and slowly curled into a ball on the floor. I didn't cry, I screamed. The scream came from somewhere deep in me, and it was physically painful, an animal howl. After howling for what seemed forever, I looked over to Mark. He didn't make a move. He just lay there in bed with a look of shock and surprise on his face. It was as if someone had pressed a button to stop him moving – he did nothing but stare at me. He had seized up and somewhere in my brain it registered – You're on your own, kid! Emotion terrified the crap out of Mark – he just couldn't deal with raw feelings. To be fair to him, he'd lost a brother when he was young, and I think the pain had stunted his emotions in some way. Whenever tragedy struck, I knew I couldn't turn to Mark for comfort. Practical things he was great at, but forget emotion. It was just the way he was. He did finally bring me a cup of tea, though. He was trying to help the only way he was able.

I called my closest girlfriend Claire and we cried down the phone for 20 minutes. She didn't try to tell me Winnie had gone to a better place, she didn't try to console me, she understood what comfort merely being around gives someone. She was the only person who didn't try to make things better; she was just there for me during that grief.

I needed to go to a church – because of my interest in the Baha'i Faith I didn't care what denomination it was – so Mark drove me to North Sydney Catholic Church. I went in on my own and basically had a right rant at God. Why had he taken Linda away? I cried and shouted and pleaded and once I'd screamed my guts out I went to leave.

Peter and I both love to see the world.

Above left: Madi was only three years old when we walked along the Great Wall of China – her little legs wouldn't carry her so Mummy's had to! I'd been invited to Beijing to address an international symposium of psychiatrists about mental health.

Above right: In Mauritius with my wonderful husband.

Below left: On safari in the Shamwari game reserve, South Africa.

Below right: Peter and I with my best friend Claire in the Nevada desert.

Behind the scenes at *The Trisha Goddard Show*.

Above: A production meeting to discuss the content of the coming day's show.

Below: Whatever is happening before the show, I never stop doing my research!

© *Peter Gianfrancesco, GALERU Photography*

Ready to roll.

Above left: About to go out in front of the cameras.

Above right: Security is an essential part of the show, just in case things get a bit too rowdy.

Below: In action, doing what I do best.

© *Peter Gianfrancesco, GALERU Photography*

Living in Norwich means I don't really do the whole celebrity circuit thing, but I do go to some fancy parties and meet other famous people! *Above left*: Peter and I with the lovely Graham Norton. *Above right*: With Sacha Baron Cohen.

Below: I don't take a great deal of time off, but when I do I like to let my hair down.

Above: This picture still makes me laugh. This was at a birthday party for Madi – and that's Peter inside the green dragon costume.

Below: The Town House TV guys – what a team!

Above: Raz, who is sadly no longer with us.

Below: With Alfie, my devoted running companion.

All in a day's work! Signing hundreds of photos for fans.

As we are. My wonderful family is the most gratifying part of my life. *Above*: With my Prince Charming, Peter and, *below*, Billie, me, Madi and Peter all glammed up for my 50th birthday bash in December 2007. Pure joy!

Above: © Peter Gianfrancesco, GALERU Photography

Tragedy

On my way out, I noticed a book for people to write their own prayers in, and I began to write about Linda. I wrote about what she was like as a child – the funny things she used to do, the ribbons she wore in her hair, the things she was good at, the games we used to play with our Barbie and Cindy dolls. And then I wrote the following:

'Linda happened to have schizophrenia. As if that wasn't bad enough our family had to feel secretive about it. There always seemed to be shame surrounding her illness and that's what helped kill her. My little sister Winnie died this morning.'

I felt that Linda had not wanted to die – I knew that she was unable to live. She had just wanted to escape the horror of her situation. She was stigmatised, held back, frustrated and ultimately didn't receive the help she needed.

Exhausted, I walked out and found Mark, who'd been looking around a second-hand record shop while he waited for me. 'Look what I've found on the top of a pile of records,' he said, handing me a copy of Barbra Streisand's 'The Woman in the Moon', one of Linda's favourites.

Linda had loved and identified with the lyrics to that song and, only a few weeks back, neither myself nor Richard Branson had been able to locate a copy of it when putting together Linda's tape. I'd been told it had been deleted. For Mark to have stumbled upon it may have been coincidence, but to me it felt like a sign – it was all so uncanny. I felt warm again, and so close to Winnie, and I was filled with a quiet resolve to fulfil the promise I'd made to Linda – *no one was going to have to go through what she went through if I could do something about it*. I knew I was going to do something to help. I wasn't sure

179

how, but I was determined to make a difference. And once I get an idea in my head there ain't nothing that will stop me following it through!

That afternoon I returned to the ABC offices and back into the arms of *The 7.30 Report* team. They didn't say anything, they just hugged me and hugged me before saying, 'OK, mate, lead story?'

I was back, and it was just what I needed. I was dressed in black, I looked like death and I was a mess, but at least I was around people who could help me focus on something else.

The 7.30 Report second-in-charge Ronnie Sinclair, a tough man who'd later become a great mate, called and asked if I'd been to the North Sydney Catholic Church and written something in the prayer book that morning. I told him I had, and he went on to explain that his partner, who was a teacher, had taken her class there on a whim about an hour earlier and one of the kids had read my entry to the others. 'Great,' I said, a little bemused.

'Well,' said Ronnie, 'I just thought I'd let you know that the whole school has just decided to raise funds for a schizophrenia fellowship.'

I remember going back to my office thinking, Thy will be done. After all my ranting earlier that day in the church, something good had happened. I'd vowed to myself I would make a difference, and this was the first step.

'Winnie,' I said out loud, 'it's already happening!'

I was back at work and I felt like shit. The only people who knew the reason were my team at *The 7.30 Report*. The rest of the Aussie media were speculating like crazy about

Tragedy

why I'd been off air for so long, and the time came when the ABC said we had to put something out to explain where I'd been. A few print journos were gathered together.

'Just say it was family sickness,' said a well-meaning publicist before I went into the room. 'Stick to that and you'll be OK. Don't say anything about the mental illness, you don't want all the shit. Just say she died of an illness and leave it there.'

By the time I sat down in front of a load of journalists, I was boiling inside. I've fucking had it with all this secrecy shit, I thought. All that playing down and hiding Winnie's 'illness' and now she's *dead* we're still at it. The publicist introduced me, saying I'd had a hard time with a death in the family, and the questions came flying at me.

I told them about the 'illness in the family' all right – I told them about the schizophrenia. I told them about the stigma Linda had endured. I told them about her frustration and suffering and I told them my sister had committed suicide as a result of it all. In fact, I went into a complete rant. I remember looking across at the publicist. I couldn't see her face – her head was practically in her hands.

When I stopped speaking, the room went very quiet. I had well and truly let the cat out of the bag. The next day the story was all over the papers. *The 7.30 Report*'s phone lines were jammed with calls. And you know what? The response was overwhelmingly *positive*. I was thanked and praised for going public about schizophrenia, and before I knew it I was doing several reports about mental illness. Several well-known Aussie faces – including a top rugby coach whose son had killed himself – came forward and spoke about their family's experiences with schizophrenia and other mental illnesses.

I hadn't expected such a response, but decided just to go with it. A highly respected ABC journalist called Anne Deveson got in touch. Her son Simon had committed suicide from schizophrenia and we had spoken about it on the quiet several times. The government wanted Anne to head up a body that became known as the National Community Advisory Group on Mental Health. She was unable to do it so she suggested me for the job. They thought it was a great idea and Anne wanted to know if I felt the same way. I'm sure you can guess how I felt. I was over the moon. So much was happening, and so quickly, it was an awesome feeling.

I went to Canberra to meet the then Minister of Health, an amazing man called Brian Howe. 'I want you to help me change the face of mental health in Australia,' he told me. 'You created this groundswell, you've got the passion and people listen to you. Will you join us?'

'You bet I will,' I said eagerly.

It was a golden opportunity. Little did I know what I was signing up for – from then on, all I did was work. Effectively my life became two careers, and it happened almost overnight. Starting in 1988, I chaired the National Community Advisory Group for ten years, working for two different governments, first Labour, then the (conservative) Liberal Party. Mark's complaint had always been that I put work before him. Well, with my new position I had to put work before him and then some! Looking back, I wouldn't change a thing.

Those ten years of work were fantastic. The Advisory

Group represented the views of people living with mental illness, as well as their carers. I became involved in so many aspects of the field and we worked in numerous projects, including the Aboriginal and Torres Strait Islanders mental-health programmes and an inquiry into marijuana and mental health. I chaired and was adviser to the government's $8 million media de-stigmatisation campaign and also worked with drug companies to better educate consumers about their medication. Also, my group and I advised on many pieces of legislation.

The work was fascinating and rewarding, and at the same time it helped me work through my grief over Linda and went a very long way towards helping me deal with the guilt I felt about her death. However, I still felt guilty when talking about Linda because I knew my parents were never comfortable with it. I got the impression they weren't too pleased about what I was doing, but ultimately I felt that the issues I was confronting in the public arena were more important than my parents' hang-ups when it came to being honest about Linda and her death. I really had to fight to arrive at that conclusion, and to this day there is still a part of me that feels guilty when I discuss what I always felt they would rather I kept a secret. 'But, hey,' I always tell myself, 'it's not like I picked up an AK-47 and said, "Right, my sister's dead, now I'm going to take out two hundred more people!"' I was actually trying to *help* people.

Instead of Mum and Dad's feelings, I was focused on Linda's pain and that of Australians with similar difficulties. I'd made a promise to Linda and myself, and my involvement in mental heath has helped others as well as me. I can look in the mirror and say that, during my time on the Advisory Group, I was doing what I could to deliver on that promise. I'm still heavily involved in mental-health campaigning today, but a little more about that later.

Right now I'll stay in 1989, for there's a story on the way ...

16

A New Arrival

'Good evening, I'm Trisha Goddard and welcome to *The 7.30 Report*,' I said to the camera from my chair in the hospital. 'I'm not in the studio tonight. You've all heard the joke "A funny thing happened to me on the way to the office". Well, very unexpectedly, I'm not going to be with you this evening...'

The camera panned out to reveal why I wouldn't be with them – I had a newborn baby on my lap. And I was her mother.

I had never wanted to have a baby until Linda died, but something about losing my sister got me thinking about my own mortality and what my next step in life could be. I had a great job, but there was something missing. I'd never really thought about having kids before, and certainly wasn't aware of my 'biological clock' ticking. As far as I was concerned, it didn't exist and then suddenly I realised it not only existed, but it was an alarm clock.

I've heard that it's quite common to want to create a new life when you've lost someone in your family. Part of my decision to have a child was certainly to do with that loss – I wanted something positive to focus on, and I wanted to give my family, who were wrapped up in so much guilt over Linda, a focal point.

In the new year of 1989, I had suggested to Mark that we try for a baby. He was all for it. He wanted a child as much as I did, but I also think he believed it would slow me down a little and turn me into a more dependent woman – hah! Three months before trying, I stopped smoking spliffs and gave up booze. In the same way that I'd been obsessive about dope at one point, I was now quite obsessive about the pregnancy, and smoking was a big issue. I was also very keen to time the pregnancy so that I'd give birth when *The 7.30 Report* was off the air for a few weeks – it would have been a breach of my presenter contract to have a child mid-season.

Throughout my pregnancy, I still went to the Rancan Sisters' Gym in Sydney's Neutral Bay. Three times a week there was me and my big tummy huffing away, doing aerobic classes next to a tall, fairly solidly built and freckled redhead – Nicole Kidman. When it all got a bit claustrophobic, I switched to weight training. I trained like mad, and discovered that I could push heavier weights than ever while pregnant.

I also power-walked three times a week to keep myself on top form, and I also went along to Ju-ju Sundin's pregnancy workshops in order to prepare for a drug-free, active and natural birth. Those workshops were great – you had to scream and shout, and it was all very cutting-edge stuff, but enormous fun. And it worked – although I gave birth two-and-a-half weeks early, my labour only lasted two and a half hours beginning to end, with no painkillers. The only thing that went wrong was that, at one point, I projectile-vomited mango everywhere between contractions. While pregnant I'd become obsessed with the stuff and had been stuffing myself with it that day. 'Ah, you'll be about ready to push then,' cooed the midwife as the mango went everywhere!

Plus, I started laughing when the midwife told me to push as, weeks earlier, I'd met Diana Ross at an after-show party. She'd told me about puffing and panting during labour. 'Honey,' she said, 'it's like shitting a fridge.' How right she was!

I was so enchanted by my beautiful bundle of joy that I'd forgotten I was supposed to be at work. My contractions had come out of the blue and, convinced it was a false alarm and that I'd be on air that evening, I'd insisted on reading all the newspapers in the car on the way to hospital. 'Oh my God, what's the time?' I said to Mark.

I realised I had missed my *7.30 Report* editorial meeting, so I called Debbie, my executive producer at the ABC. There was obviously no way I could make it into the studio, so I got dressed, put on some make-up and told them to send a camera crew round to the hospital so we could tape a piece to be shown before that evening's programme with a stand-in presenter. So, two hours after she was born, Billie was a TV star – I'm pleased to say she isn't one now, and doesn't want to be either.

I was told that there was $10,000 up for grabs for the first photographer who got a picture of Billie. There was a price on my child's head – madness! It didn't take long to deal with that – Australia's *Daily Telegraph* used a picture from *The 7.30 Report* piece we'd filmed, which killed the treasure hunt dead and gave the paper a nice scoop.

IT'S A GIRL ran the *Telegraph*'s headline the next day, 24 November 1989. I was overjoyed as I was ready to be a mother, and ready to let Mark have a go at being a father while I was at it!

Meanwhile, across town, my by then ex-husband Robert was lying in St Vincent's Hospital. I didn't know about it until, a couple of weeks later, my friend Sue Flatman, whose husband was an ABC filmmaker, called me up. After asking after Billie, Sue informed me that Robert had just died. I was shocked. Over the past year, I had heard various rumours that Robert was ill with cancer, and had called him a couple of times. Yet he was always the evasive politician and I hadn't been able to get much out of him. I spoke to him a couple more times and eventually he told me he had leukaemia. I told him I was sorry for him – which I was – and the next thing I heard he was dead. I was sad, but I wasn't devastated. It sounds a bit harsh, I know, but I had a new baby – there was a new life around and I didn't need any more death in my life.

Because I was seen as the one who walked out on the marriage, I was surprised to be invited to Robert's memorial service – I thought I'd be the last person they would want there. Nevertheless, I decided to go. It was weird turning up – once more I was thrust into the world

A New Arrival

I had run from, and sure enough the 'mourners' comprised a Who's Who of people tied up in politics and power. But this time I didn't feel comfortable. I could feel the eyes of Robert's political cronies on me and I was dreading seeing his parents, so I slipped in quietly and took a seat at the back.

Tributes were read out from all corners of the globe – even Audrey Hepburn paid her respects because of Robert's work with UNICEF. Ex-Australian Prime Minister Gough Whitlam praised Robert, as did Bob Hawke. Every speech focused on Robert's exemplary character, how he had changed people's lives and been a relentless campaigner to raise the profile of the Liberal Party. It was all true – Robert was a real champion of the underdog and had worked tirelessly for the causes in which he believed. But as I listened I couldn't help remembering the other part of Robert, and realised that no one would get up and paint a more rounded portrait of him. Then, incredibly, somebody approached the pulpit and proved me very, very wrong.

It was John Dowd, an old friend and by then Attorney General of New South Wales. 'Robert had two sides,' he began. Suddenly there was tension in the room, a few people shifted in their seats and then all was deathly quiet. 'We've heard a lot about one side – the generous, concerned international political campaigner and jurist – but there was another side to Robert that no one has spoken of.'

John paused and turned slightly to look directly at me. 'Robert's other side was altogether darker and we would be doing ourselves a disservice if we remembered the good without also remembering the bad. As Robert's deeds of good echo into the future, we have to remember to care for those who may have been damaged by his dark side.'

It was an extraordinary thing to say and I just thought, Thank you, thank you, thank you! It was a huge relief to hear someone giving a balanced view of Robert. I had never told anyone why I left Robert, and many people viewed me as some kind of pariah – in their eyes I was the girl who just upped sticks and buggered off for no reason. Now I felt someone was speaking up for me and I could have burst into tears. I've always railed against the fact that when someone dies we feel we can only say how saintly they were. I think it's fair to say that bad things happen to good people but they also happen to shitty people – how many times have you wanted someone to say, 'Actually that person was a shit, and now they're a dead shit!' I hope it's not just me!

As the congregation filed out, I thanked John Dowd for what he had done. He smiled and gave me a hug.

The next day John called me at home, wanting to know I was OK. I said I was fine, that I'd known about Robert's illness. 'I'm worried about you,' he said. 'Do you mind if I pop over?'

There was an anxious quality to his voice that made me think John wasn't coming round just to check up on me. I waited restlessly for him to arrive. Was there some twist to Robert's story I was yet to find out about? When John had spoken about a dark side to Robert, had he been referring to something I was unaware of? When John arrived I realised the answer was yes. 'What illness did Robert tell you he had?' he asked suddenly. Until then we'd just been chatting about my new life with Billie.

A New Arrival

'Leukaemia,' I answered. 'That's what he told me.'

'It wasn't leukaemia,' John said with deadly seriousness. 'I *know* it wasn't because my wife's had leukaemia for 20 years and I know what it's like. Robert just didn't have the symptoms.'

'So what was it then?' I said, a little confused. 'Why would he lie?'

'What really got me thinking about it all was when you gave birth and it was in the *Daily Telegraph*. I took the paper to Robert's bedside, and when he saw the picture of you and Billie he let out a strange, vindictive laugh and said, "She thinks she's got it all." I didn't know what he meant by it, but it sent a shiver down my spine.'

By now, I was getting anxious. It was obvious John had something very heavy on his mind. Why else would he be telling me all this?

'He worked a lot in Africa, didn't he?' continued John. I nodded. He paused for a while, and looked like he was thinking hard. 'HIV's very prevalent in Africa, isn't it?' he said slowly, solemnly. 'Ever thought of having an AIDS test?'

I went cold – it was as if somebody had tipped ice down my back. 'What?' I said as the dread starting to build up inside me.

'I think Robert died of AIDS.'

If I hadn't had Billie in my arms, I think I would have reacted how I did when Mum told me Linda had died. 'You *think*, you *think*?' I said, my voice quivering and rising, my heart racing.

'I'm pretty sure,' he said. The conviction in his voice was terrifying.

'Right,' I said. I was in absolute shock. I went numb with fear. 'Do you think he had it when I was with him?'

'I've arranged a test for you tomorrow at the hospital,' John continued. 'A car will collect you. No one will see you go in – you'll be taken in through a back door.'

After John left, I remember changing Billie's nappy – it was like I was watching myself doing it, as if in a dream. All I could think of was the disease that could be coursing through my veins, *and Billie's too*. All I could think was that I had killed my baby. I felt sick to my heart.

That day I called Robert's doctor. He wouldn't tell me anything until I gained clearance to access Robert's records. After a few phone calls, I got this, and it was then that the doctor confirmed the worst. 'Did you have unprotected sex with the deceased?' he asked before breaking it to me.

'Of course I fucking did!' I yelled. 'I was married to him!'

'Ah,' he replied.

Robert had definitely died of AIDS. Worst of all, the doctor told me that when I was sleeping with him he would have been at his most infectious.

I was given the test and told I wouldn't have the results for three weeks. *Three weeks!* I thought I would go mad in that time, and in some ways I nearly did. The anxiety was overwhelming – I could barely function and wasn't sleeping at all. My thoughts were everywhere. I was filled with a sense of dread I can hardly describe, and at the same time a million questions were flying through my mind. Did he know about it when we were together? If so, why hadn't he told me? If he didn't know till later, why hadn't he told me then? How could he have gone to his grave knowing I was alive with a newborn baby, and chosen not to inform me of the position I might be in?

How had Robert contracted HIV? I kept thinking. Did he get it from a woman, or was he gay? Had I just been a cover-up for his homosexuality? I talked to my social worker about it all. 'But surely he couldn't have been gay?' I would say. 'We had sex – how could he have been gay?'

'Do you really think that all gays have a limp wrist and speak with a lisp while mincing down Oxford Street and swinging a handbag?' she replied incredulously.

She had a point. The more I thought back to the time I was with Robert, the more I started to question everything. Suddenly I was looking at some of the things that had happened between us in a different light.

While we were together, Robert had brought up the subject a few times, telling me that if I ever heard rumours he was gay I was to ignore them. He was just 'tactile', he'd say. At the time I thought little of it – I assumed he was just making me aware of how malicious the press could be. Now, however, I wondered if he might have had a reason to worry. I remembered him saying, when I offered him a lift in my lilac VW convertible, 'People would think I was homosexual if I went in that car.' Robert was obsessed with people thinking he was gay. If he had nothing to hide, why the obsession?

I thought back to the time Robert proposed in the hotel lobby, his eyes full of tears. Who had the tears been for? Were they tears of happiness, or tears of guilt, because he knew had HIV, he knew was gay and knew he was asking me to marry him so that he had a defence against the rumours he warned me were circulating?

During another conversation with the social worker, who specialised in HIV cases, I explained how much I had admired Robert's fundraising in Africa, and she told me that it wasn't unheard of for men interested in young boys to get involved with agencies dealing with young people in the Third World. I was pretty angry at her for even suggesting it, but in my darkest thoughts I wondered if, running alongside Robert's genuine desire to help others, there was an altogether darker, more sinister motive for his involvement in Africa. I couldn't believe there was.

And then, of course, there was the fact that Robert and I rarely had sex. When we did, it felt like he was acting a part he couldn't really play. I've never mentioned it before but Robert occasionally used to try to cajole me into certain things that I didn't want to do. I've never been remotely interested in anal sex, but Robert had casually mentioned it. I realise that some heterosexual couples do it, but Robert didn't really seem interested in regular sex. After all, he'd even asked my friend Noel to service me. So I couldn't help but wonder why he was so keen to get me into *that* position. Hmm!

My life was on hold for three weeks as I slowly got through one panicky day after another. Christmas was on its way, but I had made no preparations. All I could do was wait, constantly turning the same things over in my head.

And then the call came.

I was clear. I nearly fell over with relief. The first person I called was John Dowd, who had kept in touch with me throughout the whole ordeal. When he heard my news, he sobbed down the phone. 'I'm so sorry you had to go through all this,' he cried.

'I'm scared, John,' I told him. A couple of days earlier I had received a very clear message from certain quarters of the Liberal Party. I was told that if I ever went public about how Robert died they would turn it around on me. They told me that AIDS comes from Africa and many black people there carry it, and that unless I kept my trap shut the press would say that *I* gave Robert HIV. (Remember this was the 1980s and knowledge about HIV and AIDS was riddled with myth.)

I told John all this and he was outraged. But there was nothing he could do. We both knew the system was bigger than us. But later I heard how the NSW Liberal Government had brought in legislation that made it a criminal offence for someone to have sex while HIV positive or with AIDS and deliberately withhold this from their partner. John resigned as Attorney General not long after that. I felt the whole experience with Robert really affected him. John was a good man, a very Christian man, and he just couldn't bear the fact of Robert's deception.

I was still reeling from it myself. I discovered that Robert's GP had told him it was vital that he tell me about his HIV. Robert led him to believe that he had told me, that I'd had a test and that I was clear. I was astounded that Robert could have done this. It really took my breath away. Everyone thought Robert was so fucking honourable, but behind closed doors he was able to tell such lies all the way to his deathbed.

Not long after I'd got the all-clear, I was changing

Billie's nappy (again!) with the TV on in the background. There was a report on the news about a certain politician who was facing corruption charges and was also in trouble for having used rent boys around 'The Wall' area in Kings Cross, very close to where Robert and I had lived and where I had been to the counsellor about him all those years ago. Suddenly, I heard a voice I recognised from somewhere. I looked up at the TV and froze.

It was the counsellor's voice. Her name was on the screen. I watched, transfixed. She was speaking about the rent boys she had worked with and how the men who used them were mostly professionals, some of them politicians. My memory flashed back to the day she had taken one look at a photo of Robert and told me to get out of the relationship. She had been so forceful, but had refused to tell me why. At the time I'd assumed she knew something about Robert, but I had no idea what. Watching her now sent a shiver down my spine – what if she knew about Robert through one of the rent boys who had come to her for help?

I suppose I could have approached the woman to try to get to the truth, but by that time I was utterly exhausted. I never found any absolute proof that Robert was gay. Whenever I have been asked about it, I've always maintained that I don't know if Robert was gay or not. But, going on what I know, I'd say there's a good chance he was. I certainly do not believe he was purely heterosexual.

People often ask me if I hate Robert and they are surprised when I say no. Sure, I hated him when he was giving me all that shit during our relationship, but once I'd left him all that hatred went. I think Robert did a good job of hating himself – he didn't need me to add to it. Despite the secrecy, despite the AIDS, I couldn't hate him. I only had pity for Robert. I think he spent much of his life wrestling with his demons. I don't believe hell is a place you cross over to. Hell is a living condition, and that man lived in hell – his life was spent in a conservative environment where being gay was just out of the question. The poor bastard, if he was gay it must have been torture for him. Robert probably had to live two lives and I wouldn't wish that upon anyone.

The funny thing is the amount of shit I get from certain quarters in politics every time I hint that Robert might have been gay. So what if he was? What is wrong with being gay? I don't think it diminishes Robert's good work. The sad thing is that if he thought it was such an issue I don't see why Robert didn't leave the party he was with. He could have done the same work elsewhere.

Maybe part of the reason Robert wanted to control me was that he had to spend so much time holding back from being the person he really was. If Robert had turned to me and said, 'You know what, I can't do this any more, I'm gay,' I would have told him, 'I respect that, you sleep in one room, I'll sleep in another. Just don't do the control thing and I'll cover for you.' That might sound bonkers but in many ways our marriage was a mutually convenient union and Robert leaving me alone in exchange for a cover-up would have made things much more convenient.

Somebody once asked me if I ever used Robert. My response was as honest as I can be: 'Yes, but not as much as Robert used me!'

I think that just about summed it up.

17

Married Again

Billie was my first true love affair. Up until giving birth, I never knew how mind-blowing love could be. Sometimes I would just hold her with tears in my eyes because never before had I experienced a connection like it. I found mothering a young baby so natural and I absolutely adored it. At the end of 1999 I decided that with Billie on board I would have to give up *The 7.30 Report* – there was no way I could keep up with such a punishing schedule. The ABC were thinking along similar lines, and they asked me what I wanted to do next. I suggested a programme on health and social welfare and, bingo, they gave me the opportunity to make one. In 1990, *Everybody* was born. I worked with the highly talented Giampaulo Pertosi to produce a series of 12 programmes. By the end of it, Giampaulo had another string to his bow – nappy changing! – because

Billie came everywhere with me. It was a wonderful focus to have after the pain of losing Linda.

Soon Mum and Dad came to visit. Mum fell in love with Billie straight away, and I think having a granddaughter was so good for her. Dad was quite distant initially. On the phone before they came, he had said to me, 'I've just lost one child. I'm not ready to take another on board.'

Although I understood, it hurt like hell.

When they arrived, I could tell Dad felt a little nervous around Billie, and he was clearly still racked with a load of guilt about Linda. There came a point when Mum was out of the house and I needed a shower, so I asked Dad to hold Billie. He didn't seem keen but, despite his protests, I left her with him.

Five minutes later, I peered around the doorway. Dad was cuddling her gently, eyes closed and tears streaming down his face. At that moment, I truly felt for him and the pain he was in. This is the beginning of the healing process, I thought. I knew he had connected with Billie and I knew I had done the right thing by having her.

Whether I had done the right thing remaining with Mark is a different question. It wasn't that Mark didn't love Billie, or that he didn't like fatherhood – once he accepted he had to change nappies, he took the ball and ran with it. I know that he truly loved Billie. The problem was that Mark and I were like two single people who had a child in common. While he cared for Billie, Mark couldn't wave goodbye to the high life – he still wanted to smoke dope, go drinking and live it up. That was fine for him, but as a breastfeeding mum it was no longer really my bag.

Married Again

What made things worse was that we didn't even have massive fights at that stage. If anything, we were both too apathetic to do anything about the relationship. Apathy was the problem – at least if there's conflict it shows you care and there's something to work through. Before we started filming *Everybody*, I trained in conflict resolution. Unfortunately, there was no such course for resolving the problem of apathy.

I was working hard (surprise surprise!) and by that stage so was Mark, who was working on a gardening and lifestyle show called *Burke's Backyard*. When I wasn't working I was totally focused on Billie. To be fair, I was freezing Mark out. I don't think I was fully aware of it at the time, but – forgive the psycho-speak – I wasn't investing in the relationship. Emotionally, that is. When it came to money, I had no choice but to invest in Mark!

Cash became an issue. Basically, I was earning a lot more than Mark. I've never been tight and certainly don't have a 'what's mine is mine' attitude to life, but I felt that Mark spent quite a bit of what I was earning on going out and having a good time. He'd either be out or he'd have loads of mates round to the house we were renting in the Greenwich area of Sydney.

Another problem was sex. Mark loved sex. He wasn't a sex addict, but he often said he saw it as a way of winding down. The trouble was, I wasn't too keen on 'winding down' with him. It wasn't that I didn't like sex, it was sex with Mark that I didn't like.

Most of the time, unsurprisingly, I wasn't desperate to accommodate him at every opportunity. Mark admitted he saw sex as a release from everything, so when he asked for it I often felt it wasn't necessarily me he wanted, but just sex. Sex with Mark didn't feel intimate to me, and that's what put me off. As a result, he often complained he wasn't getting enough – and he wasn't!

Looking back, I remember once finding a packet of condoms in his wallet. 'What are these for?' I asked. 'We don't use them!' Mark had just come back from a trip filming for *Burke's Backyard* in Queensland. His response was that, as a producer, he needed to make sure his cameraman and crew didn't get into trouble, so he carried condoms for them. Hah!

Many of my friends weren't too keen on Mark. At various times they told me they didn't think it would last, and even asked me what the hell I was doing with 'that stoner'. But it's funny, when you're in a relationship, even if your mates are right, you often don't really want to hear their criticisms. Bizarrely, being told I was in the wrong relationship made me stick my head in the sand even more. I did care about Mark and hearing him being bad-mouthed just made me defensive and more determined to paper over the cracks.

In the light of what I've said about Mark and I, it may come as a surprise that, instead of calling it a day with him and moving on, I did two things that would ensure we were more involved with each other than ever. In 1991, I left the ABC. My contract had come up. I'd loved all the creative freedom I'd had there, but an opportunity arose and I seized the moment to go freelance with a great producer and director called Paul Hawker. We did this in order to work for healthcare company MBF making 'Know Your Heart' advertisements to raise public health awareness on the subject of cardiovascular health. The ads won awards and led to me being offered a budget of two million dollars a year to make a series of chat shows on health and social issues. I formed an independent production company with Phil Gerlach and we called the show *Live It Up* and very quickly it became a success. Our health features were combined with celebrity interviews about health and lifestyle – Nicole Kidman's psychologist dad, Dr Anthony Kidman, came on, as did Julian Clary and a whole host of Aussie celebrities – and Mark joined Phil and I as a third partner. Things hadn't been going too well for him on *Burke's Backyard* – he didn't seem to be getting on that well with the host, Don Burke – so he was only too happy to jump on the bandwagon. In fact, he nagged me relentlessly until I gave in and somewhat reluctantly let him join us.

It was an exciting new venture. Stepping out as an independent company was a huge challenge and initially Mark and I worked together really well. He was a brilliant editor and producer and we spent a lot of time bouncing creative ideas off each other. Working on *Live It Up* was a real focus and became the bedrock of our relationship. Our problems were eclipsed by the huge task of getting a company to grow and churning out hours of television.

And grow it did. We were making lots of money, working crazy hours – Mark and I ran an office, and I'd often be producer, co-executive producer and presenter all on the same programme. However, looking back, I know I was neglecting my personal life, but at the time the only things I bothered about were work and Billie. The success of the company (and the hours required to keep it successful), my good relationship at work with Mark and my love affair with Billie meant that I wasn't giving due attention to what was really going on inside me.

Back then I was a different person, and I didn't expect much more from a relationship than what I had with Mark. He was a companion of sorts, and by and large he let me get on with my life because he was so happy getting on with his and the evenings were 'getting stoned' time. Somehow, I thought this was reason enough to take things to the next level – marriage!

These days I am fortunate enough to understand what marriage *can* be all about. Back then I had a slightly skewed view of it, to put it mildly. It sounds awful, but I can only really think of two reasons why I decided to marry Mark, and romance didn't come into either of them. One reason was that part of me naïvely thought that getting hitched would make things between us better, but don't ask me what I thought it would change – I really can't put myself back in the head of the Trisha Goddard I was then. The other reason was I'd decided I wanted another baby. I didn't want to have two children by two different men, so I decided to really try to make a go of things with Mark. Getting married just seemed like the next step. Talk about cold and calculating, Trisha, I hear you saying to yourself. But that's what I was like then, and there's no point in pretending otherwise.

Mark didn't take much persuading, and in the spring of 1993 marriage number two began for me at the registry office in Crawley Town Hall. The atmosphere felt pretty clinical and I was shocked when, in the middle of the ceremony, Mark's eyes started to well up with tears. He was holding my hands and looking right into my eyes. Oh fuck, I thought, don't do this now because there ain't no romance on my part and I can't handle this! The reason I was surprised was that I'd made all the arrangements for the wedding, and Mark had just gone along with it. Before the wedding, he'd seemed even less emotional about it than I was, and now he was full of sentiment. I just didn't get it. When he started with the tears, I must admit I did begin thinking, What the fuck am I doing here? Romantic, I know!

We had a little ceremony in the cutest little church too. Afterwards, Mum was going round hugging and kissing everyone. When she got to where I was standing, she took me in her arms and whispered something I'll never forget. 'Make this one work, Tootsie darling,' she said into my ear.

I wanted to freak out and scream. I think she'd been embarrassed by my divorce from Robert and was worried about a repeat performance with Mark. Her comment made my blood boil. *Robert had AIDS, for fuck's sake.* 'If I'd made it "work" with him,' I felt like yelling, 'I'd be fucking *dead*!'

Mum moved away and I was speechless. As all the guests came up to me to offer their congratulations, I just stood there with a maniacal grin fixed on my face, feeling very little. I was emotionally cold that day – marriage was part of my grand plan to have another baby and I don't think it even occurred to me that I didn't feel what I was supposed to be feeling about Mark. Looking back, I find it incredible that I operated like that, but I did.

So, man and wife returned to Australia to begin married life and, guess what, nothing changed. The only difference in our relationship was that we now had a bit of paper saying we were married.

It might have been easy to get Mark to marry me, but it wasn't so easy getting him to agree to have another child. In fact, it was like pushing poo uphill! I'd stopped breastfeeding just after Billie turned two, and we'd started to have a slightly better time inasmuch as I would take the odd puff on a joint again and have a glass or two in the evening. This was good news for Mark, but one child was enough for him. Although he loved Billie, I think he had sometimes viewed her as a barrier between us (and to be fair I *made* her that barrier), and another kid wasn't his idea of a laugh.

But I was determined to get what I wanted, so I hatched another plan. Mark might not have wanted another baby, but he did want sex. So I decided to let him have as much as he could handle – I took him away on a dirty weekend! We booked a fancy Sydney hotel suite and I made sure I got him drunk and stoned before getting down to it. He got what he wanted and I got what I wanted – a baby was conceived at some point during those 48 hours in early September. God, it's a wonder I wasn't laughing like Dr Evil from *Austin Powers*!

Soon after we married, I bought a house in Chatswood, Sydney, and had great fun making a *Play School* film about moving house with Billie. There was a garden, a veranda and enough room for us three plus a new baby. I had just got pregnant when we moved in. Meanwhile, Mark wasn't over the moon about there being another baby on the way, and was once more banished from smoking dope in the house, even when Billie was in bed. At 11 weeks, we found out that the baby was a girl and, when I told him, Mark's face fell. He wouldn't tell me quite why, but something he did tell me was that he'd have preferred a boy.

Mark and I began living increasingly separate lives. I didn't rely on him to fulfil my needs and we were both so busy at work that nothing seemed amiss. When I wasn't working, Billie and I would go out and explore the park together, but Mark was rarely around for such occasions. The times we did go out as a family, Mark acted like he didn't want to be there. It makes me laugh when I recall the time the three of us went out and Mark admitted he was walking ahead of us because he was worried that being seen out with a wife and kid would spoil his image.

When we did spend time together, it was obvious that things weren't all rosy between us, though luckily that didn't happen too often. Outside of the house, Billie and I had a life together that Mark knew nothing about. Later I would discover that Mark had a secret life outside of the house too.

This time, being pregnant made me sick morning, noon and night. And it wasn't just the first few weeks; it was a pukefest from beginning to end. When Mark suggested spending Christmas driving around Western Australia on a tour of the vineyards before heading to the coast to surf, I just laughed. Even the smell of alcohol was enough to make me heave, and the idea that I'd want to drive him around while he got pissed was a joke. 'You can lie around on the beach and watch me surf,' he said in an effort to get me to agree to the trip.

'Yeah, and I could also have someone put hot sticks in my eyes,' I replied. 'I'm heavily pregnant, Mark, and I'm not going.'

We ended up deciding to spend Christmas apart, so Billie and I jetted off to England to spend Christmas with Mum and Dad. They were great grandparents, and at that stage my relationship with them was pretty good. Billie really brought us all together. We had a great Christmas, with Mum getting tipsy and making us all laugh, and Dad being very affectionate to Billie. With Mark absent, I spent quite a lot of time daydreaming about what life would be like with a warm husband who wanted to spend time with us. I imagined holidaying together, camping and doing things as a family, but I would snap myself out of it by thinking, Trisha, you've made your bed and now you can lie in it.

Mark met us at the airport when we got back, and immediately I set eyes on him I felt there was something amiss. It was hard to put my finger on it but he looked totally *different* and there was something different in his manner. He was all spruced up and smelled of aftershave, something he rarely wore. Instead of his usual casual, laidback gear, he was wearing clothes I'd never seen before. Smarter clothes, and trendy shoes, whereas normally he wore trainers.

'Daddy!' shouted Billie as she ran towards him. Mark and I said hello and, once again, only in a very subtle way, he seemed slightly less relaxed. His whole demeanour was enough to make me narrow one eye and think, Hmnn, what's going on here then?

Maybe he is making an effort for us, I thought, as we walked to the car.

Little did I know there were more changes to come.

18

The Penny Drops

'Get this baby out of me!' I said to my obstetrician, Ian Symington.

It was 12 May 1994, and I was two weeks overdue. The next day was Friday the 13th, and the doc had told me that the hospital would be packed with Chinese women trying to give birth on that day, as for them it signifies good luck! The maternity ward would be completely overstretched.

I was feeling pretty overstretched myself, so Ian agreed to induce the baby. Mark drove me to the hospital. He seemed incredibly stressed out, and when another car cut him up he was effing and blinding like crazy, which wasn't like him at all. Mind you, since he'd met us at the airport after Christmas, Mark had started doing lots of things that weren't like him. First, there was the change in clothes (over the previous few months he'd totally revamped his wardrobe) and the aftershave, next he decided to drink whisky instead of wine, and then there was a sudden interest in herbal medicine – he'd brew stinking potions on my cooker hob for hours! It was all downright weird. I'd wondered what the hell was up with him, but, aside from asking him the odd question here and there, I'd been happy to leave him be with his new self.

Mark was different at the hospital too. Considering I was about to give birth to our child, he was mighty laidback. As the doctor went about inducing the baby, Mark just sat in the corner of the room reading a newspaper and glancing up at the telly vacantly. Meanwhile, I was standing there at the foot of the bed rocking and grinding and making a right racket. With Billie, Mark had been watching me with concern – we'd had a rapport going on and he'd supported me through the birth. Now, it was as if I wasn't in the room. He seemed utterly disengaged, confusingly indifferent.

Dr Symington got Mark involved. 'Try to get Trisha to slow her breathing down,' he told him.

What happened next was just bizarre.

'Yes,' said Mark, as he came over to me, 'try and slow your breathing down, Trisha.'

He said it so dispassionately that his coldness just made me think, What the fuck is going on here? Why the hell is my husband acting like such a detached robot? I didn't need those anxieties while I was giving birth, and I've always been angry with Mark for acting the way he did in that room. To me, childbirth is a spiritual, holy thing, and the way he acted messed with that in a big way.

Madi was born on Thursday, 12 May, and I was

delighted. The next day I was back power-walking and first thing on Monday I was recording a *Play School* CD with Madi in a moses basket by my side. The doctor thought I was bonkers, but it worked for me. Work and babies were all I knew.

I am sad to say that the experience of having a new child was different with Madi and there's one reason for that – Mark. Our relationship had never been amazing, but now it was most definitely stinking like rotten fish! Mark was being very distant and it was making me feel insecure – there was something up between us, but I couldn't quite figure out what was happening and why. I hadn't changed, that was for sure, so the problem lay with him. He was awkward, nervy and simpered around in his cashmere roll-necks and trousers (the Mark of old would have just worn baggy jeans and a T-shirt). We'd been together six years and, even if our relationship had been apathetic, I'd always felt safe within that apathy. I knew Mark well enough to realise something in him had changed, but I couldn't quite pin down what it was. As a result I didn't feel safe any more. I felt vulnerable.

When Madi was about seven weeks old, she started having trouble breathing. Billie had suffered from childhood asthma so I assumed Madi had it too. I went to the doctor, but the mask and oxygen machine she gave her to ease her breathing didn't seem to help. Within a matter of days there came a moment when Madi suddenly seemed to have stopped breathing altogether. The sense of sheer panic that rose in me is indescribable. 'We need a hospital, *now*!' I shouted to Mark.

I didn't want to wait for an ambulance, so Mark drove

us to North Sydney Hospital's A and E department. They took Madi straight in for assessment. Before long, she was in the intensive-care unit on the children's ward and hooked up to a ton of equipment – oxygen tanks, drips and heart monitors. I was in a right state – the anxiety of not knowing if my daughter was going to live or die made me want to scream. I'd like to be able to say I had Mark by my side, but unfortunately I can't. Mark had decided to go elsewhere.

We were meant to be at a friend's wedding that day. Dr Rosie King was a psychologist who co-presented *Live It Up* with me twice a week, and not long after we had arrived at the hospital Mark had started whingeing that we were going to miss her wedding. It was unbelievable. 'Fucking hell,' I said, 'we're not going to that now, we're in a fucking hospital!'

Mark suggested that he take Billie to the wedding to get her out of the way. I was in the middle of talking to all these doctors and didn't have time to argue, so off he went. With my baby in intensive care, I had no intention of moving a muscle until I knew she was OK.

The problem was, they couldn't work out what was wrong with her.

I was on my own, or at least I thought I was. Carefully watched over by nurses, I was in a chair next to Madi's bed, trying to breastfeed her while listening for any irregular beeps from the heart monitor, while other kids on the ward kept coming past with their parents and saying, 'Ooh, look, Mummy and Daddy, it's the lady off *Play School*!' And, would you believe it, some of the parents would begin to approach me wanting to say 'Hi!'

or get an autograph. It was pretty obvious this was *not* the place for that, but it didn't stop 'em trying! People can be utter fuckers. But for the fact that I was so petrified about Madi, I would quite happily have sledgehammered those people to death at that moment.

Madi would be lying there for a while, and then suddenly the steady 'beep... beep... beep' of the machines would either dramatically speed up or slow down. I would only have time to whimper and the nurses would come and work on her until she was breathing again. They would go away, and then it would happen again. My senses were pricked; I could not move a muscle for fear of losing my baby. I would hold off going to the loo for hours, only once dared shower and lived in my nightie.

Madi steadily got worse, and they kept on reviving her. It was hellishly touch and go.

The time came where Barry Wyeth, a wonderful doctor who had dealt with Billie as a private patient in the past, came up and told me I had to make a decision. 'We either leave Madi as she is, or increase her oxygen. If we leave her as she is there is a chance she will go into cardiac arrest, but if we increase her oxygen there is a risk she might get brain damage.'

I couldn't make such a decision, and I couldn't believe this was happening. *Brain damage*, I thought. I asked if there was another way. If they increased the oxygen just a tiny bit, was there still a risk of Madi's brain suffering? The answer was yes.

I couldn't risk it. I couldn't put my daughter through that. My thoughts were a mess but I knew I couldn't risk brain damage. I had to make the same decision time and time again, and I was forever having consent forms shoved in my face. I barely knew what they were for. I was in emotional chaos. The only other time I've felt like that in my life was when I was told I might have AIDS and thought I'd killed Billie. It's pure, unadulterated hell.

I was hysterical, but not on the outside. My panic was not visible to others. Inside I was screaming, and making *several* deals with God, one of which was 'Take me instead, for fuck's sake. Take me!' Any mother in a similar position feels the same way. The desperation you feel for your child to survive is like nothing else on earth.

The minutes and the hours merged into one. I lost track of time, taking five-minute catnaps here and there, or running to the canteen to get a bit of food (and often running back before I got to the end of the queue). And I was still getting hassled for autographs. It was an experience I wouldn't wish on my worst enemy.

At one stage, a nurse came up and put her arm around me. 'You know, you're going to have to really think about whether you want them to increase the oxygen before long,' she said.

I nodded. I knew it might have to come to that.

'I don't want to panic you,' she continued, 'and I'm not saying Madi won't survive, but are you religious, and would you want a priest to give Madi, well, you know...?'

I knew exactly what she meant – last rites.

I went cold all over as she spoke. I knew she wasn't trying to freak me out, because it was clear things weren't looking good at all. I didn't want a priest as I thought it was bad luck to ask for one at that stage. Having a priest felt like tempting fate, and I was nowhere near ready to give up on my darling Madi. Still, I was in total distress and tried to call Mark at home and on his mobile to tell him how fragile Madi's state was. There was no answer.

No answer became a bit of a theme with Mark during that period. I was there non-stop for four days, and all that time Mark popped in daily to check up on things. When he wasn't around, I would ring home but the answer machine would always cut in, but I simply thought he'd be exhausted keeping our company going and looking after Billie. His mobile phone would ring out too. I called England and spoke to Mum on the phone and told her that Mark wasn't around much. What she said has always stuck with me.

'We women have to be strong,' she said. 'We give birth and we bury the dead. You can't rely on men in these situations. Men just fall apart. Mark can't cope with this, and you have to help him cope with it. It's what women do.'

One day Mark came into the hospital unshaven and wearing the same clothes he'd been wearing the previous day. When I remarked on it, he told me he had been so tired he couldn't even get undressed and had just collapsed fully clothed on the bed with the stress of it all. This explained why the phone had been ringing out when I'd tried to call. With Mum's words in mind, I hugged him and told him it was all going to work out. He looked so rough I told him to go home and get more sleep.

Eventually the hell was over. It had been established that an unidentifiable infection had 'bloomed' in Madi's lungs. After those four agonising days, the doctors got the infection under control and sent us on our way.

I was back at home, relieved and exhausted, and Madi was in the final stages of recovery. Mark was still being weird, and then he did something really out of character. He arranged for his parents to come over from Western Australia. 'I want them here so they can support us,' he said.

There was nothing wrong with Mark's parents, and I adored his mother, but I didn't need them to support us. We had a nanny, and I simply didn't understand what Mark was thinking. I objected, but it was too late, they were on their way.

Once they arrived, Mark's mum, Lenore, said that she wanted us to have some time together. Mark said he wanted time together too. I was a bit bewildered. It wasn't like Mark and I were used to spending much time together and I didn't see why there was a sudden need. But I went along with it anyway. 'OK,' I said to Mark, 'why don't we go for a meal then?'

'I was thinking we could go to the park,' he replied.

Fair enough, I thought, and suggested we take Billie with us.

'No, I thought we could have some time alone together,' Mark said.

What? I thought. I knew something strange was going on. All I could do to find out what was to go along with Mark's suggestions with butterflies in my stomach. We got in the car, drove to Lane Cove National Park and began walking.

'What's happening?' I asked Mark as we sat down at a picnic bench. 'What's this "time together" thing all about?'

The Penny Drops

There was a pause and then he began. 'It's not working,' he said, gazing out into the distance.

I looked at him for a couple of moments. I wasn't sure if I'd heard him correctly. 'What do you mean,' I said. 'What are you talking about?'

'Well, where do you see us in five years?' he continued.

I wasn't ready for this. I'd just spent around ninety sleepless hours in hospital and now my husband was laying a load of heavy shit on me. I told him I didn't know where I saw us in five years. It wasn't the kind of thing I really thought about.

'You don't know where we'll be,' he said, 'and I think that means it's not working.'

'What are you saying, Mark? Are you saying we should split up?'

He didn't have much of an answer to that. He answered with a combination of yeses, nos and maybes, though not necessarily in that order. 'I think we should have relationship counselling,' he said.

So that's what he's been trying to get to, I thought.

I was very unclear about exactly what Mark was hoping to achieve when he suggested relationship counselling. After the ordeal with Madi, I had shit for brains and I simply agreed to it there and then.

Mark even had someone lined up. We went to see an American woman called Toby Green, a brilliant relationship counsellor. Mark was quite happy talking but I wasn't quite sure what I was there for and was reluctant to speak. And, anyway, I didn't have an awful lot to say, so the conversation was very stilted for the first couple of sessions. We attempted to answer questions along the lines of 'What do we want from this relationship?' and I remember thinking, Why am I here?

It wasn't until I was back at work that I began to find out the answer.

We were in a production meeting with all the producers and researchers, and were brainstorming for ideas to feature on *Live It Up* that week. Everyone chipped in and then Joanne spoke.

Joanne was from a tough background, and I'd employed her after receiving a letter begging us to give her a chance in TV. We always received tons of letters asking for jobs, but Joanne's had stood out and I called her to say she could have a bit of work experience with us. She came along and did well. She wasn't stunning – the boys used to joke that she was 'all teeth and tits' – but what she did have she wasn't afraid to show off. She dressed inappropriately, and I had to have a word with her about it several times in the early days. She would wear a leather micro-miniskirt and the like. Other women didn't like her, but some of the blokes thought she was sexy. Despite that, I'd wanted to give her a chance and taught her as much as I could. Eventually I took her on as a researcher.

Joanne's past openness about sex meant that it came as no surprise to anybody when she gave us her suggestion for a programme as we sat around in the meeting that morning.

'Let's do a show on sex and relationships,' she said. 'And let's do it about celebrities.'

I liked the idea – after all, it's a fact of life that anything to do with celebrities and sex tends to work on TV. I asked Joanne to expand on it a bit, which she did. 'Let's do a show on the fact that every frontwoman on TV – every successful woman who's really in charge of their career – might be up there on the red carpet, but the truth is their love lives are shit,' she said confidently.

Even though I immediately felt defensive, I was interested to hear how she thought this would work as a programme. She suggested we did a feature on Elizabeth Hayes, a popular morning-TV presenter whose boyfriend had cheated on her (according to the tabloids). Joanne wanted to compare all the other successful women on TV with Elizabeth in order to suggest what might be going on. Elizabeth was someone I totally admired and there was no way that I was going to do a hatchet-job show on her. She had already been upset enough by what had happened, and Joanne was mad to think I'd be interested.

'Don't be stupid,' I told her, 'we can't say that every successful woman on air has a partner who is screwing around!'

'Oh yes we can,' she shot back. 'Every single one.' Her attitude was strange, and rather aggressive. It was time to cut her off.

'OK, Joanne,' I said decisively. 'We're not going to go with that one, so…'

'Why not, is it a bit too close for comfort?' she snapped, then laughed.

'I beg your pardon,' I said, amazed at her audacity.

'Is it a bit too close to the bone for you?' she said tauntingly.

I had no idea what she was trying to achieve, but I knew she was pushing her luck. 'Well, I don't know if someone I know is being cheated on, but…'

'You mean you don't like the idea that your man could be screwing around on you,' she snapped, glaring at me smugly.

Joanne had gone too far, and by now I was angry. I couldn't believe that one of my researchers was talking to me like this in front of the rest of my staff. I lost my cool. 'Would you like to shut up, Joanne. In fact, shut the fuck up or get out!' I shot back, my face burning.

'I knew you'd hate the idea. Like I say, it's happening to every successful woman, *every single one of them.*'

I wrapped things up quickly, outraged by what had happened. I had to drive to another meeting and as I drove I was suddenly overcome by a horribly strong wave of nausea. I couldn't believe the way I'd been talked to. I felt humiliated. The cheeky bitch! I thought. How dare she treat me like that and after all I've done for her? I'd taught her so much about TV, encouraged her to progress in her job and even listened to all her crappy little boyfriend worries. I got so angry I had to pull off the road.

I sat there for a minute, then picked up my in-car phone and called Mark at the office. I explained exactly what had occurred and how upset I was. 'I'd like you to get that ungrateful little cow up to the office and give her a bloody good talking-to!' I said.

Mark was always good at giving staff a dressing-down when they needed it. I knew I could rely on him to explain in no uncertain terms to Joanne how out of order she'd been. I assumed he'd be as pissed off as I was about it all, but instead of jumping to my defence he jumped to hers. His voice softened and he said something that completely threw me – 'Oh, I'm sure Jojo didn't mean it.'

The Penny Drops

Jojo! Jojo? I'd never heard anyone call her that, and it had been years since I'd heard Mark use that soft voice. 'Jojo didn't mean it' – those words said it all. From that moment I knew. Mark and Joanne were screwing each other. I wanted to throw up. Then I went deadly cold.

I didn't say a word. There would be time for that later. I wanted to watch him for a while, and I would watch little Jojo too.

I said goodbye and drove on.

I hadn't suspected that Mark was having an affair. For months I had wondered what was going on with him. All of the changes he'd made to himself, the distance in his eyes and his regular absences had made me feel unsafe, but I'd always told him that if he *had* to screw around to make sure it was on a trip to another part of the country and that I'd never find out! Why? Don't ask me. It was a semi-serious joke and he was in Sydney all the time now. In many ways, I suppose, the classic signs of infidelity were all there, but I hadn't been looking for them. I'd thought I was going mad at times – I wondered whether I was imagining the changes in Mark – but it wasn't until he called Joanne 'Jojo' that the pieces of the puzzle fell into place.

All became horribly clear. At the office I started watching Mark and Joanne like a hawk. Very quickly it dawned on me that every programme Joanne worked on, Mark produced. Just days after *that* meeting, I walked up to Mark's office to ask him a question. He was working with Joanne. I poked my head around the door and we all had a conversation. As we talked, I noticed that Mark was gently stroking the small of Joanne's back – he obviously thought I couldn't see. Right, I thought, that's it.

Later I went through Mark's emails and what I found was no surprise, but it still made me feel sick. There was nothing explicit, no hard evidence of an affair, but all the 'Hi Honeys' and 'Jojos' were enough for me. Whatever was going on between them, it was far from innocent.

I decided the time had come to get the truth out of Mark. I knew it wouldn't be hard. After all, there was nothing he liked more than a night on the booze. I suggested we get the nanny to babysit and go to a jazz night that I had tickets for. He was all for it. I wasn't drinking, but was happy to indulge Mark in his newfound weakness for good scotch. Before he could finish one, I made sure there was another double waiting for him to skull back. I got him nice and drunk very quickly, and after the concert we went downstairs to the coffee shop.

'So, tell me about Joanne,' I said casually.

Drunk though he was, Mark jolted a little at my words. 'Joanne? Oh, we're just mates.' The lie rolled out pretty smoothly. Still, I wasn't impressed.

'Great. So how long has it been going on then?' I said, still calm.

Mark shot a look at me. He realised I knew something, I'm sure of it. 'Eh? No, Trish, we're just mates, it's nothing like that. I just like her.'

The lie didn't sound so smooth this time. Mark was in a corner, and he was stumbling on his words.

'You like her,' I repeated back to him, my voice a little less calm. 'You *like* her. How about you cut the crap and tell me just how much you *like* Joanne, Mark.'

The Penny Drops

Mark protested his innocence a few more times. He told me I'd got it all wrong. But, after a few more lame attempts to cover his tracks, the truth fell from his mouth. 'I think I've fallen in love with her,' he admitted sheepishly.

He told me his feelings had developed over time, but that they hadn't slept together. I wasn't going to swallow that one. 'Are you telling me that you, Mark Greive, have fallen in love without having sex?' I said. 'You, to whom sex is everything! Don't make me laugh. Let's have the story again, Mark.'

It all came out. Mark had slept with Joanne all right. He'd been with her while I was in England for Christmas, he'd been with her during my pregnancy and he was still with her now. Even though I'd worked out what was going on, having it confirmed was still a shock. Worse still, Mark hardly offered any apology. Once I'd got the truth out of him I just wanted to go home, so I stood up to leave. I was expecting him to come with me, despite what we'd just talked about. But instead he looked at me and, shrugging his shoulders, said, 'Well, I might as well go and spend the night with Joanne then.'

'What about me?' I said. By now I was beginning to cry. I had been utterly humiliated and now Mark was sticking the knife in with his coldness.

'Not my problem,' he said, and began to turn away.

I went to walk towards him and, as I did so, tripped and fell on the pavement. I was still quite big from having just had a baby, but Mark didn't move to help me up. He just stood there and looked at me as though I was a piece of shit. It was around midnight. We were in the middle of Sydney and the streets were swarming with revellers.

People walked past me, glancing down as they went. I remained on the ground, and Mark's look was so full of loathing and disgust that I just burst into tears. I felt so ashamed and hurt, and the more I cried the more Mark just stared. It was as if he was getting a kick out of it. After a minute or so, he broke his silence. 'Goodbye, Trisha,' he said coldly. With that, he walked away.

The next day was a Saturday. I'd lain awake all night, endlessly turning things over in my head. I asked myself how it had all happened, why it had all happened. I tortured myself by raking over the past few months and thinking of all the things that should have made it click that Mark was up to no good. *And as I lay there I knew that Mark was with Joanne.* It felt like a sick joke.

Despite what had happened, Mark came home in the morning. As I looked at him wearing the same clothes he'd had on the previous night, I had a flashback to when he'd come into the hospital wearing the same clothes as the day before. I remembered hugging and comforting him by poor Madi's bedside. I'd been trying to call him all night and he had told me he'd been sleeping.

Then I checked our mobile-phone bill. Mark had called the same number over and over again in the early hours of the morning. I checked our staff list. Three guesses as to whom that home number belonged to...

The penny dropped. Mark had been screwing Joanne while Madi was lying in intensive care! I took one look at him and let him have it. 'Am I right in thinking that when I was calling you up from hospital to tell you Madi might need to be given last rites you were busy screwing Joanne?'

My dear friend B once told me that a standing cock has

no conscience. Mark was one fine testament to the truth of that statement. That he'd been able to carry on with Joanne under such circumstances just blew my mind!

The argument got vicious. I wanted all the details, and Mark gave them to me. He didn't even seem ashamed. He spoke as if I'd deserved his treatment, as if he'd had no choice but to cheat on me. He stood there pathetically and told me he'd been lonely when I went away over Christmas. Perhaps he thought I was going to feel sorry for him. He told me he was in love, that he'd been sucked into the romance and couldn't help himself. He was like a Z-list actor trying to say, 'I can't live without her' and mean it. What melodrama! Basically, he fed me a load of shit and all I wanted to do was punch him out. If the kids hadn't been in the house, I may well have done it.

It was always a rule of mine not to argue in front of the children, but on this occasion emotions were running so high it all went out of the window. I felt such a fool. You've heard the phrase 'Hell hath no fury like a woman scorned'? Well, say no more.

I was all over the place emotionally, completely winded by Mark's cruelty and utterly humiliated. But it didn't stop me calling Joanne at 2.30am one morning when Mark was asleep in bed. When she realised who was on the end of the line she panicked. When she'd stopped saying, 'Oh my God,' she asked me why I was calling.

'Well, I'm not ringing you at this time of the morning to give you a fucking pay rise, darling,' I said. I was as cold as ice. 'You're fired. Get your stuff out of the office before nine o'clock in the morning or, God help me, I'll throw it out on the street! I've got friends in the industry. If you find another job in TV, you'll be a very lucky girl. I was good to you – you even told me I was like a second mother!'

Joanne told me that, while I'd been good to her, I hadn't been good to Mark. She told me he had 'skin hunger', that he was lonely and I should have been a better wife.

Joanne immediately left the company, and no one was told why. Mark kept coming and going, one minute telling me he wanted to be with me, another minute telling me he couldn't live without Joanne. It was mental torture, and the weird thing is I didn't kick him out straight away. The way I saw things, we had two children and I wanted him to stay. God knows why, but I did. This put Mark in a position of power, a position he wasn't used to having in our relationship. In the past, I'd certainly worn the trousers – one of the things that always antagonised him, though I've always said that if I hadn't worn the trousers they wouldn't have stayed up! – but now the tables were turning.

It wasn't like I was thinking, Poor me. On some level, I could cope with the fact that Mark had had an affair. What did my head in was the way he did it, who he did it with and the way he behaved once I found out. Instead of doing the sensible thing and leaving – or indeed staying, as he did have that option – he simply played mind games, and at one stage expected me to counsel him about his feelings for Joanne. 'She's angry you and I are still having sex,' he whined. 'How dare she! After all you are my wife!' It was bizarre.

We took the children with us on a trip to New Zealand to try to work out what to do, but made little progress. I had been humiliated and, looking back, I was only deepening the humiliation by allowing Mark to carry on fucking with my head once I'd found out what was going on. I should have cut him off straight away. That's what I'd advise anyone to do these days.

Instead, I let him torture me and I also tortured myself. I couldn't sleep or eat, and became so distracted I would find myself doing the clumsiest of things – my mind was simply elsewhere most of the time. Work was as busy as ever. I dragged myself through each day and Mark was always in the office. There was no escape from him. He came and went to the house as he pleased, and when he wasn't around either he or Joanne would call up. I was becoming physically, mentally and emotionally drained. It wasn't long before my tank was running on empty.

I started seeing the counsellor Toby Green again, and it was only through her that I finally told Mark what I wanted. We arranged a session for Mark and I. Toby sat us down and asked me what it was that I wanted to say to Mark. 'I want him to get out,' was my reply. Toby asked me to explain to Mark exactly what I meant. 'I want you to pack up and go. I cannot deal with your comings and goings. I don't want any more phone calls and I don't want you to come back.'

Once Mark realised how final I was being, he changed his tune. When we went back home, he tried to hug me. 'I'm so, so sorry, Trish,' he whimpered.

'I don't care, you can get out,' I said.

It wasn't until Mark was packing his bags that I said I wanted a divorce. He was really shocked, and asked me why. I was gobsmacked! 'There's nothing to think about,' I said firmly. 'I want a divorce and that's it.'

Trisha - *As I Am*

Despite everything that had happened, it wasn't an easy thing to say. There was so much raw emotion on both sides. As Mark packed, things got ugly again. We screamed at each other, our words filled with bitterness, anger and confusion.

And then, finally, he left.

19

In Pieces

My head was everywhere and nowhere, and I didn't know what the hell was going on any more. All I knew was that I couldn't take it. Mark shut the front door behind him, and I sat there feeling absolutely good for nothing. I had never been so low. All the energy had been drained from me. My mind was a jumble of pain, anger and exhaustion, yet it would not stop whirring. I hadn't slept properly for weeks, and I couldn't think straight. In fact, I could no longer think. *I didn't want to be thinking.*

I poured myself a brandy. Its warmth seeped into me slowly. I felt slightly woozy. I could feel myself collapsing inside, as if my mind was crumbling gently. There was nothing I could do to pick myself up. I was spent.

I had already been prescribed anti-depressants – my GP knew what a state I was in and had urged me to take them. So far I had resisted, but now I realised I needed them. I knew I'd have to be on them for six weeks before they began working, but I didn't care. I examined the packet, took one of the pills out and swallowed it.

Then I poured another brandy and knocked back the pill. More warmth. But my mind still wouldn't stop racing. I just wanted it to shut up. I started get angry with myself. The last time I'd been this angry was the night when Robert had kept talking at me and I had grabbed the knife...

Shut up, head!

This time I swigged the brandy straight from the bottle. I was getting angrier and angrier. I couldn't stop thinking about the shame of Mark's betrayal. I wondered if anyone else knew what had been going on behind my back.

More brandy. More pills.

Something in my consciousness broke the spell – the survival instinct perhaps. I snapped out of my furious self-talk long enough to remember I had taken pills – exactly how many I wasn't sure – and that I may be in danger. I called the National Health poisons advice line to ask them how many pills were an overdose. The woman on the end of the line would not tell me, but kept repeating, 'What have you done? How many have you taken?' I couldn't tell her. I wasn't thinking straight. I just wanted an answer to my question. She wouldn't give me one, so I hung up.

I started to feel really strange. My limbs felt weak, the room was going in and out of focus, and I felt like I might be about to slip away into unconsciousness. My coordination was going, but I managed to call Rosie King. 'Rosie, I think I've done something really stupid here,' I said. 'The girls are going to be on their own...'

In Pieces

It wasn't Rosie who turned up first. It was Mark. He lived closer to me than Rosie did and, knowing it was an emergency, she must have called him. When Mark arrived, I was trying to make myself sick, but I was feeling dizzy and out of it. He lost it and began calling me a stupid bitch and shouting. The more he went on, the more I began to give up again. I started to shut down, to go to another place, just as I used to when Dad would have a go at me all those years ago. But now I had brandy and however many pills to help me on my way.

It's warm, I remember thinking. Nice and warm, and I don't fucking care any more. The warmth descended upon me in calming, heavy waves, and Mark's shouting began to seem a long way away. I'm letting go, I thought. At last my brain's shutting up. I don't have to think any longer...

I came round a little on the back seat of Rosie's car. 'She's still breathing,' I heard her say before I fell unconscious again.

I was in and out of consciousness. I remember sensing the bright lights of the A and E department, and I remember the feeling of being in a bed. I remember being in a wheelchair and entering another building. There was a person behind a desk, and then there was nothing.

I woke up in a bed in a sparsely furnished room. I was cold, and I didn't know what had happened. *Shit!* I thought. *I'm still here. I'm still thinking.* A nurse came into the room. 'You're not very well and you're in hospital,' she said gently. It sure didn't look like a normal hospital room. 'You're in Northside Clinic.'

I knew where it was and what it was. It was a private psychiatric hospital.

I was confused, angry, disappointed. I was scared, frightened, ashamed – not of what I'd done but of where I was. But most of all I was just so tired. I'd never been that tired in my life. It wasn't like being knackered and fancying a sleep; it was an overwhelming sense of heaviness, of exhaustion. I could hardly find the energy to lift myself up in the bed – it was as if gravity had just got stronger and was pulling not just my body, but my mind too. It's hard to describe, but I could barely cope with the stark reality of being conscious. Noises jarred me, the white of the walls made me wince, my senses were pricked but at the same time I was like lead.

But I couldn't let myself lie in bed. Sleeping during the day had always been something I regarded as grubby, so I moved to the edge of the bed and sat there, still as a statue. If I sit very, very still, I remember thinking, if I don't talk and don't move, then everyone will go away. All I wanted was to be left alone, and within my distorted logic I thought the world would go away if I acted as if I didn't exist. If I wasn't there, I reasoned, I couldn't be kicked around any more.

I would hardly even move my eyes. I thought that if I moved my eyes they'd work out I was still there. The nurse was right, I wasn't well. I needed help, whether I knew it or not.

I was beyond coherent thinking. I would have the beginnings of thoughts, but never see them through. After the events of the past few weeks – Madi's illness, Mark's infidelity, the rows, the sleepless nights, the crazy hours at work – my mind had finally said, 'Enough!' Once alone again I moved around the room, examining in a daze what little there was within it. There was a shower rail that was bendy to the touch. I realised that it was designed to stop people hanging themselves from it, and then I noticed that everything in the room was suicide-proof. I felt disgusting. *They think you're going to kill yourself*, I thought. Later I learned I was indeed on 'suicide watch'.

I had never taken the decision to say goodbye and kill myself. When I had taken those pills and drunk that brandy, it was not because I wanted to die. 'Suicidal' is a word that is often misused. I have never been suicidal. People think that doing what I did was a deliberate act designed to end it all, but that's where they get it wrong with me. I just couldn't take it any longer. I merely wanted to be able to sleep without a baby crying, some bitch on the phone telling me I was a shit wife or Mark's behaviour implying, 'You'd better sleep with me because if you don't want to fuck I can always go and sleep with Joanne.' I wanted everyone and everything to fuck off out of my head. I wanted peace, and in those desperate moments I had associated brandy and those pills with peace. I had wanted to get to the point where I could sleep for a long, long time with nobody bothering me.

Nowadays, when I talk with people with mental-health problems, be it on or off my show, I ask them if they are suicidal. If they say no, I'll ask them if they are at the point where they just want peace, and more often than not I receive a resounding yes in response. What I did was an example of how far some people are prepared to go to attain that peace.

When people 'attempt suicide' – for want of a better phrase – irrespective of whether they succeed or not, they often come under fire from others for being selfish. 'How could someone do such a thing, knowing the pain it would cause those left behind?' people say. In my case, I would have left behind two young daughters and my parents would have lost yet another child. If I had died the devastation would have been horrific, as it is for so many families who lose their loved ones in such a tragic way. But I was in a very dark place in my head. I would soon learn I was suffering from depression and, at the point where I did what I did, *I was past the point of thinking straight*. I wasn't thinking clearly enough to have selfish thoughts.

Trying to end your life may *appear* selfish, but the point is, when a person is in such a bad way emotionally, selfishness has nothing to do with their actions. Almost anyone who takes such drastic action is suffering from terrible clinical depression, and when you're depressed your thinking is far from rational. Everything seems utterly pointless, impossible, you feel like nothing will *ever* work out (in fact it's more than a feeling, it's a conviction), your self-esteem has disappeared and so too has your ability to feel for yourself and others. A depressed person is not thinking rationally – if they could think rationally, they wouldn't be depressed.

Suicide is a desperate measure. Rather than being selfish, it's a heartbreaking act of despair. When in the throes of depression, your mind is everywhere and nowhere – other people don't even enter your thoughts because your mind is shutting down. You're distanced from your real self too. If you can't think about yourself or others, you can't act selfishly. That word itself suggests an ability to think of your own interests – well, ask yourself this: does a person who tries to kill him- or herself really have their own interests at heart? Are they really being selfish, or just suffering in a way that is hard to imagine? Can getting rid of your 'self' really be 'selfish'?

I hardly said anything for a week. I had shut down. My head was foggy, and the tiredness never left me. Even looking out of the window became too much to bear. I'll never forget looking at a tree outside, and somehow just the movement of the branches, the fluttering of the leaves in the wind, caused me to panic. Suddenly something so commonplace, such a part of everyday 'reality', caused my chest to tighten, my breathing to quicken and my heart to race. In a matter of seconds, I could hardly breathe and I was shivering uncontrollably. I had to look away from the window and try to calm down.

But, whatever I did, I couldn't escape my own thoughts. And, as far as I was concerned, people could see my thoughts. It's hard to describe such skewed logic, but I was convinced people could know what I was thinking if they saw me. So because of this I spent a lot of time sitting still on the bed, pretending I wasn't there.

The people at my office were informed I was ill, but not given details. Mark knew what had happened, and he turned up regularly with Madi so that I could breastfeed her. I lived for those feeds, as in some small way they began to reconnect me with the world. The devastating thing was I had to breastfeed her with the door open because they were worried I might do something 'stupid' to my children. How wrong they were. It was my children who helped me more than anything else.

Only when Mark was around did I talk. I was trying to act sane. During the long hours of silence, I'd been doing a lot of rocking forwards and backwards, but when Mark was there I had to keep it under control. The effort was exhausting.

Soon, though, Mark's visits were discouraged. The counsellor Toby Green had come to see me a few times and realised Mark's presence was only causing me further distress. He had to wait outside while I fed Madi or he'd leave both girls with me for the afternoon. He threatened to take me to court to stop me harassing Joanne (now and again I had phoned her asking, 'Why? Why?'), and at the time I was so fucked up and felt so weak that I believed he might have a chance of taking my babies. It may sound surprising, but the person who supported me most during my anxieties about the kids was Mark's mum, Lenore. We spoke on the phone, and she sweetly vowed to support me in any way she could.

The days and weeks passed in a drawn-out blur. Then, one step at a time, things began to improve. My mind had disappeared, but after a while I could sense parts of it re-emerging from the black hole it had dropped into. One of the first indications that I was coming back was that I began writing again. I wrote out my thoughts. I wrote poems. I began to reconnect with myself.

I hadn't been eating and had lost a lot of weight very quickly, but gradually I began to eat small amounts again. I'll never forget, about two weeks into my stay, one of the nurses urging me to eat, especially because I was breastfeeding.

'No, I can't,' I said.

'OK,' she replied, 'you don't have to eat at the prescribed

mealtimes but we'll leave your tray in the kitchens for when you are hungry. You needn't worry that anyone else will eat it, because this floor is full of anorexics!'

The nurse's comment must have been one of the first things that made me smile. Every psych ward has its fair share of 'gallows humour' and there plenty of jokes about us 'depressives', and it was with humour that someone had made contact with me again. There was another nurse called Elaine who also managed to connect with me. She arranged for me to have a TV in my room and, although I couldn't concentrate for very long on whatever I was watching, it made me remember the world outside. There was a Billy Connolly show where he travelled through Scotland, and because of the holidays I'd spent there as a kid I got lost in that programme whenever it came on. It was an escape from my mind. Elaine would come in as I watched Billy and comment on what he was doing. I would never say anything in response. Then, cleverly, she started saying things like, 'Oh, Trisha, I've missed a bit. What happened?' and I would tell her. That was how she got me talking again. Elaine helped me so much while I was there.

Not that I sprang back into action. Far from it. I merely began to function again in small but significant ways. I was still very depressed and I just felt that I was nothing but shit. Nothing I'd achieved meant anything to me. As far as I was concerned, I was nothing more than a waste of space. I spent huge amounts of time just sitting still, filled with self-loathing. I didn't want to do anything or see anyone except my little girls.

One day a stunning vision of a man stuck his head

around the door. It was my friend B. B was a fantastic bloke, and we'd become very close over the years. He was always coming on to me jokingly, but I'd never succumbed to his advances, gorgeous though he was. He had too many problems of his own. Now he was looking at me on a psych ward and all I said to him was, 'Go away.'

'No!' he replied firmly. 'I'm not going anywhere.'

Part of me wondered if I was imagining him being there, so I asked him a pretty odd question – I asked him if he was really standing there! Once I'd established that he was, I told him to go away again.

'Why do you want me to go away?' he asked.

'Because I'm shit,' I said. 'I look like shit, I feel like shit, I *am* shit. You shouldn't be near me.' I didn't even want him to look at me.

But B knew what was going on. In the past, he'd been through some tough times himself. He'd been in this hospital before, but as a patient, not a visitor. B reminded me of that. 'You came to see me when I was a mess, remember?' he said. 'I too was shit once, and you sat with me. We didn't talk, we just sat. And now I'm gonna do the same for you. If you like, we won't talk, but I'm not going anywhere.'

So we sat there. We didn't speak but I didn't feel uncomfortable. After God knows how long, B broke the silence. 'You know something, Goddard,' he began, 'you are beautiful. You're a beautiful, beautiful person.'

'No I'm not,' I protested. 'I'm shit!'

'You might think you're shit in the place you're in right now, but you are beautiful and you'll think you're beautiful again.'

We carried on sitting there, and occasionally B talked.

He would reminisce about the past, about good times we'd had with friends. I would listen and the warmth of those memories brought some comfort. B was amazing. He didn't push me to respond to him. He didn't talk too much, and he didn't mention the problems that had brought me to the hospital. Because he'd been to some terrible places in his head, I think he instinctively knew how to bring me out of myself a little. He came in several times and showed me nothing but kindness and patience, which is more than I can say for some people.

Another welcome visitor was my dear friend Judy Hardy. She worked with me as the consultant of the mental health advisory group I chaired and she made it her duty to ensure that I was being treated well.

After four weeks in the hospital, I was still very shaky. *Live It Up* was finishing for the season and there was a wrap party, and I decided I had to go to it. Everyone at work had been told I was ill, but they didn't know the details. Determined to show my face at the party, I arranged to be smuggled out of the hospital for a few hours. I made myself look presentable and hired a taxi. I had to lie down in the cab because looking out of the window and seeing the world flying by just made me panic.

The party was at a Balmoral Beach restaurant. Mark was gobsmacked when he saw me, and, although I was bloody fragile, I managed to hold it together. I didn't eat or drink much, but stayed long enough for the speeches to come around. Mark got up and told everyone how great they were, and what a great season it had been. And then it was my turn.

'Hello, everyone,' I began. 'You've all been brilliant, as

always. In fact, you're the best staff anyone could hope for, which makes my next announcement really sad. I'm afraid I've decided to shut down *Live It Up*. From now on I will no longer be doing it.'

Everyone was stunned, speechless.

'Please don't worry,' I continued. 'You're all great and I'll do all I can to get you jobs in the industry.'

'But *why*?' people began to ask, clearly shocked and upset.

'Well,' I told them, 'Mark's been having an affair with Joanne for some time. This is why Joanne left the company. I haven't just been ill, I've had a breakdown and as I speak I'm in the psych hospital.'

Mark was utterly shocked and embarrassed, and fled outside, where I'm told he remained for a while on his mobile calling Joanne to let her know their secret was out. (Apparently, when he came back in, some of the guys had a right go at him.) Some of the girls began to cry. I explained that I was only able to be out of the hospital for two hours and that I had to leave. I apologised again to everyone and left.

Back in the cab, I felt that a weight had been lifted from my shoulders. I had realised that life just couldn't go on in the same way, and I had decided to shut down *Live It Up* as well as the production company. As we sped back to the hospital, I felt vindicated for having been absent from work, and it felt like I had some of the power back. I was taking control again. I'd shocked Mark with my strength, and there was no way I would let him carry on kicking me while I was down. I got back to the ward exhausted, but knew I had done the right thing.

During my spell in hospital, I hadn't even thought about

the press. I'd forgotten my life outside. Then one day I was catapulted back into the media. A nurse told me there was someone on the phone for me. I assumed it would be Mark and I braced myself for yet another shitty conversation. But it wasn't Mark's voice that greeted me.

'Hi,' said a man whose voice I didn't recognise. 'You don't know me but I'm a journalist. I hear you're on the psych ward there, aren't you?'

Oh shit, I thought, here we go. 'Who the fuck told you that and how did you get hold of me?' I shouted.

It turned out that one of Mark's mates had told the journalist where I was. 'You can talk to me,' said the journalist. 'Tell me what's going on.'

I told him to fuck off and slammed the phone down. Suddenly, I got really scared. The idea of publicity hadn't even crossed my mind. They're going to say I'm mad, I thought. They're going to make up all sorts of shit and I'm going to lose my kids. I had no choice but to try to kill the story, and the only way to do it was to do the story myself. I called the head of publicity at Channel Ten, a fantastic Brit called Cathy, and she organised for a journalist called Leigh Reinhold to do the story with me. The result was a balanced article that said I'd had a breakdown, and that I was very scared but recovering. Mark's affair was mentioned, but I didn't slag him off.

If it wasn't for that journo ringing me up, I would never have 'come out' about my problems. People often remark on how open I am about my breakdown and depression, but if I'd had my way nobody would know about any of it. I went public about my problems for very specific reasons. I simply didn't want my story to have a price on it, or for the press to get it wrong and call me a loony. Rightly or wrongly, I was ashamed about what was happening to me. I didn't want any pity. The piece would come out soon after I left the hospital.

The day I was discharged I went to an awards ceremony I'd been invited to ages before. I needed to prove to myself I could function. A dress had been made up by my dressmaker, who knew I'd been ill. I'd lost loads of weight, and while she was measuring me up she said, 'I'm going to make you look fabulous. Fuck 'em all, darling, fuck 'em all!' I couldn't help but smile at that.

I went home to change into my dress and have my hair and make-up done, and though I say it myself I reckon I looked pretty fabulous considering what I'd just been through. I didn't feel on top of the world, but something about being dressed up and dignified again brought some warmth back into my heart. I was ready to leave the house with just a hint of a spring in my step. As Mark watched me leave, he burst into tears. Whether they were tears of guilt, remorse or just plain unhappiness, I will never know, but it shocked me to the core.

A limo awaited me. The driver, George, graciously opened the door for me. 'Would you like some champagne, Miss?' he asked.

It was so nice to be talked to normally again by someone who had nothing to do with psychiatric units. Why not have a little champagne? I thought. 'Yes please,' I said, and George poured it out before we set off.

The limo stopped outside a block of flats. My friend B had arranged for one of his friends to accompany me to the party. I'll call this guy James. A minute later I was clinking glasses with a gorgeous, sandy-blond-haired man. It was all a bit surreal. I was being treated like a lady again, and I laughed when James said, 'By the way, B told me that, if I fuck with you, I'm dead. I'm just gonna be here for you tonight.'

And what a gentleman James was. B had told him my situation and James completely understood. We got to the awards and he didn't leave my side for a second. Even though I was still feeling pretty brittle, I had a great time. I didn't drink much, and as James and I walked around the room I began to remember what it was like to be me. Sounds a bit corny, but it's true!

Afterwards, we ended up in a nightclub called Sugar Reef on Bayswater Road. My beautiful gown was a touch out of place amid a crowd in their clubbing gear, but I didn't give a shit – all I wanted to do was dance. I so love dancing! As I moved around that dance floor, I felt the misery of the past few months start to drain away from me. I felt good for the first time in ages, and I didn't want that feeling to go away, which is probably why I danced all night, sometimes on my own, sometimes with James.

Before I knew it, it was six in the morning. It was daylight, and it was Sunday. At first I felt a little guilty about having stayed out all night, but that feeling soon faded and was replaced by something much more positive.

There was no traffic. With my shoes in one hand, and the hem of my dress in the other, I walked along the middle of Bayswater Road. All I could hear was early-morning birdsong. The sun was rising, and the air smelled clean and fresh. I threw my head back and drank up the atmosphere, and a wave of happiness and relief washed over me.

This life ain't so bad, I thought, swinging my shoes by my side as I walked. I might be able to make it after all.

20

The Ascent of Man

Sometimes it's hard looking back at who I was. It seems incredible to me now that I ended up in such bad relationships. After all, some of the things I put up with were pretty shit. When I talk about it, I feel like I'm talking about another person. Don't get me wrong, though. I don't sit around thinking, Poor little me who suffered at the hands of all those bastard men! Rather I think I got the relationships I deserved at the time. I might not have beaten anyone, I might not have tried to change and control others and I was always faithful, but I *was* damaged goods, and people who are damaged goods tend to attract partners who are also damaged.

During all the years I've written about, I was often an emotionally shut-down unit. Sure, I had a great career and was highly successful, but at the same time my ambition and drive meant I didn't have to focus much on my feelings. I was always too wrapped up in my career to be in love. In fact, I'd go further than that. Until Billie came along, I don't think I really knew how to love. From a young age, I'd learned how to shut myself off from people. I didn't want to let anyone in – if they couldn't get to me, then I couldn't get hurt. Also, I learned to be fiercely self-dependent. I never leaned on anyone financially or emotionally, and didn't expect the men in my life to lean on me.

I know now that all of those ultimately disastrous relationships happened for a reason, and I think the men were attracted to me for my distance and aloofness. The trouble was that the distance and aloofness didn't go away as each relationship progressed. I was a thoroughly defensive person. I didn't mean to 'treat 'em mean, keep 'em keen', but that's what I was doing without realising it. It was always work that came first, and blokes used to feel that I didn't need them. And, within the system I ran my life by, I suppose I didn't need them. This was another problem, because most of the men I was with were pretty needy. It wasn't that I didn't have needs, it's just that I wasn't in touch with myself enough to even know they were there. My emotional needs were buried. After all, everyone has a need for closeness, intimacy and love, but from an early age my take on love had been messed up, so as an adult I got a lot of things wrong. The fact that all was not well deep down in me eventually came out when I had a breakdown.

I wouldn't have realised any of this if it hadn't been for one thing. Therapy. A condition of being released from the hospital was that I attend therapy, and from then on I went up to three times every week. I was very reluctant at first – it was the first time I'd ever really had to take a good look at myself, and it was tough – but, at the end of the six months for which I had to attend therapy, I carried on anyway. I had to examine my own behaviour, talk about my childhood. Through therapy, I made the connection between childhood and adulthood for the first time. I didn't end up blaming my childhood for everything that was wrong with me, but I realised that my father's apparent disapproval and his constant criticism and smacking, which alternated with bursts of humour, sent me very mixed messages about love. Add to that my mother's effusive pride about what I did rather than who I was and my focus became to 'achieve' at all costs. I also realised that I had perfected the art of dissociation – I had learned to deal with conflict by just going somewhere else in my head, and as an adult I had continued to 'opt out' of situations in a similar manner.

When conflict arose, or when there were problems in relationships, I pretended they didn't exist, or went to work in order to distract myself from them. In other words, I carried on our family tradition of secrets and lies. This meant I wasn't the easiest person to communicate with, and I probably didn't have much time for the neediness of my men.

I had three types of therapy – psychotherapy dealt with my past, Cognitive Behavioural Therapy helped me deal with day-to-day problems in a practical way and relaxation therapy (which at first I thought would be a load of wank) helped me, well, *relax*! All three proved invaluable, and made me realise I had to change if I ever wanted to be happy with myself and my relationships. As far as men were concerned, I thought, Trisha, my girl, if you can't change the fish you're catching, you'd better change the bait.

And, lo and behold, as I began to change the bait, I started to catch much better fish!

Immediately I left the hospital, my life changed almost overnight. *Live It Up*, and the generous salary that came with it, was history, as was Mark, and I was back at home with the pressures of work greatly reduced. I was still involved in my mental-health work, but for now I had said goodbye to the world of TV and its people. For the first time in my life, I had time to take stock of things and focus on myself and it was scary!

Life was pretty weird during my days of single-motherhood. I'd often fall apart and friends would sweetly drop by to see if I was OK and either help with the girls or just sit and listen. My obsessive nature also came back with a vengeance. Before we had split up, when Mark and I had been at loggerheads, I'd go out clothes shopping, see an outfit in a shop window and go in to buy it without even trying it on. Half the time, I didn't even unpack the bags or take the labels off the clothes and, when I later found them stuffed in my wardrobe, I'd only vaguely recall buying them. It was retail therapy taken to the extreme! Now, though, I didn't have the money to do that.

When I went power-walking, I'd tell myself I had to get to the next lamppost before a car passed me or else someone I loved would die. I'd almost be in tears as I raced to beat the car as if my life depended on it – because, as far as I was concerned, my life *did* depend on it. And I truly believed something even worse would happen if I trod on the cracks in the pavement, so I had to dodge them too. Thus, the runs I did on my own often left me mentally drained and feeling almost traumatised.

Money was a real worry. I'd forever be promising someone I'd pay them later. I had to pay for Billie's school, doctors and my brilliant solicitor Barbara. I was about to go under when my bank acquired a new female manager with a heart of gold – she was a genius at refiguring and rearranging loans.

Our nanny stayed with me long after I could afford to pay her and would make meals for me, cover them with cling film and leave them in the fridge with a note about how long to reheat them in the microwave.

Going out and about with the girls saved me. I'd put Madi in a baby back-pack and Billie in my giant running stroller and power-walk all over my neighbourhood come rain or shine. We'd either sing 'We are the Goddard Girls' or *Play School* songs at the tops of our voices and I wouldn't give a stuff about the cracks in the pavement or racing passing cars. Gradually, I met all the people I never knew existed in all the houses I'd never bothered to notice: I got to know my community and started to feel less isolated. The walking also lifted my mood in a way that no medication ever could.

I'd always made time for my kids, but now I was with them almost 24/7. It was a beautiful bonding period. We would shop in Sydney's open-air food markets together, go to the park and do everything on the cheap. I gradually sold all of those designer clothes to help finances, and sometimes got some pretty confused looks when people recognised me in discount shops. It was embarrassing. But it didn't matter – I was slowly on the mend from a lot of pain, and being with my kids was all that mattered.

But I had a social life too. My darling best friend Claire and I became even closer. She confessed to me how glad she was that I'd finally got rid of Mark, and even told me that, from the moment she met him, she couldn't stand him. I remember asking her why she hadn't told me before, and she just looked at me and said, 'Yeah, like you would have listened!' She was right, of course.

Mark would take Billie and Madi every other weekend, and that time gave me a chance to do what a lot of people do in their late teens and early twenties – a time in my life when I was already a workaholic. In my late thirties, I went out and partied!

I wasn't hanging around with the media crowd as much now. Instead, I was introduced to a whole new segment of society. Since the awards night when I went clubbing till dawn, B's friend, James, had stayed in touch and began taking me out. And, when James went out, it was no-holds-barred clubbing.

James and his pals were wealthy bad boys who loved a good time. They were heavily into ecstasy – 'eccies', they called it – and eventually I decided to try some. James hadn't put any pressure on me to do it, I just wanted to see what all the fuss was about. James was great, and talked me through exactly what to expect when I 'came up'. I remember taking a pill and waiting for a while. For some time, I felt nothing, and then suddenly I was 'loved up' in a way I'd never been – I was off my face on E and it felt great.

James was a gorgeous, kind but messed-up man, and we

ended up having a bit of a thing. We were in love in the way that great friends can be in love. He never made me feel that I'd fallen from grace on TV, he never judged me for having been in hospital. Once, we were standing on a balcony and James said, 'I've never loved anyone but I love you.'

I was having a great time with him, but his comment frightened the shit out of me! 'What do you mean?' I asked, worried he was going to get all heavy.

'I mean you never demand anything of me, you don't nag, you're never in my face and you just let me be. You're the only person I've met who just allows me to be me.'

I realised he meant it, and I realised I felt the same way. James didn't want to change me, and he wasn't a pain in the arse. Both of us knew we weren't going to last for ever – we just appreciated that we loved each other as great friends, and that's what made things work.

During this period with James, I went back to the UK at Christmas to see Mum and Dad. I was pretty much out of work, and used my time there to take some video tapes of me in *Live It Up* to a few TV stations in the hope it might lead to something. I'll never forget being at the Living Channel offices. I persuaded some people there to watch the tape and, once they'd had a look, one of them said to me somewhat sarcastically, 'And what makes you think you can make it on British TV, huh?'

I made my excuses and left. It was so dispiriting. At Meridian TV (which incidentally was later swallowed up by Anglia TV who made the first *Trisha* show), a fab guy there made encouraging noises but couldn't promise anything. After that, I cancelled all the other interviews, thinking I didn't have a hope of breaking into British TV. Little did I know...

Talking of British TV, it was odd when I was watching *The Tube* on Channel Four that Christmas and I heard a reference to myself – from Russell Crowe! Russell was being interviewed and had just been asked if he'd ever sworn on TV. He said that he'd once said 'fuck' when he was being interviewed by 'this bird' (me) while promoting *Romper Stomper* in Australia many years ago. It was true that I'd interviewed him when I was standing in on Channel 7's *Tonight Live* show, but my recollection was not that he said the 'F' word. 'Shit' is what I thought he'd said.

After the show, I had invited Russell, his parents and my other guests to the Green Room for a drink and we'd all got pretty merry. He changed from his 'moody' actor persona and we had a laugh and a bit of a flirt. The trouble was, Russell obviously hadn't wanted the partying to stop. As I had a horrendously early flight back to Sydney the next morning, all I'd wanted to do was sleep. Flattered as I was by Russell's attention, I had been firm but polite – no more partying for me! The flirting was definitely not going to lead anywhere.

But now, all these years later, here was the interviewer asking Russell how I had reacted when he came out with the 'F' word. He said something along the lines of, 'Dunno, mate. But it didn't do any harm. She obviously fancied me!'

There I was at Mum and Dad's, squealing like a teenager. Yes, I'd almost had my moment of fame with Russell, except that he didn't seem to remember my bloody name! Thinking I had fancied him when, to me, it had seemed the other way around. Giggling, I tried to ring Channel Four to leave a message for Russell, to tell him that 'the bird' was watching. I don't hold it against him and, years later, he married the gorgeous Danielle Spencer, the daughter of my dear *Play School* colleague, Don.

Christmas came and went and I went back to my crazy new life in Sydney. Clubbing around Kings Cross was great, and I got pretty keen on ecstasy. Then one night I freaked out on it. I became all shaky and edgy and just didn't feel right. I knew I shouldn't have taken it that night because I'd been feeling quite fragile and vulnerable, but once it was in my system there was nothing I could do. I didn't want to make a fuss, though, and tried to blend in with the crowd. But I can't have being making a very good job of it, because as I stood there, rooted to the spot, someone soon approached me and said, 'You're not safe, are you?'

He was a gorgeous, dark-haired guy with piercing blue eyes.

'What?' I said, slightly taken aback.

His name was Andrew and what he said was amazingly perceptive. He told me that he knew another ill person when he saw one, and that I was a 'silly girl' for having taken the pill. It turned out that Andrew had been through very similar mental-health experiences to me, so I guess it was a case of 'it takes one to know one'.

We became great friends. Andrew was a bit of a posh boy, and confused about his sexuality. He was gay but not entirely comfortable with it. He'd had a tough past and was a damaged person. But that damage had turned him into someone filled with empathy and insight. He started hanging out with James and I, but soon I was going to gay clubs in Oxford Street with just Andrew. Through him, I got to know an entirely new side of Sydney, as we went to some clubs that were just worlds apart from anything I was familiar with.

There I ended up hanging around with a crowd of 'non-specific-gender' clubbers, strange-looking people with no hair, no eyebrows, dressed in gothic rags and big clumpy shoes. I couldn't tell the girls from the boys – fascinatingly, most of them had been abused as kids and didn't want to identify with either men or women. Sex-wise, they weren't gay or straight, they were just into bodies. I got to know about 15 of them. It was strange. I was oddly drawn to people that society considered freaks – perhaps because I felt a bit of a freak myself – and on many occasions ended up sitting cross-legged on the floor talking to a whole group of them about their lives.

They all had problems, and it turned out that many of the men were rent boys. We would talk about all sorts of issues, including male rape and the possibility that some of them had become gay as a result of gay rape when they were young. I got to know a lot of drag queens too, and all of these people were the most fascinating, decent people who had adopted a certain way of life in order to survive. What's funny is, it got to the point where I would turn up and they would all say, 'Oh, it's Trisha, I wonder what we'll all end up debating tonight.' Little did I know that by leading such groups I was in some way preparing myself for the *Trisha* show!

I loved those guys, and they showed me a lot of love too. James didn't really get the gay scene, and Andrew didn't get James's scene, but I kept on jumping between two worlds. I was embracing my newfound freedom and having a ball. I kept on taking ecstasy until I eventually realised that the low that inevitably followed a night out on pills just wasn't doing me any good. As for dope, that was history. I associated it with Mark and with my breakdown, and never touched it again.

I don't see the point in denying my experiences on drugs. I know some people hide their pasts from their kids and tell them to just say no. But I don't think that really works – you can't get round the fact that your children will be offered drugs at some point, so I've told my kids that if they want to smoke dope it's up to them, but I remind them that we have a family predisposition to depression and that drugs often play a big part in bringing mental-health issues out in people. But I get the feeling that they're not too interested – when you can remember how stoned and boring your father was all the time, it doesn't really make dope that tempting.

It's good to talk to your kids about drugs, and I'm glad I had the experiences I did, otherwise I'd be like a priest talking about sex. I hate it when politicians get slated for having smoked dope, and personally I don't want to vote for one who hasn't. I want a politician who has shagged, smoked, got pissed and fallen down. Then, at least, when they come at us with policies about such matters, they know what they're bloody well talking about!

I loved that period of clubbing. In those clubs, whether I was on ecstasy or not, I felt liberated. I wasn't 'her off the telly', I wasn't 'black', I wasn't a 'single mum', I wasn't a 'nutter' who'd had a breakdown. For the first time I was just me, and it felt wonderful. I was saved by the people and the music of Sydney's gay and alternative scene.

In between looking after the kids, I was still involved in mental-health work. In 1995, I was asked to chair Australia's Community Awareness Project, a board intended to deal with national community attitudes to mental health. The idea was to try to get rid of the stigma surrounding it, and we had been allocated $8 million for a massive ad campaign.

Through my dealings with the advertising agency handling the project, I ended up agreeing to meet up with a very posh British guy called Steve. He'd kept trying to get me to go for a drink with him, and eventually I agreed. He was a real pretty boy with a cut-glass accent. I fancied him, and we had a fling. What was great about Steve was that he was going through a divorce too – his wife had been shagging his best mate – and we had a fine old time bitching about our exes.

Steve was great for me. His little boy met the girls, but, as far as they were concerned, we were all just friends. We became more than that, though. Steve was a pretty gentleman, and emotionally we just clicked. The thing is, I wasn't ready to commit to anyone at that stage. I was enjoying myself, which is why I was able to see Steve at the same time as seeing James and going clubbing with gay Andrew. There were no secrets, and the great thing about those guys was that none of them wanted anything from me and they weren't needy or possessive, but they could communicate and enjoy themselves.

And then I met someone else!

It was Billie who set me up with him. I'd taken the girls

skiing in New Zealand (thank God for the frequent flyer points I'd gathered over the years!), and Billie introduced me to some little friends she'd made in ski school. John was their father, and Billie and her friends decided to suggest that we go out on a date together. Billie had said she didn't have a daddy and Alice had said she didn't have a mummy, so they thought it was the perfect solution. A senior Qantas captain, John had been through a nasty divorce. He was a little overweight, but a really attractive, kind and charismatic guy. And, what's more, like Steve, he had a brain. He was a great dad, and we ended up pretty serious about each other. John took me to wonderful restaurants and we had fascinating conversations. He was interesting, passionate and sensitive, and I learned a lot from him. He was a proper grown-up, a real man, and a complete contrast to the men I'd spent most of my life with. The great thing about seeing John was that it often revolved around the kids – and he was happy about it!

I'd been seeing James, Steve, another guy called Chris (who was really just a bit of a handbag) and John all at the same time. They all knew about each other, and all of them opened my eyes to the fact that there are men in the world who actually give a shit about whether a woman enjoys herself or not. Each one of them was passionate about life in his own way, and each one I met was more inspiring and affectionate than the last, which is why I jokingly refer to that period as 'The Ascent of Man'. During that time, I also met two men who are still incredibly central in my life – Kevin and Madison. Both became such amazing friends.

John ended up taking priority. I couldn't get enough of the guy, but eventually it went wrong. We'd been seeing each other for about a year and, though things were wonderful, he seemed to want more commitment than I could give. I loved the way we had quite separate lives and saw each other when he was over from New Zealand or when I flew to see him, but he wanted more. Basically, I got dumped. It wasn't bitter, though, and John was a gentleman about all of it. We wanted different things and in June 1996 it was all over.

I was a bit hurt over John. Certainly I loved him, but I wasn't in love enough to commit to him. After it finished I realised just what a positive period I'd had with all those guys.

I'd done what I should have done in my teens. I'd learned a ton of things about men, and discovered they could be pretty wonderful creatures.

I'd been off work for a while, and began to think it might be time to go back. But when I received an offer from good old SBS, the channel I'd started with all those years earlier, I was apprehensive about accepting. I was still in therapy and learning to deal with my panic attacks.

The offer was for part-time work presenting the medical section of a show called *Second Opinion*, and Dr Lena Saffra, the woman who'd made me the offer, was very understanding about my anxiety over returning to work. She gave me a desk in the office where I could see everybody and everything, and I was always given the same camera crew. She also let me work a lot from home. All of this made me feel secure, and once I got started I relished being back in the saddle. The difference was, the balance between work and life was better now. I worked hard, as always, but knew where to draw the line, and I didn't burn myself out.

The Ascent of Man

During this time, I was also asked to join the Geneva-based World Psychiatric Association and, as a result, ended up taking Billie and Madi along with me when I was asked to be part of a select working group, meeting in Boulder, Colorado. I was there to represent the views of those with mental illness and their carers and was the only woman on the entire committee, which included experts from all over the world, such as the late Dr Anthony Clare. I worried that I might be out of my depth, but I spoke passionately and confidently and everyone seemed to take on board what I said. I felt strong and assertive again. I was contributing to international mental-health policy and I had some credibility.

Once the conference was over, I took the girls for a little skiing holiday in nearby Winter Park. We hired a log cabin and set ourselves up with a six-inch plastic Christmas tree. The girls took the double bed and I had a sleeping bag in front of the log fire.

One night, as the girls slept in the next room with the door open, I was lying there staring into the fire. It was Christmas. All was quiet. Snow fell gently outside, softly adding to two feet of drift.

I remember thinking that I didn't care if I never had another relationship. By then I'd been single and without sex for six months. I didn't care because I was at peace just as I was. I was utterly content.

It was normally when I was relaxed that all the usual angst would creep into my mind and make me think I was shit, I was a single mother, I'd never make it, I would go bankrupt, I was a bad person.

But the angst wasn't there to disturb my peace. All I

could think was, I've got my girls, I've got my health (just about!), and that's all that matters. If I lose my job or my house, I will start again.

It was at that moment that I knew I was no longer scared.

I didn't need a relationship other than with myself and my girls to feel whole. A couple of months later, I was dating the man who would become the love of my life.

21

My Prince Charming

I think Peter and I were meant to find each other. It was as if our coming together was part of the grand plan.

The first time I met him was in 1996, quite a bit before my trip to Colorado. He was going for a senior government job in mental health and I was on the board that was interviewing him. I already knew about him because I had read all of his papers on the subject and been impressed by how innovative and challenging they were. He wrote quite radical pieces suggesting that sufferers of mental illness should be shaping the services available to them, rather than the professionals and psychiatrists and, back then, his work certainly rattled a lot of cages in the mental-health world. His honesty and openness in the interview impressed all of us. When the board asked me what I thought of him as a candidate, I replied that I wouldn't kick him out of bed for eating biscuits! It got a laugh, and I meant it too.

But, even though I'd thought he was dark, brooding *and* intelligent, I didn't see Peter again for quite a while.

After I got back from Colorado, I was involved in a focus group to promote mental-health issues in the media. We were a bunch of well-known media names, and most people were bringing along someone from the mental-health field who would support their ideas. I was particularly interested in mental-health users' rights and was racking my brain as to who I could get to accompany me. Then it hit me – Peter Gianfrancesco!

By then, I knew he ran Ryde Mental Health Service in North Sydney, so it wouldn't be a problem tracking him down to ask him along. The problem was, I was inviting him to a dinner – it felt a bit like a date in a way – and I'd never asked a guy out on a date in my life. I asked six mates if I should ask Peter. Three said yes, three said no, so eventually I just went for it.

The dinner went amazingly. Peter was incredible with everyone – a range of Aussie actors and celebs – and afterwards he drove me in his banger of a car to Neutral Bay, where we drank all night. His was a coffee or two and my tipple was peppermint tea. We talked and talked about anything and everything until it got light. Then he drove me home.

The girls were staying away with Mark, so I asked Peter in. He was nervous, sweet and natural and I adored him from the word go. I was comfortable with him right away, impressed by his passion about mental health, and blown away by his intelligence. He hadn't had an easy life. By the age of 13, he was living semi-independently in a caravan in his older sister's back garden, and yet by the age of 19 he had finished his first degree. He was well travelled and fascinated by the world. He was very moral, very male, but not frightened of his feminine side. And I realised all this on the first night!

Needless to say, I wanted to see more of this man.

About six weeks later, he came to the beach with Madi, Billie and me. Apart from John, I'd kept my boyfriends away from the girls up until now. I watched Peter like a hawk – if anyone was going to come into my life, it was paramount that they got on with my girls. He did more than get on with them. He was amazing with them. He asked them tons of questions, and I could tell he actually wanted to know their opinions on things. He talked to them on their level – he didn't talk down to them or put them down, but treated them as equals. As the relationship progressed, he soon became all the things I could wish a man to be for the girls. He'd get up in the night for them, he'd deal with the dirty nappies and the tummy aches. He was tender with them, and just so solid. We'd go on camping trips – the kind of camping trips I'd dreamed of going on when I was alone in England the Christmas Mark had begun his affair with Joanne. Later Peter would say that one of the things he fell in love with me for was the way I was as a mother. Well, one of the things I fell in love with him for was the way he was such a brilliant father-figure for my children.

In those early days with Peter, I was living for the moment. I wasn't thinking, This is the man I'm going to be with. I was just thinking, *Wow, this is too good to be true!*

Looking back, what really made me realise that this man was doing a Heineken number on me – reaching the parts of me that no other man could reach! – was when I

was learning to rollerblade. I'd always fancied rollerblading and, thinking it would help get me out and about,
I bought a pair. Every Tuesday evening I went to free
classes at Centennial Park's floodlit tennis courts and,
along with teenagers, a granny and a couple of cops, I had
enormous fun learning to skate.

We were told to practise between lessons, and that's
where Peter came in. With me gripping on to him for dear
life, first he walked up and down my driveway with me
clunking along beside him. Then he encouraged me to go
around the block, again helping me stay upright.
Gradually we went further and further with him praising
me, telling me not to give up when I fell arse over tit,
laughing and getting excited when I finally managed to do
it on my own. He stuck by me day in and day out until I
was confident enough to go rollerblading around
Centennial Park on my own while he cycled, cheering me
on. I'd never had that level of intimate, practical devotion
from a man before. Peter would later write in a card, 'May
you rollerblade happily through life without the threat of
twigs to trip you.' So sweet!

Rollerblading in the park with a crash-helmeted Madi in
a special huge running stroller was how I met and became
best buddies with Australian-based American singer
Marcia Hines. She's a huge star down under, but to me she
was just a fun, laugh-a-minute, 'you go girl' kind of mate.

The night Peter told me he loved me was the most
romantic moment of my life. The girls were with Mark,
and Peter had invited me over to dinner. I arrived at the
house and the front door was slightly open. Inside it was
dark, but on the floor there was a candle burning with a

red rose and a piece of parchment which had been charred around the edges. On it, in beautiful calligraphy, were written the words 'When I look at you...'

I walked along the corridor. Sure enough, another candle, another red rose, another piece of parchment.

'...My heart stops...'

There was no sign of Peter. I moved down the corridor to the next candle.

'In your eyes I can see the future...'

Eventually I arrived at the last candle. It was on top of a place setting on a table set for two. I sat down and read the last one.

'I love you.'

Peter stepped out from the darkness. I was completely overwhelmed. Nobody had ever done anything like that for me in my 39 years on this planet! I was gobsmacked. I didn't tell him I loved him because the old impetuous Trisha was gone. This was serious. I needed time to *think*!

Peter cooked an incredible Italian meal and we drank gorgeous wine. What a sweet, sweet man, I remember thinking.

Within six months of dating Peter, I was in love. It was a love that grew over time, and because of all the shit I'd been through with men it took me a long time to throw my caution aside and truly accept how much I felt for him. But eventually I realised that I'd kissed a lot of toads and had finally got to the prince!

Soon afterwards, things began to happen quite quickly. I was having to ask Mark for money towards the children, school and medical bills, but it wasn't always easy to get him to cooperate, which was pretty stressful. One day the phone rang and Peter answered it. Mark was on the end of the line. I'll never forget Peter telling Mark not to worry about any of it any more. He was going to cover it all. Mark was delighted about the money bit but assumed Peter was trying to stop him having contact with the girls. 'I wouldn't dream of it,' said Peter calmly. Since then Peter has always worked hard to ensured the girls see Mark. Peter grew up with an absent father and would never want the same for Billie and Madi.

Nowadays, the girls have their own (differing) relationships with Mark, and he and I operate on a level of civility. Things have improved since he got together with a fantastic girl a few years ago. As a result of my being in the public eye, Mark is forever being confronted with the misdemeanours of his past, the poor sod! But, for the record, I don't hate him. We didn't fulfil each other's needs emotionally or otherwise, and that's that. I'm glad he's found happiness.

Having not really worked for two years, I was in pretty deep financial trouble. Peter must have recognised this. He sold his share of a house he owned and helped to bail me out of my most pressing financial problems. He kept the wolves from my door. I couldn't believe it. Peter's argument was simple. 'I love you and I love this family,' he said. 'If it works between us it works, and if it doesn't we'll deal with it. You're an amazing mum and you don't deserve to struggle.' He said I didn't owe him anything.

Then one day Peter's behaviour made me think it was all about to go wrong.

22

The Happiest Day
of My Life

Peter turned up at my house one afternoon, and he looked nervous. Very nervous. 'Can you come outside for a minute?' he said. 'I've got something to tell you.' We walked outside, out of earshot of the girls.

Oh, God, what's going on here? I thought. I braced myself for whatever the bad news was.

'I just wanted to ask you,' he began.

Here we go, I thought.

'I, um, wanted to know...' he continued.

Spit it out, I thought! And then he did.

'I want to know if you'll marry me!' he said.

'Oh my God, Peter, I thought you were going to dump me!'

I thought about what he'd said and became teary. I'd been married twice before, remember, and more to the point, I wasn't going to marry anyone again without consulting the girls first. My reply was probably not what he wanted to hear. 'I'll have to give it a rain check,' I said. 'I have to ask the girls. This isn't just about me, and I don't want to sound silly, but I need to talk to Billie and Madi first. It's not a no, I'm just not quite ready for it yet.'

'Oh,' said Peter. I could tell he was a little disappointed, but he seemed to understand.

Once Peter had left that evening, I spoke to Billie. 'What would you think if Mama told you she was going to marry Peter?' I asked her.

Billie wasn't keen. She liked Peter but wanted it to be just us. I told her how much I loved Peter and how nice he was, but Billie was very wary. 'You will always come first, so we'll wait and see how you feel about him,' I reassured her.

For the time being I waited.

A few months later, Peter called me to tell me we were booked into the Intercontinental Hotel in Sydney. It was another one of his gorgeous, romantic surprises (of which there have been too many to mention in one book!)

'I'll check us in and I'll meet you in the bar between 7.30 and 8pm,' he said. 'We'll pretend we don't know each other, I'll chat you up and we'll have a romantic weekend. You can dress up if you want.'

I certainly did dress up. I did as I was told and arrived at the bar on time. 'Can I buy you a drink?' said Peter as he came over.

'You may,' I giggled, and we 'got to know each other' as if we were strangers. It was hugely romantic and we had a wonderful night.

The following evening, Peter suggested going for a run.

The Happiest Day of My Life

We ran around part of Sydney Harbour and then into the botanical gardens. It was twilight and the sky was a beautiful lavender colour. Peter stopped for a moment to tie his shoelace. Or at least I thought that's why he'd stopped. But when I looked at him I realised he was down on one knee! 'Right,' he panted, slightly out of breath, 'the first time you said no, and now I'm asking you for a second time. Will you marry me?'

My eyes welled up with tears. 'Yes, I will, I will. Of course I will,' I said elatedly. 'Now get up, for God's sake!'

I knew Peter was right for me. In the months since he had first asked me to marry him, Billie had become even easier with Peter being around – he loved watching *The Simpsons* for a start! I knew it would all be OK.

This time, I was going to do it my way. The wedding would be all about Peter and I celebrating our love, and nothing else. I didn't want my family there – the memory of Mum saying, 'Make this one work' when I'd married Mark was bad enough, but in addition to that I couldn't face the hassle of family politics – all the 'must invite so and so' bollocks that can come with weddings. Also, I didn't have enough money even to walk down the road and get married. Peter would be paying for everything and there was no way I was going to burden him with flying my family around the world. I didn't care what Mum and Dad would think.

Two years previously, my parents had flown out to spend Christmas in Sydney with me and the girls. I'd interrupted a petty outburst from my father by saying, 'The shit stops here, Dad.' With the help of therapy, I'd finally decided to break away from being the obedient, compliant daughter.

I'd managed to stop berating myself so much whenever I didn't do what Mum and Dad wanted.

We decided to get married in Italy – with Peter being an Australian-Italian, it made sense, and, besides, we wanted to avoid the media. On the way there we spent Christmas with Mum and Dad in the UK, but we didn't tell them what we were up to next. We just said we were going skiing in Italy and kept sneaking out to have my wedding dress made. The girls knew we were engaged but even they didn't know that our wedding was just around the corner.

I think Mum and Dad liked Peter. More to the point, they respected him. Whether he realises it or not, Peter is the only man I've ever been with that my father hasn't referred to as a boy. Mark had been a 'nice boy', but Peter seems to be a 'man' in my dad's eyes. Peter witnessed the Goddard family in full swing that Christmas – there was a spectacular screaming match with a touch of chair wielding between Mum, Dad and one of my sisters, and both Peter and I were annoyed that the girls were around to witness it. The amazing thing was that Peter stood up and did something about it. He took Mum aside and told her that he didn't want to be around arguments and he didn't want Billie and Madi to be subjected to them either. He wasn't nasty about it. He was firm and polite. I'd never heard her apologise to me in my life, but Mum actually apologised to Peter. It was truly incredible the way he dealt with things that Christmas. 'To be honest,' he told me later on, 'I thought you might have been exaggerating about what your family's like. You weren't. From what I've seen you were playing things down!'

The Happiest Day of My Life

Arguments aside, though, we had a 'skiing holiday' to go on, so what did we care!

We were staying in a chocolate-box painting of a ski lodge on the outskirts of Cortina d'Ampezzo, a town in the Dolomite Mountains in northern Italy. The big day had arrived.

I've already described a couple of other weddings in this book. And what dismal, depressing events they were! In fact, they were such dismal happenings that I can hardly think of them as weddings at all. I've always said that Peter is the only person I've ever *really* married. He's the only man I've ever truly loved, and the only person I've stood at the altar with for the right reason – love. So, when I talk about this wedding, do join me if you will by thinking of it as my *first* wedding, and of Peter Gianfrancesco as my first husband!

I was wearing a floor-length, dark-purple velvet dress with a shimmering veil and a headdress made of winter apples and vines – all very Shakespearean – and the girls had long blue velvet dresses with sprigs of winter flowers in their hair. Peter wore traditional Italian dress, a high-collared suit with a pin from Cortina. We were dressed in real style and I'll never forget the marvellous feeling of standing together outside the ski lodge awaiting our carriage. And what a carriage it was. We were taken down into Cortina by the hotel owner's son in an old Transit van!

There, in the ancient town hall, we were married by the Mayor of Cortina, and the service was absolutely spot-on. It was conducted in Italian but translated for us as we went along. The vows the Italians have for new families are beautiful. We had to promise that we would look after each other and nurture our relationship for the good of the family. Billie sat on Peter's lap and was the ring-bearer, and Madi was involved too, sitting on my lap, cuddling the nervous bride! Both of them were made to feel very important.

It was the first time I understood why people talk about getting married as the happiest day of their life.

I felt so warm and glad to be alive. It sounds corny, but that room was so full of love it was just magical. I felt like I was sparkling all over and when I look at the photos I can see that we were all sparkling.

Once the service was over, the massive doors to the town hall were thrown open and for a few seconds we just stood there blinking in the brilliant sunlight. There was fresh snow everywhere, and the air was cold and crisp. I looked across to the snow-covered pines on the hills in the distance and was so happy I could have cried. But there was no time for that – some of the villagers had got wind of the fact that ours was only the second foreign wedding ever to have taken place in Cortina. Word had got around, and as we stepped out of the hall we were greeted with the cheering, clapping, jumping and whooping of dozens of locals.

Rice and confetti filled the air and it was all just absolutely heavenly. Peter leaned to me and told me that everyone was shouting for us to kiss, so we did, and everyone went wild. It was incredible – we'd never even met these people in our lives, and yet they were all so excited for us. We walked through the village hand-in-hand, and more and more people came out of the shops to cheer as we went by. I'm sorry, but I'd take that reception over family politics any day!

We got back in the van and zoomed up a little winding road to a tiny restaurant in the mountains where our reception had been arranged. The restaurant was next to a huge frozen lake that sparkled like diamonds. It was a wonderland that looked like something only Hollywood could make happen. I'd never had an experience like it.

I was married in spirit, soul and mind, and just thinking of that wonderful day still gives me the warmest glow inside.

After a few days, the girls flew back to England to be with Mum and Dad so that Peter and I could go on our honeymoon. We hired a little car and after negotiating the perilous Italian roads arrived at the walled town of San Gimignano, where we stayed in a tiny apartment. It was nothing flash – we were on a shoestring budget – but we had a ball wandering the winding streets at night and just being together. It was all that we wanted to do. One night a horrible snarling dog followed us wherever we went and we spent the entire evening giggling and trying to get away from it. At one point we even parted to try to confuse it, but nothing worked – I felt like we were in the film *Don't Look Now*.

It seemed that the gods were smiling on me. I'd had an amazing wedding and an amazing honeymoon, and I felt better than ever. Things can't get much better than this, I thought.

And then they did.

23

Opportunity Knocks

'I'm going to take you to England and make you a star,' a man called Malcolm Allsop had said to me in the Sebel Townhouse Hotel restaurant in Sydney in late 1997, just before I was due to be married. Malcolm was one of the bosses from Anglia Television and had travelled from the UK to meet me. He'd been given a VHS tape of me presenting *Live It Up* (so it *had* been worth touting my tapes around TV companies that Christmas!) and he liked what he'd seen. He thought I'd be the ideal host for a new daytime show they had come up with called *The Ladies Room*. It was to be a show along the lines of *Loose Women*.

Yeah, right, I thought.

I told Malcolm I hadn't worked much in three years. I told him I had panic attacks. I told him I was a bit of a mess. I told him I was damaged goods.

'Great!' he said. 'That'll make you an even better host. You've lived and you're not afraid to say so.' I think he must have liked me.

Malcolm flew back to England and we stayed in touch but it wasn't until the honeymoon that I heard from him with a firm offer. I was calling Mum from Italy every day to see if the girls were OK, and she told me that Malcolm had been ringing the house wanting to speak to me. I contacted him and he told me they definitely wanted me. They weren't yet sure what for – *The Ladies Room* idea had been dropped – but they wanted me to come and be a presenter on British TV.

It was a massive decision for me to have to make. Right from the start I'd made it clear to Malcolm that I wasn't going to give him an answer until I'd spoken to Peter. There was no way I was going to go to England unless he was in agreement.

Peter and I were in the one relationship I was not going to put my career in front of. I asked him what he thought and straight away he said I should go for it. Still, I wasn't so sure. I'll never forget what he said next. 'Trisha, this is *England*, what an opportunity!' he began. 'You go for it and I will be right there behind you. I will come to England. You need to know you've got what it takes, so this is your time, and it's the time for you to find out if you can still do it.'

Peter assured me he had no doubts, so I just thought, OK!

It turned out that Anglia were looking for a replacement for Vanessa Feltz's *Vanessa* show, and they thought I was the woman for the job. I'd done a pilot screen test four months earlier when in London for a mental-health conference, and when Malcolm had seen it he'd made the decision he wanted me. In August 1998 he called me and asked, 'Can you be in England by the end of the week?'

End of the week! I thought. *Bloody hell!*

I told him it might be difficult to arrange. 'How long do you want me for?' I asked.

'Well, if you're as good as I think you'll be, you may end up doing the show for a while!' he said.

Blimey! I thought. *This is it.*

I spoke to Peter again and decided to take the plunge.

I needed to be sharp and focused, and once I knew I had the job I decided it was time to come off my anti-depressants. Along with therapy, I'd been on them for about six months and they had helped me out of a very bad place, but with Peter in my life I felt stronger than ever. The pills had worked, but they had made the world a little blurry at times. If I was going to front a TV show again, I had to be right on the ball, all pistons firing, and I no longer wanted to be anaesthetised from the world. I needed to be able to access the adrenalin that makes a live TV presenter think on their feet. So, with my psychiatrist's help, I stopped taking them. It was a horrible experience. I got the shakes, I had panic attacks, my vision would unexpectedly go completely blurry. The day before I got on the plane, I told my shrink Paula I wasn't sure if I could cope, as coming off them was just so awful. She said she knew it was awful but to stick with it.

'But how am I going to present this show? People will see I'm damaged goods!' I said.

'Well, maybe they want people who've been through

hell,' replied Paula. 'Think of the insight you'll be able to bring to the show. You won't be glossy and untouchable, you'll be real. You'll be you.'

And then Paula said the sweetest thing. 'Think of all you've been through,' she told me, smiling. 'Think of all we've talked about and remember that, despite all the shit, you've made it. You've got insight now. I set you free.'

Paula was right, and I had a plane to catch.

24

Trisha

Peter couldn't leave Australia right away. He had a high-powered job in mental health and needed to work his month's notice, so I went ahead with the girls. Everything had happened so fast. One minute I was enjoying married life in Australia, the next I was on a Qantas flight reading British newspapers and seeing my face in every single one! Oh my God, I thought, everyone knows about me, and the British press has found out everything, warts and all! I was nervous, for sure. I knew nothing about British TV and had never heard of Vanessa. It transpired that she'd parted company with Anglia and I was to take over. My show would be called *Trisha* and I was due to begin filming in a matter of days!

I was given some *Vanessa* tapes to watch so I could get an idea of the show's format. One of them was about a guy who had anorexia and Vanessa was saying, 'Can't you see your mother crying? You should eat for her... Will you promise to go home and have a meal for your mother?' Then came the applause.

I couldn't believe my ears. If the guy with anorexia could have eaten a meal, he wouldn't have had a problem. Moreover, if he had gone off and forced down a plate of food it might have had adverse effects. Suddenly introducing a load of food into the stomach of someone who's been starving themselves could be like feeding roast beef and Yorkshire pud to an Auschwitz survivor – the body might not be able to take it.

As I watched the show, I thought, I can't do a show like that because I've got too much inside information. My background in mental health would stop me from doing anything so crass. I actually think Vanessa is very talented. She's a bit manic, but she's an extremely bright girl. But when I watched that show I just thought she obviously doesn't have a clue about mental illness. And why would she? I'd spent years involved in trying to educate people about it and that included journalists and TV presenters too.

I knew I was going to do things differently.

A couple of days later I met the staff I would be working with and told them how things were going to be. 'I realise a lot of you don't know me,' I began, 'but my background is in mental health and this is going to be a very different show from the one you've been working on. A lot is going to change. On my show we won't be pointing fingers at anyone. We'll be coming at people's problems from a psychological point of view, and trying to understand what lies behind their issues, in order to help them. It's not just about entertainment, and, if you're not happy about it, that's cool with me, but say now because you'll have to go. And you'll have to go now. If you stay and you want to do things the way you did Vanessa's show, I'm not gonna want to know and you'll be in deep shit. This is your opportunity to go if you want to, no hard feelings.'

They were strong words, but I had nothing to lose. I wasn't interested in having a show with rhyming scripts and puns, and I wasn't going to take the moral high ground with any of my guests. I made myself very clear about that. A few people left and joined Vanessa at the BBC, but those who stayed were great at adapting to my way of operating, and some of them are still with me ten years on.

And so began *Trisha*. I loved the show from the start. I was able to put my training in conflict resolution into practice (God knows what I would have done without it!), and my own experiences, coupled with my knowledge of mental health in general, meant with the help of the show's counsellors I was well equipped to deal with and help my guests. I never went after ratings but luckily they were fantastic from the word go.

It was hard work, but I wasn't the Trisha Goddard of old. I had a family that I loved and there was no way I was going to drive myself into the ground and neglect them for a minute. When I'd negotiated my contract I'd been very clear about wanting school holidays off, along with other time to rest (to this day, I still make sure I have plenty of time with Peter and the kids).

I also needed time to 'sort myself out' a little. After

months of being on anti-depressants and feeling sluggish (despite my power-walks), I arrived in England at twelve-and-a-half stone – I weighed as much as I had when nine months pregnant with Madi. So one of the first things I did was to hire a personal trainer, Darrell. Back then, Darrell Greaves was one of the few other black people I was to encounter in Norwich, and over the years he became a good mate (and task master!) to both Peter and I. Darrell knew his stuff. 'One thing,' I told him when we first met, 'I don't do running. Power-walking, yes, but you'll never get me to run, so don't even try!' I was 41. Eighteen months later I was three stone lighter, lifted weights that had other guys in the gym stunned and I was totally hooked on running – and have been ever since!

I imagine that, if you've picked up this book, you've a fair idea about the general format of my show, so I won't bore you with too many details. Over the years we've dealt with a huge variety of people and a wide range of issues – family breakdown, infidelity, depression, domestic violence, eating disorders, weight issues, drugs, prostitution and sexuality, to name a few – but have always tried to approach each case on its own merits. *And we've always tried to help.* When you see people on my show, you may wonder what 15 minutes can really do to help them, and it's a fair enough question to ask. For many of the people that come on, 15 minutes can actually make them look at themselves differently. Many of my guests do not have access to therapy and, more to the point, wouldn't know it even existed. I see the time they have with me as the closest they are likely to get to it, as we live in a country where NHS resources are so stretched that counselling can be very hard to come by.

For other guests, 15 minutes isn't enough, and we always offer them as much time as they need with our qualified counsellors who work off the set. Often it takes a lot of bravery for people to get up and talk about what they've been through, and I could not live with myself if I thought we were just making good TV and leaving someone with no more insight into their problem than they had before they stepped in front of the camera. I need to know I've helped, or at least done my best to help, and that's a feeling shared by everyone who works on the show.

My show was the first in the UK to incorporate lie-detector and DNA tests into the format. I adapted the concepts from shows I had seen on foreign TV. The tests are hugely helpful in establishing paternity among other things, and I believe they are a good thing, though some people may dispute how proud I should be of using such techniques on the show. One person who wasn't happy about the DNA tests was my mum! Up until we began using the tests, in all my years of working in television, my mother had only ever commented on whether she liked my outfit or my hairstyle. No matter what I asked her about the content I got the same quick 'Yes, good, darling, but I loved that blue top you were wearing...' That all changed when I started doing *Trisha* shows where a parent was either trying to prove or disprove that a child was biologically theirs.

I'd never seen Mum so angry about anything I'd done on television. 'It's disgusting!' she snapped. 'Why do you have to do those DNA shows? Awful! Awful! They shouldn't allow people to do those tests!'

There were many media commentators saying similar things, but they usually also had a problem with the lie-detector programmes as well as guests coming to blows or screaming at each other. Mum didn't have a problem with those elements at all. But she really had a bee in her bonnet about anything to do with the question of paternity. Even then, I suspected her reasons for this had little to do with any moral issues. I wondered if it was a subject that hit a raw nerve with her for other reasons.

When people accuse my show of exploiting vulnerable people, I just can't take them seriously. I love doing what I do, I'm genuinely interested in mental health, but I'm also a professional TV presenter. I see being able to help people *and* make TV that interests viewers (and maybe even helps them too) as a win-win situation. Anyway, how come celebrities with problems can air their dirty laundry in public and get paid, but critics snobbishly sniff at 'ordinary folk' who might do the same on my show but for free?

Unsurprisingly, people often ask me what I think of ITV's *The Jeremy Kyle Show*. The answer is, 'Not much.' I think that show has totally different priorities from mine. The prime motivation for getting guests on seems to be to create drama and to give Jeremy an opportunity to give someone a mouthful and call them every name under the sun! On his show, the studio audience tend to be more like spectators, whereas on my show, the audiences are very heavily involved, often using their own experiences to help or advise guests. Jeremy Kyle is a moraliser who seems all too happy to have a go at guests. Maybe I'm wrong, but each to their own, I suppose. It's just not my scene.

I take my job very seriously, but along with the emotionally charged nature of what I'm doing, the release of laughter has always been there. Many times I'm very moved by the bravery of those who come on – a lot of them are true survivors – but sometimes I have found it hard to keep a straight face.

I'll never forget the girl who came on my show years ago believing it was her right to be naked. We had to find a way of covering her up, but she simply refused to wear clothes. In the end she compromised but insisted on being wrapped up in cling film! Now, she wasn't a small woman, and cling film on skin under hot studio lights just isn't a good combination. Part of me wanted to laugh (but I didn't) and the other part of me was just trying not to show the horror on my face. I constantly had to check my reactions and tried to focus only on her face – every time I found my eyes straying towards her profusely sweating body and what was covering it, I had to quickly look away.

Another unforgettable show was with a guest called Costas. Costas was in love and writing to a prisoner in America. He had a photo of this gorgeous, 37-year-old blonde woman and told us she was serving ten years over 'a little misunderstanding'. We had tried to get in touch with the governor of the prison to find out exactly what that 'misunderstanding' was. Unfortunately, we were shooting the show when the information came through – Costas's sister was on the set trying to drum it into him that he was making a mistake thinking he was in love with this woman on the other side of the world and that he was going to marry her. While this was going on, the producer spoke to me through my earpiece and said we had the details on the prisoner. Sarah, the producer in question, came on and read them out.

The 'misunderstanding' turned out to be several crimes. Costas's sweetheart had committed kidnap using explosives, and was also a murderer. We'd also located a picture of the woman. She was in the hospital wing of the prison, severely arthritic, and she wasn't 37, she was 57. The worst thing was, she was in prison not for ten years but for life! Poor old Costas, he'd been completely taken for a ride by his woman, and sent her loads of cash into the bargain. I'll never forget the poor guy shaking his head over and over again in total disbelief. We'd had an inkling that she might have told a few fibs, but never guessed the truth about his woman would be so far removed from what Costas had told us. Needless to say, he broke things off.

Aside from the violence and the swearing, we do get the odd rather unsavoury guest on. Sometimes their hygiene is, shall we say, a little lacking. Put simply, they stink! In the early days of the show, we were all too polite to say anything. These days I'm getting bolder and am quite likely to tell someone if they stink – not doing so is doing them a disservice, right? Mind you, some people can't help it. One day there was such a bad smell in the studio that we had to evacuate the audience. It turned out that an old man had come in wearing a colostomy bag and it had burst. Yuk.

One guest I found it very hard to take at face value was an

Irish dwarf who was very serious about gnomes and fairies. He was dressed as a gnome, and that was how he spent his professional life. To him it was no joke. He was shaking quite a bit on the show, so I asked him on air if he was nervous. 'No,' he said bluntly, 'I've a neurological disorder.'

It sounds awful but I was so embarrassed I got a fit of the giggles. The whole situation was just so absurd and it took me a few minutes to compose myself before being able to ask the next question.

It wasn't much easier to keep myself under control when a man came on who'd cheated on his wife with a goat. What made things worse was that I'd just been told the goat had eaten the furnishings in the hotel room we'd put them up in!

But there have been lots of moving moments too. One of my favourite 'success stories' was a show where this terribly violent, very bad-tempered bloke came on. Matthew was an electrician who'd been electrocuted and burned so badly that he could no longer use his hands. Not only could he not do his job, but also he couldn't continually get aggressive as he'd done in the past! He was full of so much pent-up anger that it was painful to witness. We talked for a long time to work through his frustration. A few months later, Matthew came back on the show having gone on to work with young people with burns. He's done so well he's since been back on the show to give advice to another guest about dealing with anger. When that kind of thing happens it's a total buzz.

The key to solving the problems of many of my guests is to show them that they matter as people. I rarely get angry with anyone who comes on, but sometimes there is a place for it. I remember a really self-destructive drug addict who came on. He was obviously bright and capable but was completely ruining himself with whatever he was taking. I remember saying to him, 'You know what gets me? My late sister suffered from schizophrenia and had voices in her head, auditory and visual hallucinations, and all she craved was sanity. You've got clear sanity if you want it, but you're pissing it up the wall trying to get into the very hell she was trying to escape from. She killed herself because of it and here you are trying to induce that hell. Part of me thinks that she should have been given your sanity and you should have been given her insanity. Would that make you happy?'

Sure, I ranted a bit, but a year later that guy came back on the show and said my comments had really hit him. He'd gone into rehab after the first show and had been clean ever since. Being shown that someone on the box cared about him and listened to him seemed to have made all the difference, and it made me, the woman on the box, proud to have helped. And it's not just me, it's the wonderful team that work with me that achieve so much.

In 1999, I got to present a show called *Celebrity Heartbreak*. It was a great show. I interviewed George Best talking about his relationship with Alex. He was full of that Irish blarney, but most interesting because of what he said off camera. George Best was definitely trapped in the legend of George Best. I don't know why all those women went for him in the later years. For a start, he had a temper on him and, secondly, I'm guessing he couldn't even have raised a smile in bed by that stage!

Coleen Nolan and I had a cosy chat at her house and she told me the whole story about her split with Shane Ritchie.

She really spilled the beans on his philandering, and Shane didn't like it one bit. I reckon he must hate me because he put me in the box on *Room 101*! I've got no problem with him – I think he's pretty funny really – but I adore Coleen to this day. She's feisty and tells it like it is. My kind of girl.

Patsy Palmer was a different kettle of fish. Interviewing her was like trying to get blood from a stone. I found her totally impenetrable and felt like saying, 'You know what, let's not bother!' When interviews don't work you just end up thinking, Why am I doing this? But I've since learned that Patsy was going through problems with addiction that no one knew about at the time. She wasn't ready to face them at that time so I can understand why she was so difficult.

In 2000, I agreed to appear on a show that turned out to be the most terrifying experience of my life. There's a theory that all black people can sing. Well, let me tell you I'm living proof of how wrong that theory is. So why the hell I agreed to do *Celebrity Stars In Their Eyes* I can't say. I was interested in the free singing lessons, and I did get a few tips on breathing that have helped me in TV presenting. But, as for the singing, I was simply terrible. I came on as Dionne Warwick and I was petrified. When you have to go through that door the smoke and dry ice mean you can't see a thing. Sherlock Holmes would never have come across a pea-souper like it. To make things worse I was wearing high heels – a rarity for me – and I nearly tumbled down the stairs. Once on the stage I did a good job of moving like Dionne, but all I can say is, thank God for the clever machines they use to tune your voice as you sing into the microphone.

Matthew Kelly was genuinely fantastic to work with. He was a truly nice guy. We were with each other for three days and evenings and in all that time he was a gentleman both on and off camera. I got such a good vibe from him and when those paedophilia charges were brought against him I just thought, Oh, for shit's sake! He was hung out to dry by the press before he'd even had a chance to defend himself. I thought he handled it all with so much dignity, and he's turned into an amazing actor too, so, good for him.

Another show I loved doing was *Loose Women*. I was invited on in 2003 and did four episodes with Kaye Adams and Kerry Katona. I called it *Loose Dogs* – after all, there was quite a bit of bitching behind the scenes. I tried not to get involved, but it was funny being invited into various dressing rooms and hearing presenters talking behind one another's backs. Women in groups get a bad press sometimes, and for good reason – we love to gossip about each other!

I left ITV in 2004, partly because they wanted to change my contract, which would allow them to move production away from Norwich if they wanted to, and there was no way I was going to do that and risk my family life there. Also, there were all manner of unpleasant internal politics at ITV, and certain individuals that I can't be bothered to name were really pissing me off. I never hated ITV per se, but the behaviour of that tiny handful of people made me realise that staying would continue to damage my mental health. And I'm not the only ITV presenter to walk away for those reasons.

Channel Five made me a very good offer and, after a

very stressful 12 hours juggling phone calls between ITV, my Australian lawyer and Five, I decided to go with them. Malcolm Allsop and I had already set up a production company to produce other programmes, naming it Townhouse TV (Malcolm was the Anglia TV boss who had brought me over from Australia, and we named the company after the hotel in which we'd first met), and I decided to go for it. From then on *Trisha* became *The Trisha Goddard Show*. When we started Townhouse, we always said we didn't want to produce anything on the scale and complexity of *Trisha*. We were keen to make short, six-part shows and to nurture new talent, but Five suggested we produce *The Trisha Goddard Show* and we decided we'd go for it after all. In truth, we realised that, daunting as it was, it was too good an opportunity to miss.

At ITV I had been on a very tight exclusivity deal that greatly restricted me in terms of other TV appearances. Once at Five I was much freer to do more. Much to my delight, I ended up being able to accept invites to appear on all sorts of shows. The first time I went on *Have I Got News For You* it was pretty scary. But Ian Hislop was wonderful to me, and I had a great laugh with him. Paul Merton was impenetrable and I'm not sure he liked me much. In fact, I'm not sure if he likes himself very much – who knows? To me, he always looks like he's got a bad taste in his mouth. The best bit was meeting Jack Dee. I've a thing for Jack, you see. He's a gorgeous man. He had a beard when I was on and several times I couldn't help telling him how sexy he looked.

It was a bit intimidating being around all those

comedians and trying to keep up with their banter. But I must have done something right because the offers to appear on comedy shows kept on coming in. I think it's because I'm willing to have a laugh even if it's often at my own expense. I've had a ball doing *Never Mind The Buzzcocks*, *The Kumars* and *Little Britain*'s *Comic Relief* sketch (where Vicky Pollard came on my show!) but of all the comedy shows I've done my favourite has to be *8 Out Of 10 Cats* with Jimmy Carr. I've been on several times and Jimmy is a wonderful guy to work with. Beneath all the dark, sick jokes lies a very moral man indeed.

Going on Trinny and Susannah's *What Not To Wear* was a great laugh. They're really not as brutal as they can sometimes seem. When it came to picking out my outfits, I'd deliberately choose the ones I knew wouldn't work so they could give me a proper slagging off – it was pantomime horridness. There's nothing nasty about them, but I don't think they were over the moon when I nicked their freelance stylist, Zoe Lem. I quickly worked out that Zoe was the one with most of the styling knowledge, so I asked her to come and work for me as my stylist on *The Trisha Goddard Show*. After all, business is business!

Anyway, I won't go on in case people start to think of me as some kind of rent-a-celeb! Suffice to say that I love being in a position where I can accept invitations on to other shows, and I especially like doing stuff where I can have a laugh. But don't think you'll ever catch me on *Celebrity Big Brother*!

Malcolm Allsop promised to make me a star in 1998. He came good on that promise, but did it in a way that's always allowed me to follow my interests and do things my way, which is why over the years he and his wife Elaine have become good friends. I love *The Trisha Goddard Show*. I'm proud of what I do for a living and, second to my family, it's one of the most gratifying parts of my life.

25

Happy As I Am

Since I married Peter and started *Trisha* in 1998, it's as if my life has been blessed. The happiness I have experienced and the love I have been surrounded by are a million miles away from anything that came before. I have watched my girls change and grow into strong, confident young ladies. Billie is a gregarious and passionate 18-year-old, a real champion for the underdog, and at 14 Madi is zany, hugely inquisitive and has an amazingly committed social conscience.

As for Peter, well, he is the absolute icing on the cake. Since arriving in the UK and joining the local branch of mental-health charity MIND (initially as an unpaid volunteer), he has devoted himself to his work and is now the Chief Executive of Norwich MIND. I have also continued my work in mental health as a patron of both Norwich MIND and Norwich Home Start, a charity set up to help parents with young children. Our interests are closely intertwined, and Peter's devotion to his job and our family is nothing short of inspirational. He is a wonderful father, and I often envy the relationship the girls have with him. When I say envy, I mean it in the nicest way. Seeing them together I sometimes get choked up with gladness – I just wish it could have been like that with me and my dad, and I'm so deeply happy that Billie and Madi have Peter in their lives. In truth, I guess what I have now feels more like my real family because they are truly where my heart is. I know I will be emotionally safe in this family, and I'm sure I'm not the only one who feels that way.

My parents often made me feel I couldn't do anything right in my personal life, and so often I didn't feel appreciated unless it was my mum going on about how talented I was and my 'star' status. Well, nowadays Peter and the girls give me more personal appreciation than I could ever wish for, and I do my best to give it back. If nothing else, I think I must be doing something right as far as my family is concerned. Together we've created a home in Norwich that truly feels like home. Luckily, it's big enough for us to respect each other's privacy, but when we come together we more often than not get on like a house on fire. We laugh and tease each other, we debate fiercely and there's nothing we can't be open about as a family. Sure, there are arguments, and it's not always easy not to preach to my kids, but I try.

If you ask me, anyone who says they are a faultless parent deserves a slap! Parenting, like life, is a work in progress. I'm no supermum, I'm sure, and I'm still learning. Probably as a result of my childhood, I've gone to great lengths to create relationships and situations in our family that I wish I'd had as a kid. I refuse to compare my children with one another, hit them or continually criticise them. All I want for my kids is for them to be happy with who they are, and it's for who they are that I love them. Not that I believe in unconditional love. Some people say they love their kids whatever they do. Well, I reckon that's bollocks. We all have conditional love whether we like to admit it or not. Someone whose kid has just murdered 20 people may say they still love them, but in my opinion that's the wrong attitude. If people let their children cross boundary after boundary and give them so-called unconditional love, they're messing them up by encouraging them to do the wrong thing again and again. Similarly, as a parent, you can't expect to cross boundary after boundary and expect your kids to carry on loving you. At the end of the day, it's a matter of respecting each other's boundaries, and that's what we try to do.

I have the sweetest little godson, Hugo – the result of my dear friends Ian and Colette paying me the greatest compliment ever by telling me I'm a parent they admire. It meant so much to me, even though I'm still absolutely crap at taking compliments. I'm far more comfortable being criticised, even though I remain very sensitive about it. I've realised that, over the years, I've learned to be comfortable with emotional discomfort while I'm still scared of being praised. Work that one out!

I've talked about my parents quite a bit in this book. They certainly made some mistakes, and I've tried not to pass them on. But I've always maintained that they did their best. In 2004, my poor, non-smoking mother died of lung cancer. There was an awful lot going on at the time at work, but she immediately became the focus of my life. In the final months of her illness, we spent a lot of time just being together. We didn't talk about anything negative from the past. Instead, we focused on the good memories and talked about the present too. We even planned her 'celebration of life' together. Mum thanked me for having given her such wonderful grandchildren, and I thanked her for being their grandma. We laughed together as she lay in her house and I will never forget her telling me she wasn't scared of going. She felt safe with us.

I was holding her hand when she finally went.

It's impossible to describe how it feels to lose your mother. Despite all the differences between us, I loved her. Perhaps I sometimes had trouble showing her, and perhaps she sometimes had trouble showing me. I never knew exactly what she thought of me, but I know there was love there.

When she died I was left with grief mixed with anger.

I was angry with both myself and my mother and it centred around one thing: my father. At the beginning of this book, I wrote that I always felt different, and I explained why. But there is another reason for that feeling – I have never been sure if the man I have called Dad for all these years is my real father. My father is white, and my mother was lighter-skinned than me, as are my sisters (my hair was frizzy, my sisters had curls). People often thought my sisters were Indian and were incredulous if I said my dad was white. Yet even on her deathbed my mother didn't tell me the truth, and I know she was aware of the doubts I had because I'd voiced them many times throughout my life – often in pain and anguish. I was angry with my mum for this, and I was angry with myself for never asking the questions I wanted to before she died.

During Mum's illness, another tragedy happened. Our good mate and personal trainer Darrell died suddenly from brain injuries after falling from a moving car. He was only 35 and there was a lot of mystery surrounding his death. It made an already shocking death even more traumatic for his poor family and friends. Needless to say, Peter and I were devastated.

Something else happened after my mum died. My dad began to hug me. It still feels odd to this day, but I guess he's trying to show me what he's never been able to put into words.

I think this generation has been brought up to believe that life should be like a Disney film from start to finish. People expect a lot of happiness from life, but if you expect everything to be great all the time then you're setting yourself up for a fall. Shit happens, and I've been through a fair amount of it. Some have been through more than me, some less. But in the end it's the way you deal with it that counts.

What doesn't kill you makes you stronger and, when I look back on my life, I wouldn't change a thing. If I hadn't worked the way I did, if I hadn't gone through all those shitty relationships, if I hadn't hit rock bottom, I wouldn't be the person I am today. And my breakdown? I now see it as the birth of the new me.

Believe it or not, despite the obvious exceptions, these first fifty years have been a rollercoaster. There have been exciting bits and parts where you just want to scream, interspersed with moments of laughter and sheer bliss.

Trisha – *As I Am*

I've got more to learn, for sure, and I've got more to give too, but, as I run around the park with my dear doggie Alf each morning, come rain or shine, I know I've arrived at a point in my journey where I'm finally happy as I am.

Epilogue

How weird. On the very day I finished writing, a big brown envelope arrived in the post. I knew what it was the minute I laid eyes on it. But I was in a hurry to get to the gym and sensed it contained something too important to just glance at quickly.

I hardly thought about it during my workout. When I did I just tuned it out, pushed myself to exercise even harder.

But I got home and there were no more excuses. The envelope was just where I left it in the kitchen. I braced myself and opened it.

I pulled out a Certificate of Ancestry from DNA Worldwide. On it were the results of a DNA test taken from a swab I sent them eight weeks earlier.

Trisha – *As I Am*

My genetics are 90% Sub-Saharan, and around 10% European. I've European ancestry in there somewhere, but nothing as recent as from a parent.

In other words, the white, red-haired man I've called 'Dad' all these years has no biological connection with me.

I was dizzy for a moment. I was shocked. But I wasn't surprised.

After all, I have spent most of my life hung up on why I was the darkest person in my family, why I had frizzy hair and dark features when my sisters had either curls of straight hair and what can only be described as a light tan. Those deep-rooted feelings of not fitting in were for a reason. I can almost laugh about it now, but only with irony.

All those years I thought I was mad, or just imagining things. I had to come up with bizarre explanations to others for why I looked nothing like my sisters. Some people would laugh in my face; other black people would call me stupid for thinking I had 'white' in me. Often I would be left in tears about it all. All those years I was teased about being 'the adopted one', and all those years my mother brushed aside my questions when I asked about why I was so different. 'Don't be so stupid,' she would say when I challenged her. Well, I wasn't being stupid. The only thing that might have been stupid was not pursuing my gut feeling earlier on. I could have insisted on the truth from my parents a long time ago. If there's one thing life has taught me, it's that, when I ignore my intuition, it's at a price.

Am I angry? Yes and no. There's a lot I can understand and there's a lot I can't. As I've said, I think things

Epilogue

happen for a reason. I've always listed betrayal as the one thing guaranteed to derail me. I've been through it with Robert and his lies about HIV; I've been through it with Mark's infidelity. It was horrendous at the time, but perhaps those experiences of breakdown and recovery have helped me to deal with this now. Breakdown, therapy, the road to a more balanced version of my old self has resulted in my salvation. The thought of the person I was years ago opening that brown envelope is too terrifying to contemplate.

Perhaps it is only now that I have the tools to handle the new knowledge that my real father is out there somewhere...